MY LIFE AND LABOURS

IN LONDON, A STEP

NEARER THE MARK.

MY LIFE AND LABOURS

IN LONDON, A STEP

NEARER THE MARK.

BY

JAMES INCHES HILLOCKS,

AUTHOR OF "LIFE STORY: A PRIZE AUTOBIOGRAPHY;" "THE SABBATH-SCHOOL
FROM A PRACTICAL POINT OF VIEW," ETC.

Dedicated by Permission to the

RIGHT HON. W. E. GLADSTONE D.C.L., M.P

"The web of life is a mingled yarn."
"If I one soul improve, I have not lived in vain."
"Thanks be to God who giveth us the victory ."

LONDON:
WILLIAM FREEMAN, 102 FLEET STREET.
1865.

TO

THE RIGHT HON. W. E. GLADSTONE,

D.C.L., M.P.,

AS ONE WHO HAS EARNESTLY DEVOTED HIS RARE GIFTS TO

THE SERVICE OF MANKIND,

WHO IS LABOURING HARD IN BEHALF OF HIS COUNTRY,

WHO MANIFESTS A DEEP INTEREST IN

THE WELFARE OF THE TOILING AND SUFFERING MASSES,

AND

WHO CAN APPRECIATE THE EFFORTS OF OTHERS,

HOWEVER HUMBLE,

This Record

OF STRUGGLES TO BE USEFUL

IS, BY PERMISSION,

RESPECTFULLY AND SINCERELY DEDICATED BY

THE AUTHOR.

PREFACE.

"READER, for the present we part. It is not the life of an old man you have read; it is simply the sad story of one who has not passed the prime of life; of one who is as anxious as ever to be useful; of one who, though he has not reached the 'far up height,' is willing to climb the steep, yet determined as ever to rally round

'The banner with the strange device—Excelsior;'

of one who is yet waiting for work—may God, through good friends, send it soon!" Such were the words with which I closed "Life Story."* Hence, doubtless, it is that whilst one celebrated critic was pleased to say, "It is real and unexaggerated, yet reads like a novel;" another critic, perhaps referring to this statement, says, "It *reads* like a novel, but does not *end* like one: to the grief and anxiety of the admiring but saddened reader, the curtain falls too quickly; and before this life drama is finished, What has become of the author? is the question without an answer."

This unavoidable absence of the " happy ending," which so generally crowns the stories of romance, was not only observed by intelligent critics, it was also marked by careful readers; and many of both classes proved the interest they felt in the work and its author by sending letters of earnest inquiry.

One correspondent—with a dash of that freedom which honest-hearted friendship would only permit—would ask,

* "Life Story" is a first-prize autobiography. The late Professor Nichol was one of the adjudicators. The narrative is genuine.

"Has *little* HILLOCKS now grown into *large* MOUNTAINS?" Another—with an Irishism, the result of intense ardour—would add, "Whether dead or alive, write to say if you are to be *tashed* about the world till your hairs are gray, and your fire burnt out." A third would ask this question, "*Have you had to confront any more of those terrible forms of hard and stern fate which, in Scotland, ran along, and so frequently intercepted your path?*"

In relation to this last question I may simply say, that I did not expect, when I came to London, to gather up heaps of sovereigns in "Golden Square," or florins, or even shillings, in "Silver Street." Nor was I so foolish as to suppose that, even though the silver and the gold had come into my possession, my difficulties would have been over. In former times I suffered in body—and that frequently—from the want of the common necessaries of life; but the suffering in mind was greater, and that because I was often prevented from being so useful as I otherwise might have been. Ever since I began my labours amongst the people,—whether as a social or moral reformer, as teacher or lecturer, missionary or evangelist,—I have found that success has to me been dangerous, frequently causing envy, then jealousy, then backbiting, then opposition, then slander. All of these arrows being aimed at one person, it is not surprising that he should fall, or at least for a time fail. But in addition to this, I have been what some are pleased to call "stubborn;" that is, not becoming "all things to all men," in the sense in which *they* would render these words. Neither flattery, promises, nor threats could prevent me from thinking for myself, and doing that which I perceived to be my duty. This firm resolve—to be true to God and my convictions—was frequently converted into a kind of virulent poison, with which to cover the points of such arrows, the result being to lower my position in life for a time at least, to lessen—and sometimes entirely take away—the means of support, and so steep me and mine in poverty. Now though I have in England as yet escaped some of the *more* " terrible forms" of what my correspondent calls " hard and stern fate," yet the same causes have not been altogether absent. I have been, and I mean to be, as firm, when truth or principle or usefulness is involved; and my firmness has been tested. It would be flattery for which the honest—who know life in England, as in Scotland—would not thank me, were I to say that there are not any, even in this our bright and glorious South Britain, mean and cowardly enough to become envious, jealous, and unscrupulous. Much as I love England, greatly as I admire the nobility and worth of her hearty and useful workers for God and for man, my experience would condemn me if I tried to convey such an idea. The bad get mixed up with the good everywhere but in heaven. I have thus suffered here, but not so much.

But I should have misunderstood the object of these kind inquiries—on the part of the rich and poor, the great and useful, from the throne downward—proving, as they did, that "the tale of a human being has to every human being a very deep interest,"—had I for a moment supposed that those who wished to know more of me were merely interested in relation to my struggles *for bread.* I was not left to conjecture here. I knew from the letters that the inquirers were also anxious to learn if I had gained " a step nearer the mark,"—if, in the providence of God, I had, more than ever, been enabled to help those in need of help,—of being more extensively useful. Believing this, I have undertaken the work, and in it endeavoured to give some idea of my *life* as connected with my *labours*, since I closed the " Prize Autobiography " in September 1860.

I have endeavoured, as far as possible, to preserve the narrative character of the work, yet I have not altogether overlooked the important question,—*how best* to reach and improve the people ?—and I trust the remarks interspersed throughout the book will be received in the spirit in which they are given. I have spoken freely, but not without consideration.

When referring to my plans, and what measure of success with God's blessing have attended my efforts, I do not mean for a moment to convey the idea that they are all *new*. I aim at usefulness rather than originality. With the words and ways of Jesus before me, I am seldom at a loss to meet a case, or a class of cases, but I would not think twice of partly, or even entirely, borrowing a plan from others who may very likely have constructed it upon the same basis.

So far as the transferring of the incidents and remarks to paper is concerned, the effort is spontaneous. I am aware that I need not have aimed at rhetorical embellishment or elaborate eloquence. What is called fine writing, that which astonishes and dazzles, is beyond my pen. That which has filled my mind is my subject; and I am content if I am able to inform, to say what I think, in a manner in which I may be fairly understood.

Though I have adopted the title given to this book as a poet often names his volume, by the principal poem it contains, yet I have not neglected to name some of the incidents which occurred previous to my leaving Scotland ; nor have I omitted my visits to the country since I came to England, and the thoughts thereby suggested.

That this portion of my humble life may be also blessed is my ardent wish and earnest prayer.

34 STANHOPE STREET, REGENT'S PARK, N.W.

CONTENTS.

CHAPTER VII.

CHAPTER VIII.

CHAPTER IX.

CHAPTER X.

CHAPTER XI.

CONCLUSION.

MY LIFE AND LABOURS IN LONDON.

CHAPTER I.

MY LATTER DAYS IN SCOTLAND, EMBRACING SOME OF THE INCIDENTS WHICH OCCURRED PREVIOUS TO MY ARRIVAL IN LONDON.

I. MY HOPES.

T was at Edinburgh that I penned the words quoted in the commencement of the Preface. In the second edition of that "Prize Autobiography," the last sixteen words of that quotation were omitted, not because the intervening time—three months—had brought to me the "work" for which I had longed so anxiously, but at the suggestion of a dear friend, Mr Logan, editor of that admirable volume entitled, "Words of Comfort for Parents Bereaved of Little Children." Writing to me, he said, "Perhaps it would be better not to insert the last two lines of your Autobiography in the new edition. Doubtless you will succeed; and, besides, 'Life Story' will be read long after the author is gone beyond the grave."

Little did this Christian friend know, when he wrote the words, "Doubtless you will succeed," what share they were to have in helping to give to me the encouragement, then so much needed,

A

once more to rouse my hopes. In this case, my friend's plain and honest letter told for good, proving that to write properly and at the proper time is an important duty, the happy result of which can only be fully known to Him who notes the fall of the sparrow.

"Is it possible I may yet succeed?" was a question I often asked myself after reading this letter; and, generally, the answer was, "Doubtless." So I looked up, and pressed on in faith and hope. Nor were my hopes without foundation. True it was, I had been long very ill of a dangerous fever, and was not yet convalescent; nor could I entertain the idea with sufficient confidence, that I should ever be so strong for work even as I had been; but I knew that God in His mercy had blessed the means which had raised me from what was supposed to be my deathbed, to the surprise of even the kind and skilful doctor who so carefully attended me during this severe illness. This, and for nearly the hundredth time, led me to feel assured that I had been spared to be useful, perhaps, more so than ever. It was also true that long, lonely, and anxious watching had done much to undermine the constitution of her whom God had graciously given to bless me. She could not expect again to enjoy health, yet she was still spared to help me, and to nurse our darling children. I had been frequently trodden under foot, and crushed almost as flat as a beetle; but that which gave to me the elasticity, of which the critics were pleased to express their astonishment and commendation, was the conviction that I failed not because I had taken a wrong step, but often because I was overwhelmed by a power which ought not to have existed, it being generally wielded for this purpose by those from whom another influence might have been expected. I was aware that, even where visible success did not crown my efforts, perseverance had overcome many and great difficulties. Often had I severely felt that my labours for bread and labours of love were too much for my physical strength; yet I had seen and enjoyed their results in after-years. Frequently, from these causes, and others less agreeable, had I been thrown down to the bottom of the social scale, and there left to rise as I might; but glad was I to find that I had, even in the midst of my trials and struggles, been the humble means in God's hand in raising others in the moral scale. In short, whatever the result was, I could thank Him, and congratulate myself that the motive was right.

All this made me hope on and press forward, and it enabled me in some measure to realise the fact that he that hopes helps himself; that, especially on such occasions, the promises of hope are sweeter than roses in the bud. Besides, I could with confidence rely upon the continued help of God, who, amid all my sufferings in body and mind, had graciously and mercifully enabled me to realise the precious meaning, and to feel the pleasant force of the cheering idea so plainly expressed in these simple lines :—

> " Earthly friends may pain and grieve thee,
> One day kind, the next day leave thee,
> But this Friend will ne'er deceive thee :
>   Oh, how He loves !"

II. My Fears.

But fears, numerous and strong, would dash in amongst the most refreshing and strengthening of hopes; and I found that though " when the desire cometh it is a tree of life," yet "hope deferred maketh the heart sick." This I felt, but never more keenly and sadly than when I was not trustingly and sensibly leaning on the arm of my heavenly Father. If by any means the eye of faith had been turned aside from Him, as the Giver of every good and perfect gift, fear would creep round me, and cling to me as feathers to tar; and though what I have stated was enough to inspire hope, even in my condition, yet this fear would at times drag me down almost to despair.

But, it may well be asked, why did I allow fear at times thus to predominate? The pages of "Life Story" can best answer that question, but a few sentences touching that point may not be out of place here.

The hopes referred to were not of the kind to allure; my desires were neither unreasonable nor beyond the bounds of probability; but experience, sad yet useful, had taught me that it was scarcely possible for an active and earnest man to escape the keen edge of the venomous tongue of slander, and its all but fatal effects, even were he to try—if that were possible for *him* —not to offend prejudice, nor to provoke envy; and I had resolved, as before, that, if spared to usefulness, I would be as earnest and as active, as honest to my conscience and to my trust as I had been. This being the case, I might look for the opposition that met my former struggles and efforts.

Again, I had written "Life Story" to gain a prize, and it had been published that it might be the means of aiding my course. I honestly confess these were prominent motives, though there was also the ardent desire that the effort might prove useful to the reader as well as the author. But after I had posted the manuscript which was to complete the last sheet of that book, I asked myself the question, Will it, or will it not help me to a congenial situation? As is stated in the note to the new edition, " I had told the truth, and nothing but the truth; yet not the *whole* truth, and it was this omission that made me " run the risk," as has been frequently stated, " of throwing myself open to the charge of being at times something like imprudent." This was my only choice: either to run such a risk, or to mention names and tell of deeds in relation to important incidents and changes, which revelations would instantly rouse the just indignation of the thoughtful reader towards the parties concerned. To do so, I had strong provocation, for the most sensitive parts of my heart had been probed to the very quick, and that by many of whom better things might have been expected.

" This affront will make you angry," said a person to Diogenes, as a fellow had spit in his face. " No," said the philosopher; " but I am thinking whether I ought not to be so." So in like manner, if I did not yield to the force of provocation, I considered whether I ought not to do so. I confess I was not undisturbed amidst the sallies of passion, which came up one after another, during this conflict with resentment. And just as I was about to put a stop to something like anger, my counsellor broke out thus : " Surely you have suffered plenty. Let them have it. Let the reader know the whole truth. Your error and my error has been to misapply that idea, ' Charity thinketh no evil ;' and now you would make a double error by screening the guilty at your expense. Let them have it. It may be to them a lesson. Many in their time have suffered, and your speaking out may help others."

Such a statement from the lips of one who, on reflection, would not injure her worst enemy, had some influence on my mind, but only for a short time. After a little conversation on the words and ways of Christ touching this point, we resolved to act as I have done, and for these two as well as other reasons :—1. Because, after all, we had no wish to heap more punishment upon those who, without cause, had checked our usefulness and lessened our comfort, than their own conscience might inflict ; 2. Because, to have told the names and exposed the deeds would have lessened the chances of the future usefulness of the guilty parties in proportion to the influence of the book, which has become considerable, because of its wide circulation.

But, as may readily be supposed, the carrying out of such a resolution, especially under the circumstances, was a source of much fear, and often the means, together with other causes, of all but extinguishing the last rays of hope. Hence no language can detail the nature and force of the conflicting emotions which struggled for the mastery. If my reader was ever over ears in downright honest love,—if the object of his affection was more than all the world to him,—if he has felt this so that he must ask her if she would become his till death do them part,—if reflection has proved that the more he thought of her beauty and worth, he felt the effort to put the question required more and more courage,—if he has overcome this difficulty, and has waited for the reply,—if every moment was as an hour, and every hour as a day,—if he has felt the blood come to and run from his face,—if he at such a time had glanced into the looking-glass and seen his own countenance, now brightened up by the joys of hope, and then overcast by the shadow of fear,—if he has experienced all this, especially the latter, then he knows something of the emotional confusion which often made me reel like a drunken man.

And what frequently gave a keen severity to such a conflict, was the conviction that the moments of inward peace and solemn stillness, in which my fevered soul found a transient rest, had become fewer and further between than they had been before this crisis.   Day after day I felt I was becoming so much more sensitive to the terrible pangs of fear, and that which caused it, that I became astonished at, and afraid of, my mental state.   It really seemed as if the all but mortal sufferings of the past had at last so weakened me that I could no longer bear up under the crushing pressure.   Even when the blessed intervals enabled me to reflect upon the past proofs of God's matchless tenderness and soothing sympathy, I would all of a sudden sigh, as if I doubted His many precious promises.

Nor was I always alone in this state of mind.   We had often noticed, and rejoiced in the fact, that when I was weak, my helpmate was strong, or at least not so weak, and when she was weak I was the stronger, and so we were able to help each other; but at this stage we more than once seemed to give way together.   "I feel I am sinking," had been the suppressed ejaculation of each heart; and on one occasion, being much depressed, and fearing lest I had been depending more on man than on God, she, observing the depression, said, " Surely we are not to sink now. What would become of our *bairnies* ? He who has brought us through the past, is able and willing to help us in the future. He is the same yesterday, to-day, and for ever. We do not know what another week may do."

These were precious words, and timely spoken. God blessed them, and by His help we were enabled again to look our difficulties in the face, and to become as determined as ever to do battle to the last moment, in the hope that we, in some measure, might again be the means, in God's hand, of helping " to loose the bands of wickedness, to undo the heavy burdens, and to let the oppressed go free."

III. SYMPATHETIC INQUIRY.

At last some copies of my new book—the " Prize Autobiography "—came from the binders.

I had a number of private subscribers as well as booksellers' orders, and I resolved to supply the former out of " lot the first ;" but how to get them posted was the question.

To my joy, one of the Edinburgh booksellers gave a practical answer by incidentally offering ready cash for five per cent. off. Most gladly did I comply, and lightly did I come home, not only with postage-stamps, but cash besides. With all freedom of conscience we could apply those few shillings to our own use, because they did not interfere with the orders given in security to the paper-manufacturer and the printer.

After supplying " the trade " and the subscribers, I sent copies to the press, and anxiously, almost impatiently, did I look for the notices. Perhaps it was weakness on my part, for the strongest are weak at times. I felt as if I should fall under adverse criticism. However, I was not put to the test, for hardly could a book meet with a more unanimous approval. Amidst this rare harmony, there was only one jarring note, and that was sounded after I was able to listen to it. This was not so much in relation to the book as to the " self-educated struggler," as the critic was pleased to call me ; and even he declared the work " possessed the interest which must needs attach to all ' simple annals of the poor.' "

A few copies were also posted—1. To those who had shewn a willingness to help me in my previous struggles ; 2. To those for whom I entertained a high respect because of the interest they manifested on behalf of the working classes ; 3. To those who I hoped might be able, directly or indirectly, to help me to obtain employment.

Finding I had one copy left of the number laid aside to give away, I asked my private counsellor to whom she thought I might send it. " To the Queen, she will read it," was the ready reply ; and, suiting the action to the suggestion, the copy was soon wrapt in paper and addressed, per book-post, " To Her Majesty the Queen, Windsor Castle."

With few exceptions, the copies thus sent were acknowledged, but some there were who manifested a deeper interest in the narrative than others. It was then that " the postman's knock " would make our hearts beat quickly. I use the plural here, because our boy, though young, had had his wits sharpened by poverty, so that he, and even his sisters, at times joined with their mother in the anxiety I felt when the rat-tat would make me start as if frightened. All had learnt to take a considerable interest in the correspondence. Sometimes the young ones would rush to open the door, even before that important messenger, the postman, had time to give the usual rat-tat. It was an interesting sight to see them peep curiously at the letter before giving it up.

In all cases in which I sent a note with the book to either of the parties named, I made it my duty most distinctly to state that it was *work*—and, if possible, congenial work—that I looked for; and hence it was with trembling hand the seal of each letter was broken, and with eager eye the lines were scanned. How I longed to be able to clear off all liabilities, to stand upright!

Most of those who had written to me, had expressed a wish that I might get the work most congenial; and many said I would certainly succeed, not a few building their hopes on the fact that Dr Guthrie and other great and good men were now deeply interested in my welfare. Among those of this opinion was his Grace the Duke of Argyle. Nor was he mistaken as to the great preacher's heart, and intentions and efforts. Even when I did not know of it, he was using his influence in my favour. In one of his letters to a friend of his were these amongst other sentences: " Perhaps you could help him in some other way. I wish you could, for he is really worthy of a kind hand like yours. . . . I feel an interest in him, as a good and able man who has had great difficulties to fight with."

The situation referred to—a secretaryship—was just being filled up when the doctor's letter referring to me reached those concerned. It was too late, as his friend said, but that was because he had not before heard of the vacancy. His goodness was as much evinced in the writing of the letter as if I had obtained the place—and a suitable place it would have been.

It was congenial work I wished for, but I would have done anything so as to bring in cash honestly. If an opportunity of operating on mind would not turn up, I was willing, nay, anxious to *operate on matter*. Often did I apply for a " *light porter's* place," (even to carry *heavy burdens*.) I shall only name one of many failures. I observed in the *North British Advertiser* that a person's services were required in connexion with a newly-opened bazaar. I forget what designation was given to the office which the successful candidate was to fill, but it entered my mind that I might try, because I thought I could perform the duties specified. As is generally the case, I had to call frequently before I could see the person to whom it was my duty to apply; but at last I saw the "party."

"There are so many after the situation that I have no time to hear their application," he said, and was about to leave me. But I was not to be put off. I thought of the wants at home, and said, "Surely I can perform the duties mentioned in the advertisement?"

"You might do that, but you cannot answer my purpose," he added, and made off again.

"There is some mistake somewhere," I replied, and followed him. "I can write a fair hand—there is my notebook; I know something of business habits. I have an unstained character as to honesty and activity; I shall give names to any amount from amongst those with whom I have done business, and for whom I have laboured—what more is needed?"

"I know all that, but you are not the *person* for me," he rejoined, and was again off.

I became as one trying to stare through a mystery, and at last I said, "Beg your pardon, sir; tell me *why* I am not the person?"

"I 'd rather not," he said, making a step or two more towards his desk.

"Perhaps you will," I said, still following him and looking him straight in the face.

"Well, if you *will have it*, you are too little," and by this time he was at the small door which led into what was called the "counting-house."

"Too little to write, to do business, to be honest!" thought I; "that is rather strange—the man is surely crazy." And after these reflections, I put such a series of questions as caused him to solve the mystery. What he wanted was a man of mighty stature, to wear a long overcoat with clear buttons, and able to wield a great cudgel—in short, a large man to stand at

SYMPATHETIC INQUIRY. 11

the bazaar door, and frighten the boys. So he was right, I was " not the *person*."

I had often suffered because I could not be " all things to all men " in the sense that too many define these words, because I would venture to exercise my own mind and to be honest to my convictions. I had lost situation after situation because I was " a Dissenter,"—" *a Dissenter on principle*," as a minister of the Established Church worded it,—but never before was I an unsuccessful candidate because I was too little to be a policeman. And well it was, for I should have been as much, if not more out of my latitude as Burns the poet was when made an exciseman.

However, when such disappointments would combine with other circumstances so as to overcast my pale face with a dark cloud, the mother, as wife-like as it was mother-like, would bring her hand across baby's brow and look in its lovely eyes, and add, " As Mrs Brunton said at Sir James's, ' Rome was not built in one day.'" So we hoped on, for the letters still continued to come. But the first one which increased and strengthened our hopes, was that from the veteran pen of Lord Brougham. It was not long, but it proved that he had perused the book, for he was able to characterise it as " most creditable." He also stated that he would do all he could to " further " my " desires," when he had seen the secretary of the Social Science Association, (Mr Hastings,) " which cannot be before he comes to London, a month hence."

" A month hence,"—how these words made hope rise degree after degree ! So high did it become, that I could see, in imagination, at the end of that time, the beginning of a career of increased usefulness. And what castles were built by our boy and his mother ! It was not that " papa's " portrait would fill a space on the academy wall, nor that his bust would be seen in the sculptor's studio ; not that he was to be lionised, nor to have his *carte de visite* " sold by the trade " for sixpence ;

not that he was to have D.D., or LL.D., or M.D., or F.R.S., or M.P. appended to his name; not that the *Court Journal*, or the *Court Circular*, would announce that her Majesty had recognised his humble efforts. No, these were none of the elements which composed this aërial castle,—it was simply what "papa" might yet be able to do to help the people, the poor and the needy, to help to lead them so that many might become sober and happy, good and useful,—how he might yet be enabled the better to help "to fill the schools, and empty the jails," and, having finished his labours for God and man, lay aside his weakly frame, and ascend to heaven, "leaving George to follow the same path of duty." And then there was the idea of it being possible that "papa, and the whole of us, might have to go to London." Only think what an idea the going to London—for, in imagination, they were on their way—must be to a boy of about seven years of age; the glow of anticipation brightened by the enthusiasm of a naturally hearty and cheerful mother, the chief of whose earthly wishes was to see her family comfortable and her husband once more engaged at work in which he might be most useful.

"You know what we've been saying, papa?" was a question often put to me when I came home after making some fruitless effort, for I had resolved to leave no stone unturned, lest Lord Brougham might not be able a month hence to do what he wished for me. Of course I replied in the negative, and asked, "What?" when George would record the rearing of such pleasing structures as I have just indicated, appealing to his sisters, all of whom were younger, for proof in confirmation of what he was saying. The tales were such as I could not help smiling at, but I must confess, too, they gave something like inspiration to my soul, and often did they brush off much of that languid weariness which depresses one anxious honourably to sustain his responsibilities amid sad reverses, and to perform his duties even when the limbs refuse to comply with the will.

"Here, my dear, is a letter that will do your heart good," was the salutation which met my ears as I went home one day. It was from Professor Blackie.

After reading my little book, this worthy scholar and liberal educationalist sent to me this letter. I give it entire, because it is short, characteristic, and representative :—

"DEAR SIR,—I have read your 'Life Story' with great interest and pleasure. It is what old Goethe used to call 'Ein stäck leben,' (a piece of real life,) and such things are often of more value than many sermons. With the experimental remarks on the philosophy of education, scattered through various parts of the work, I most heartily concur. On the whole, I would say your book is a real, true, and good book, full of the bones and sinews of a sturdy reality ; and I am sure no man will read it sympathetically without being the better for it.—Sincerely yours,

"ROBERT S. BLACKIE."

But this good man did not only write, he actually did us the honour to call at our humble home, there to console and to encourage, proving, as I have elsewhere said, that he knew human nature as well as Greek. Imagine, if you can, my astonishment when I entered and saw the eloquent professor seated, quite at home, at the fireside, talking fluently to " Auntie Maggie," as he said—the name by which Mrs Hillocks was first introduced to the readers of " Life Story." He received me as cordially and heartily as if I had been his equal in station and learning. After exchanging of a few questions and answers as to our present condition and future prospects, he delivered an extempore clear and sound dissertation on biography and autobiography. This discourse arose because of his renewed praises of my humble effort. I learnt much from his remarks. He also invited me to his residence to have a conversation, and to get from him some elementary Greek books, previous to my entering his classes, to which he had previously given me an honorary order, a mark of his respect for " persevering endeavours."

This was a kind offer well meant. It was blessed to me more

ways than one; and one way was, it enabled me the better to make the best of things. Whilst in the expectation of employment to procure bread, I laid hold of the chance which the kindness of Professor Blackie put in my way of acquiring some of that learning for which I had longed, and, as I thought, necessary the better to prepare me for the object of my life—to become a preacher of the gospel.

Agreeably to invitation, I went to the professor's residence, and pleasant were the hours I there spent with him and his kind lady. This was soon followed by my introduction to his students—an introduction of a kind not easily to be forgotten by me. He asked me to meet him in an apartment adjoining his class-room. This I did. He begged me to be seated for a short time, when he appeared, dressed in gown, &c., ready for work. "Come this way," was the next injunction, and I obeyed. He ascended a few steps, entered by a door, and in a moment we were on the rostrum, facing a great mass of students waiting for more enlightenment in classic lore from their teacher. There I had to remain, and, instead of commencing his lecture at once, the professor first introduced me as his friend, "the author of 'Life Story,'" followed by a panegyric earnest and eloquent. This was an honour, a mark of respect which I could not have looked for. I can assure you my face was not pale during this my introduction to the students. But in a short time my mind was trying to follow him in his grand and graphic lecture on Homer.

Now, said I to myself, was the opportunity I had longed for. All that was needed was something to do in Edinburgh that would permit my attendance at college; for we should have been content with small wages to have had that opportunity, and I would have worked and kept up my studies. But this did not turn up, yet I lost no chance of benefiting by my friend's kindness. As long as I was in Edinburgh I attended his junior and senior classes, when nothing came in the way to prevent me.

Words cannot express how thankful I am to Professor Blackie for thus evincing his native kindness.

Again the postman knocked. "Who is this James Miller that has promised to be so kind?" was the question put after I had read his letter aloud. I was able to state that it was no other than the Professor of Surgery in the University of Edinburgh, and author of "Alcohol, its Place and Power." The sentence in his letter which called forth this question was, "I shall be most happy to help you to any situation suitable that may come within my power."

"Another professor, I suppose. He wishes to see you," was another salutation as I arose from a kind of sleepless rest which I had been endeavouring to get because of exhaustion and sickness brought on by anxiety and fatigue. The conjecture was correct. It was from Professor Aytoun. I went at the time appointed. We had a long and pleasant conversation. He had read the little book; and having asked some questions, I had the opportunity of clearing up to his satisfaction what to him—as to other careful readers—seemed doubtful passages—that is, those referring to my leaving places of usefulness without giving in full the reason why. I was glad he did so; and I shall never forget the glow of righteous indignation which stamped the words he uttered in relation to the manner in which I had suffered by many who ought to have helped "an aspiring soul bent on good" —I quote the last six words. He, too, assured me that it would give him very great pleasure to see me in a situation in which I might get vent for the good I wished to help forward.

But these were not the only friends who thus recorded their sympathy,—thanks to feeling hearts and Rowland Hill's penny postage! Nor can I here withdraw the impulse to name yet a few more who added to the number of the postman's knock. The letter from the Right Hon. Lord Kinnaird was kindly and encouraging. It was followed by others from Sir George Ramsay, Sir John S. Forbes, Sir John Ogilvy, M.P., and George

Kinlock, Esq. of Kinlock, all of which were encouraging and calculated to keep hope alive. There was also the friendly advice and good wishes of Robert Chambers, of *Chambers's Journal ;* the expressive words and kind sympathy of Duncan M'Laren, ex-Provost of Edinburgh ; and the Christian expression of a sympathetic heart from Thomas Cooper, author of the " Purgatory of Suicides."

And to represent the ministers of the gospel, there was a letter from the Rev. Dr M'Gavin, under whose pastorate I first commemorated the death of my Saviour ; one from the Rev. Principal Tulloch, who, because of his readiness to express his mind, was amongst the first to speak publicly of me, so as to help to gain that popularity as a teacher which never left me so long as my health permitted me to follow that " delightful task ;" and there was the familiar handwriting of the Rev. George Gilfillan, my dear and constant friend, the same yesterday and to-day.

Nor did the Tweed bound these expressions, proving that " man is dear to man." England was well represented by some of whom I had not heard before. I may here, in passing, refer to two of the latter class,—both in London,—one a master baker, and the other a journeyman gardener,—one a Scotchman and the other an Englishman, but both were moved by the same cord—that of humanity ; both shewed the same spirit—that of kindly sympathy ; both are engaged in advancing the same heavenly work—the glory of God and the happiness of man. Both had read my Autobiography, and they must each send a letter, in both of which reference is made to " Auntie Maggie," and in a very touching manner ; and both, like others, remembered the children, proving that they had kindly, manly, goodly hearts. The one says, " Go on in the strength of God ; " the other says, " I commend you to God." The one says, " ' Excelsior ' is your motto, and stick to it ; " the other says, " God will soon make way for you, and give you what you need to make you, your good wife, and dear children comfortable."

Here, thought I, is a union of sentiment, a union of hearts, a union of action—most remarkable, and yet the writers of these letters may not have seen each other, *but both are British*—both are representatives of two great and united nations, trusting in God and good work.

Nor was Ireland behind in this respect. I have before me expressions of sympathetic inquiry as kind as any ever uttered in Scotland or England. The writers I have not yet had the pleasure of seeing face to face, because I have not yet visited the " Green Isle ; " but I long to see it, especially as I then may meet with my friends in Erin, which gave us Curran and his wit, Grattan and his eloquence, Moore and his poetry, and many other splendid and glorious gifts which have helped to bless the United Kingdom.

III. WHY I VALUE THE QUEEN'S LETTER.

Often have I read this bundle of letters, and as often have they filled my heart with gratitude to God and the writers; but I may be allowed here to refer more particularly to one— that indited by her Majesty the Queen.

Never had I better reason than at this time—even whilst yet waiting anxiously for work, and feeling severely pinched from want of a steady income—to believe in that strong and grand humanity which is implanted in our nature by our heavenly Father; that humanity which tells of one human heart, and is ever enhanced, because it is elevated and sanctified, when brought in contact with the light and love of Christian principles. It may be crushed, it may lie as all but dead, yet let the pressure be removed—let the filth and mist of wickedness and prejudice be scattered—let the rays from the Sun of righteousness but shine upon it, and then its tendencies manifest themselves to the happiness and usefulness of all concerned.

Nevertheless I was yet in the midst of trials, for never were envy

B

and malice more determined to crush me than at the moment her Majesty's letter came to hand. Some say they care not for the world, nor what any one can say concerning them; but I cannot say so. I wish to be in favour with man as well as to be in favour with God, and that because I can then be the more useful. Some declare that the abuse of certain people is ineffectual; but they forget that there are others whose word, whose *gossip*, has some weight, and who are ever watching to catch something as it flies; which something, however petty and groundless, is retailed with all attention to particulars, followed by the words, " I could not have thought it." This goes a little further up, till its baneful influence begins to tell against its subject as well as usefulness. How galling to meet one whose friendship was valuable, whose kindness had been evident, whose heart was all right, but whose opinion had been thus suddenly changed, and had therefore become cold in his manner! Such a change I had felt and lamented, and that the more keenly and sadly because it had been thus brought about. In comparative prosperity and crushing adversity, in good report and bad report, amidst struggles and temptations, I had endeavoured to maintain an " irreproachable character; " but, to the uncharitable,— those who judge prematurely,—poverty and its attendant evils rouse suspicion, while the inventions of wickedness and the ear of the thoughtless too frequently give to airy nothings " a local habitation and a name." This I had experienced, as all do who are surrounded by like circumstances, and who earnestly and fearlessly declare war against the vices of the day; but this letter opened the eyes of not a few, and hence I am not only thankful because of the Scotch caution of our good Queen in causing an inquiry to be made, but I am also deeply indebted to those who were able and willing to forward the required information to Windsor Castle.

With the press, I felt that the value of this letter was greatly enhanced, because " the gracious act was followed *after due in-*

quiry was made, and the results *proved* "*perfectly satisfactory.*"
Here are the words :—

"SIR,—Her Majesty the Queen received, at the end of the
month of October, a little work which you forwarded to her
Majesty ; and I was commanded to make some inquiries with
respect to you.   These inquiries, which have taken a longer time
than I had expected, have proved perfectly satisfactory ; and I
have received the commands of her Majesty to forward to you
the enclosed cheque for five pounds, as a mark of her Majesty's
appreciation of your attention.—I am, sir, your obedient servant,

"C. B. PHIPPS.

"Mr James I. Hillocks."

"Her word is law," said a forcible writer, lately, referring to
the influence of her Majesty for good.   And I could not help
noticing the fulfilment of this in the simple act referred to.
Even the immediate result was to me astonishing.   Not long
before this I was laid low by fever, and the most of those with
whom I had co-operated in labours of love had forsaken me—
some intentionally, others not knowing where to find me in the
ruins to which we had crept, and where I had been all but
buried.   Not many days before there were those who passed
me by as if I had committed some crime.   True, my hat was
not the best, my coat was far from being glossy, and my boots
were not waterproof ; but I was the same man in hope, in trust,
in love, and intention ; the same man in the sight of God, perhaps a little nearer to Him, perhaps even more anxious to serve
Him ; but these knew it not.   They looked at the pale face,
the feeble step, and the sorry dress, and passed by as if afraid
lest some one might see them even slightly acknowledge the
helpless invalid.   But when the press informed the public of
what the Queen had done, some of these passers-by begged "to
compliment" me "on the event."

"How remarkable !   A very few weeks before this, hid in a
miserable hovel, and now recognised and countenanced by the

highest personage in the land!" said a friend, referring to this letter. He was correct, it *was* "remarkable," and I was able, with thankful heart, to recognise in this act the merciful interposition of a gracious Providence.

The readers of "Life Story" are aware that I never was a worshipper of rank and titles, as such. Therein I stated, at the very commencement, and quoted from the poet, that with me

> " The pith o' sense, the pride o' worth,
>   Are higher far than a' that."

I admit and also admire the powerful influence of well-sustained rank; but I am aware that it is recorded on the best authority that it is not easy for a rich man to enter the kingdom of heaven, and the same may be said of the influence of rank, often perverted and converted into a means of successful intrigue and tyrannous usurpation. In both cases the power of mischief is great; and human nature, in its pride and its blindness, is so ready to yield to temptation all but omnipotent. And nowhere has this been more sadly manifested than by those elevated to thrones—to the highest places of earth. Hence, as a rule, " uneasy lies the head that wears a crown;" hence that sensitive jealousy and that want of confidence which bring about so many troubles culminating in revolutions, blood, and death. But how different it is when the crowned head is useful as well as grand, when glory and grace are blended, when the august and the serene are united, when the secret influences are exercised for good, when a subdued earnestness is manifested in quietude and moderation, when a pleasing placid dignity gives evident proofs that its source is from the rich and graceful elements of true moral greatness, and when all this is true of a queen, (as it certainly is of our Queen,) then the people yield that full confidence and enlightened admiration which personal virtues gently enforce; and as one of the people, born in their midst, reared at their hearths, and ever interested in their temporal and spiritual welfare and happiness, I feel as they feel towards our Sovereign, not so much because her queenliness is genuine, as because she is true to womanhood—tender, gentle, faithful, loving, and good.

Such are two of the reasons why I so highly value this letter, but I may name another. I should not be faithful to facts, nor just to myself, did I convey the idea that I thought light of the " pecuniary honorarium,"—her Majesty's tangible " mark of appreciation." It was a seasonable gift, a timely help, which God blessed to me and mine. And " a timely help," who can tell its worth, or what it may prevent? How many even of the honest poor suffer and fall from the want of timely help! And, alas, when they do fall, how few, even of the virtuous, rise to usefulness!

V. Leaving Scotland.

But with this recognition, with these and other proofs of sympathy, I was still without a steady income. Though I had by this time got some little things to do,—about two days' work in the course of a week,—yet I felt anxious to get more to do, in order that, as soon as possible, I might be enabled to see more domestic comfort in our home. And whilst anxiously praying and earnestly using the means within my power, events were transpiring which were soon to cause me to bid adieu to *auld Scotia,*—events which ended in an invitation to London.

Having resolved to accept this invitation, the question was how to get the means to enable me to undertake the journey. The " mark of her Majesty's appreciation," which accompanied the letter already given, had enabled us to clear off some of the more pressing claims, and helped us to taste a little of the comforts of life, which the body requires. There was a balance left, and this went to help to pay my way to London.

The amount being made up, then came what some would call the sentimental part,—the thought of leaving the

> " Land of brown heath and shaggy wood,
> Land of the mountain and the flood."

The readers of my Autobiography know that I could, in more ways than one, exclaim,—

> " O Caledonia! *stern* and wild."

Yes, but I also knew her to be a

> " Meet nurse for a poetic [struggling] child."

And hence the thought of leaving her made me weep like a child about to be torn from its mother. True, there are those who, in a strange kind of stolidity, speak of Scottish civilisation as very modern; who speak of the sons and daughters of Scotland as rude, though hardy, having lately crept out of the bogs of barbarism; and such may be at a loss to account for attachment on the part of one who had there endured so much; but there is no such astonishment on the part of those who know Scotland best. By the latter her stamina and endurance, enterprise and courage, agriculture and architecture are regarded as sublimely protesting against those who, in their self-sufficient ignorance, try to make their hearers or readers believe that whatever is Scottish is boorish. True, some there are who, by labour and skill, have to extract a precarious subsistence from a sterile soil, and the climate may not be suitable for those brought up in fashionable hothouses; but there is careful and persevering industry. And who that have traversed her valleys and climbed her mountains have not felt strengthened and invigorated? Her industrial arts, together with her facilities of transport, and many other grand and self-made opportunities, wisely and perseveringly applied, have placed her in a position to meet the contingencies of life and the vicissitudes of a society in which civilisation, in its highest and best sense, is evident and active. Was it strange, then, that I should listen to the poet's question,—a question indicating the impossibility of an affirmative answer,—

> " Breathes there a man with soul so dead,
> Who never to himself hath said,
> This is my own, my native land?"

Was it strange that I should silently but positively reply, I am not the man? The sublime and beautiful in nature, and which on this occasion stood enhanced before me, carried my mind back upon the past, and brought in review the stirring history of the strange old forms of the " dark-brown years." Yes, renewed were many of the feelings I had experienced when on her towering mountains gloomy night had spread her dark mantle, and the vivid lightning darted along as on the wings of the wind; when the hoarse moan in the hoary cliffs had been replied to by the sullen roar of the distant stream, dashing in its foaming course from crag to crag; when in sunny days I had traversed her lonely valleys and sequestered shades, by the side of her placid lakes and crystal streamlets, through her green woods, and under her leafy bowers, watching the flight of the lark, and listening to the song of the blackbird, admiring the shaggy thistle and wild daisy. All these sounds rushed into my ears, all these sights flashed before my eyes. And to me they had been not only endearing but useful, because of the interesting association and overwhelming thoughts they bring up and suggest. To none do I yield in my thorough admiration of rural life, but I had also learnt that the most beneficial, and hence the greatest study of mankind is man, the history of nations, the biography of the leaders; and never were such themes more worthy of attention than in Scotland. I refer not now so much to the day of dun shields and gleamy spears, when her veteran warrior's voice rang through the echoing isles like the thunders of heaven,—when the son, stately in his youthful locks, was bright as the morning, fleet as the roe, and brave as the lion; to the stormy days when the shaggy brows of her heroic children bespoke their gathering rage, their eyes sparkling with fire. These were stirring times, and they yet stir the soul of him who gives them even a thought; they were the days of trial and preparation, a training for that hardy energy and daring heroism which afterwards gave effect to her unshaken zeal and noble patriotism. I refer as much, perhaps more, to the glorious triumphs of peace, manifesting, as they have done, that persevering industry which has enabled her to tower to the utmost heights of knowledge and honour.

All this was not likely to escape the mind of one so roughly cradled, but there were also other ties less remote. Not only was I about to leave friends as true and kind, as my foes had been false and cruel; but also the ground whereon my parents had struggled, in the dust of which they are resting, waiting the sound of the trumpet that shall call them to put on immortality. A mother, whose beauty and purity and affection to me were all the more lovely, unsullied, and tender, because I had never seen their decay; to this day they are as attractive, as humanising and elevating as when I first heard of them from the lips of my poor dear father. And what feelings try to get vent when I think of him! the "brave tar," who, in his happy moments, and with emotion, would sing,—

"All in the Downs our fleet lay moor'd."

One of those who were proud of the gallant Nelson, of those who made our grim bulwarks terrible—one of the oceanic lifeguards who manfully defended our noble isles. This poor weaver toiling from early morning till late night, that he might support his family; enduring the ills of poverty, and dying in their midst.

These were no mere sentimental emotions. They were real, they are lasting; but they were deepened by others springing from the same fountain. For a time, at least, my departure was to take me many miles from my sweet children and their dear mother,—of those whose lovely faces and loving kisses had given energy when strength was all but gone,—of leaving her with whom I had co-operated in every good word and work. "He is everywhere present, in Edinburgh and in London," were her parting words. What a consolation, thought I, as the train started from Princes Street!

VI. How the Invitation to London was brought about.

With my heart thus filled to overflowing, I left, saying,—

> " *Land of my sires!* what mortal hand
> Can e'er untie the filial band
> That knits me to thy rugged strand?"

Some sleep, some amuse others, some read, some observe on the rail, and some there reflect on the past. I could not sleep, and my chief work was thinking, and the leading theme was, *How the invitation to London had been brought about.* Often before this had I rejoiced in the conviction that I was ever under the watchful eye of Providence; but never did I perceive this more clearly than when I retraced, step by step, the incidents which had run into this one, as a series of links in a chain, each link being essential to the whole; never before had I a more distinct view of God's mysterious ways and kind purposes than when I looked from the beginning to the end—from the time when a kind friend, placing his hand softly on my head, said, "You may be a minister yet;" from that time to my leaving for London I had not forgotten, never shall I forget, the affectionate tone and assuring look of that dear friend when he uttered these words. The incident encouraged me in adversity, and urged me onward in prosperity.

But that which also had a share in this result was my meeting with a gentleman in a railway carriage. Our conversation was pleasant, and to me it proved to be profitable. That which occupied the greater part of our time were the duties and responsibilities of the preacher and pastor, and the difficulties which a poor man finds in attempting to rise to that position, because of the long and expensive course prescribed by the United Presbyterian Church, to which I belonged, and to which I had adhered amid many inducements to leave its communion. But my new acquaintance incidentally informed me that he was a Congregationalist, and afterward endeavoured to shew that it was possible in that body for a poor student, especially if he had experience in public speaking, to gain his aim, and yet share the advantages of the education and training necessary for such an important position.

This induced me to give the whole matter, from this point of view, a careful and prayerful consideration. Years passed with the ups and downs of life, but no amount of adversity could cool the desire of my life, it followed me throughout all its joys and sorrows. Hence I ventured to write to the Rev. Dr W. L. Alexander in relation to the subject. He kindly gave me some wise counsel on the point, and I resolved to put his hints in practice whenever Providence might place an opportunity in my way.

Again years rolled on, yet only to increase my desire, till shortly before the attack of the all but fatal fever, when comparative prosperity and positive usefulness once more seemed to attend my efforts, and, as usual, my hopes rose some degrees. At this time I revealed my mind to my dear pastor, one of the most loving and lovable of real friends, the Rev. William Reid of the Lothian Road United Presbyterian Church, Edinburgh. I told him all that had passed in my mind in relation to Congregationalism. He encouraged me, and related an instance of successful aspiration on the part of a young man who had felt as I felt.

The events which surrounded that fever passed off, leaving their results, and one was a *stronger desire* thus to serve my Preserver and Redeemer. How wonderful are the links, and how nicely fitted the chain, God in his providence makes! As is stated in "Life Story," before I left the breakfast-table, to which Dr Guthrie had so kindly invited me, with a large company of other friends, he thoughtfully gave me a note to the editor of the Edinburgh *Witness* newspaper. This note gained for me the good wishes of a new friend; and when that little book appeared he read it with such an interest that he thought of treating a London friend to a copy. This gentleman, to the editor's surprise, soon wrote to say that the author was not altogether unknown to him. He further stated that, as he perceived by the book that I was still aiming at the ministry, he might be able to help me. The editor's friend was no other than the Rev. James H. Wilson, whom I had incidentally met years before in Aberdeen, where I, by invitation, had gone to lecture. Then Mr Wilson was there labouring to reclaim the " Moral Wastes," by his Ragged Church and School, and other means of evangelisation; but by the time my little book appeared he had gone to London and become the Secretary for the Home Missionary Society. But Mr Wilson did not only write to his friend, he sent a letter of encouragement to me; and whilst he stated his willingness to aid me, he honestly and carefully told me that he was in connexion with and labouring for those known as Congregationalists. This led me to tell him what had been transpiring, and how I was prepared for the charge of church fellowship; that though previously, and up to that time, no inducement, no pecuniary benefit, not even situations promising usefulness, could draw me from that body to which I first attached myself, and in which I had derived so much spiritual benefit, yet the reasons which had led me to remain were not to be found in this case, that here I did not and could not see any sacrifice of principle, the only difference being the recognising of a governing power in the assembly of representatives from the churches of the body to which I belonged, whereas each of the churches of the body which I was now proposed to join governed itself.

Having said so, because I felt it, and having also sent to Mr Wilson the letter with which Dr Alexander had sometime before favoured me, I waited the result, believing that God would sooner or later answer my prayer, to give me increasing opportunities of real usefulness. Where my lot might be I could not conjecture, I was willing to go anywhere to be useful and provide for my family. Imagine if you can my joy, and perhaps I should even add my surprise, when I read this paragraph in a letter written by Mr Wilson, addressed to our mutual friend: "As regards Mr Hillocks, if he could find his way to London this week, I could send him to one of our mission stations for a month on probation. It is in Kent, and I think he would find it a very suitable sphere indeed for a beginning."

This was the way by which my invitation to London was brought about. How remarkable! Truly "God moves in a mysterious way," said I to myself as I crossed the Tweed for the first time, and felt I was in England.

CHAPTER II.

I. FIRST IMPRESSIONS.

READER, having come thus with me, I can easily anticipate some of the questions you would ask were we face to face. Doubtless one such would be, "*What think you of the great metropolis?*"

There is no question more natural. Were I in your place, most likely I would put the same question. Who that has heard —and who has not heard?—of the absorbing, interesting, and subjugating influence of London, has not wished to see it? And who that can write his own name, and has had this longing desire gratified, is not expected to say something, or write something touching his first impressions of the great centre and mighty source of commerce and civilisation? "This is the realisation of a life-long dream, and I do not know what to think—I am overpowered," said a gentleman to me lately, referring to his visit to London, and was yet staring in wonder at every person and thing with which he came in contact.

"What is your impression of London?" I asked this stranger.

"I cannot tell you," was his reply, *emphasising* every word.

So I felt, realising the force of De Quincey's words when he said, "No man was ever left to himself for the first time in the streets, as yet unknown, of London, but he must have been saddened and mystified, perhaps terrified, by the sense of desertion and utter loneliness which belong to his situation. No loneli-

ness can be like that which weighs upon the heart in the centre
of faces never ending, without voice or utterance for him; eyes
innumerable, that have no 'speculation' in their orbs which *he*
can understand; and hurrying figures of men and women wend-
ing to and fro with no apparent purpose intelligent to a stranger,
seeming like a mass of maniacs, or oftentimes like a pageant of
phantoms."

Such I believe to be the feeling of most people on their first
entrance into London; but I feel convinced that most people
have their peculiar as well as general impressions; though, as
with me, they may not be easily defined; or it may be, as it
often is, that there is the absence of that descriptive power
which characterised the writings of De Quincey. As it is, how
varied the records which we have of such first impressions!
This is not to be wondered at when we recollect the fact—a
natural tendency—that many, very many, if not all, look at this
world emporium from that point of view which is nearest to
their own position in life and condition of mind. This being the
case, how different must have been the impression made on the
mind of her Royal Highness the Princess Alexandra, when passing through London to become the Princess of Wales, from that
of a deserted, penniless woman from the country, entering London
in search of a cruel, faithless husband! The story of the sign being
regarded by one as gold, and by another as copper, because the
one only looked at the golden side, while the other kept his eyes
upon the copper side, is often repeated by those who have written
about London. This accounts for the various shades of opinion
touching London at first sight, and perhaps it had something to
do with my first impressions. I cannot say it had, but I endeavoured to look at things as they were, or appeared to be, apart
from my relation to them. And yet I must say the reality did
not come up to the imagination. True, I saw not a few places
of interest and curiosity,—many places, the names of which have
been long and frequently recorded in hundreds of story and other

books, and were thereby as familiar as " household words;" but I must say I was greatly disappointed in the aspect as a whole, so much so that for some time I felt difficult to believe that I was in London.

Perhaps I had done that which was not correct in forming some notion of London, from the fact of its being frequently compared with other cities which had been, or still are, great centres. " Modern Babylon" is an appellation frequently applied to London, but where are the lofty walls, the brazen gates, and the hanging gardens of which we read as associated with the splendid Assyrian capital? Again, London is not unfrequently compared to Rome; and the former is, as the latter was, the vast centre of a powerful empire, able to sway the land and sweep the sea; the one is upon the Thames as the other is upon the Tiber; but we look in vain throughout the British capital for anything approaching the vast beauty and grandeur which wealth and a favourable position insured to the Eternal City. The magnificent architecture, the marble edifices, the glorious columns, the lofty arches, the lifelike statues, and all that united to form the sublime and beautiful of the ancient city upon the Tiber, are not, at least in any great number, to be found in the modern city upon the Thames. The truth is, the most intelligent and best informed cannot say to what London may be likened. Though in it there may not be so much of prominent beauty centered in any given spot as may be visible in other great cities, especially such as may have been under the sway of an autocrat; yet there is that vastness and variety which could only exist in a country like ours, where thousands of minds as well as hands are at work. There are not the pyramids, but there is the pavement; there is less of the ornamental, but more of the useful. And notwithstanding our practical ideas touching utility, to which our unparalleled commerce gives birth—that which tells of magnificence unequalled in the world, stands out in London in bold relief. This is not only evident in its palaces

and parks, bridges and docks, but also in that grand spectacle—
the people at work.   The truth is this, the imperial city is only
like unto itself, both in relation to influence and construction.

And if ever it was difficult to give in words one's idea of
London, especially in its physical aspect, it is now.   No letter-
press picture can be presented so as to leave a permanent impression of its size and form upon the mind of the reader; and
even were it possible so to spread out the conglomerate map of
London *as it now is*, there are a variety of means at work which
threaten not only to destroy the present aspect, but also at no
very distant day to demolish London as a city *to live in*.

From what I have seen and heard, I can easily believe that
it is long since the wealthy of London began to go out of town.
Nor are they to blame.   Those who know, and have the chance
of acting upon the knowledge, that lungs were formed to take
in *fresh* air and let the foul go out, are very likely to go to the
suburbs, and, if need be, to the more outlying villages; and
hence London is continually stretching into the country, and
colonies of the wealthy are being formed further and further off.
And besides the natural desire to escape as soon as possible
from underneath the carbon-loaded cloud which canopies the
metropolis, a multiplicity of railway schemes threaten to blockade
her thoroughfares, choke the river, and make the city one vast
central termini.   These beleaguering armies do not only threaten
to invade, even already they are daily turning up her streets and
houses as a labourer turns up his lime and sand.   While I write,
this great metropolis is being so changed by the shovel and
wheelbarrow, that if one is laid aside, or goes into the country
a few weeks, on returning, he is led almost to doubt the existence in him of that organ called " locality."

And let it be remembered that whilst I was at first disappointed with the aspect as a whole, I confess that I had not then
visited all the places, and examined all the points of attraction
to which sight-seers go.   Not that I passed by any of them as

unworthy of notice. No, I love the grand and the interesting wherever seen, especially as seen in London. Who that has any of the emotional within him could pass St Paul's Cathedral, Wren's greatest monument, without being overwhelmed in unutterable astonishment as he marked its solemn grandeur and stately proportions? Again, if I were to give way to the flow of my soul touching the various sights I have seen, and their associations, I might write a volume on the poets' corner in Westminster Abbey, for let me say that, like many other young men, I once thought I was a poet.

Again, what author—be he ever so humble, and his production ever so small—has not visited "The Row" on his reaching London. Of course, I do not mean the "Rotten Row," but Paternoster Row—that street, which those who have not seen it may be led to regard as broad, clean, and commodious, but which, in reality, is narrow, dirty, and inconvenient. But though the shops are not magnificent, though the windows cannot be regarded as large, yet there are strange associations connected with this emporium of letters—associations which cluster round every corner—the meetings of authors and publishers, artists and engravers, printers and bookbinders, and the immense issue of publications on all conceivable subjects, all tend to bring up to the reflecting mind matter interesting and instructive.

And to leave literature and come to the commercial, there is room not only for amazement but instruction—at least so *I* felt. I refer to the varied and ever-changing scenes which surround the great and crammed storehouses along the Thames ; the immense traffic and rushing masses at Cheapside, Leadenhall, and other streets, through which lofty piles of precious goods pass and repass ; and allied to such reflections are those connected with the great extent, the peculiar construction of the Docks— the great centre of attraction of the four quarters of the world— the mighty mart which ever presents a scene interesting to the curious, and a source of healthy reflection to the thoughtful

C

—the blessing it is to mankind that this centre and source of a world-wide commerce is open to all the tribes of man—

> " From where the orient sun salutes the morn,
> To where he dips his golden beams in night."

These, and a thousand others are pleasant and inviting themes upon which to enlarge, but I must leave them to other pens, only adding, that I soon felt that the vastness of London is overwhelming; its greatness is immense—morally as well as physically importing and exporting not only for the citizen, but for the stranger; not only for the British public, but for " the great globe itself." But one needs not be long here—with eyes and ears open, and mind given to reflection—before he finds, that whilst the grandeur is beyond description, the wretchedness cannot be described. Yet, to behold the strange elements of human character, as seen in the various phases of the restlessness of this mighty city, is to listen to the sublimest of sermons, touching the evolving and eternal purposes of life. Every step has its purpose, every look as well as every word has its meaning, every faculty as well as every nook of space is occupied—the intensity is as grand as the diversity is great.

II. HOLIDAY-MAKING.

Amongst other sights which helped to fix my *first* impressions of London, were those I saw during what is called Holiday-making.

I refer not now to the doings of such roughs as are mixed up with what are called London mobs. By these every consideration, save savage selfishness, is lost sight of. I speak of what one would suppose to be the best chance of seeing the best behaviour of Londoners in their holiday attire and holiday temper.

Though, even yet, I do not find myself so sufficiently versed i the *Acta Sanctorum* as to be able, off-hand, to name all the canonised and popular English holidays, yet I have carefully watched the various developments of disposition as manifested on such occasions, and my impression is far from being favourable. In London, I find that Easter-Monday stands out amongst the chief days for holiday-making. The truth is, all the "saint" days put together—St Andrew with his thorny thistle, St Patrick with little shamrock, St David with his green leek, St Valentine with his love letters—are not equal to this Saint Monday. Weather wet or fine, it is sure to present a moving mass — some of whom are bound for the country, some for the surrounding fair, some for the parks, and the rest seem to move with the mass anywhere. Then it is that the million is effervescing. All is bustle, for every one is brimful of excitement.

As a whole, holiday-making did not produce on my mind a favourable impression. True, the unfavourable aspect is greatly and happily modified by the appearance and general behaviour of many of the better paid of the working classes, who, as well as the rest, are evidently determined to be happy and merry; anxious with "squibs and cracks and wanton smiles" to make others like themselves. There they are in lively groups as neighbours, comrades, friends, and relatives, frequently manifesting some of the noblest characteristics of the true British workmen. There is "father" and "mother," with their boys and girls not far distant, indicating something like a desire to be free from a healthful restraint, yet yielding to paternal control. And there, too, is the young wife, (often very young,) a little way before her gallant but youthful spouse, who carries that sweet charmer, the "first baby" in his arms, somewhat awkwardly, but as carefully as he can. Yes, and not far distant, indeed, looking with something between envy and hope on the young mother, is that smart, smiling creature, somewhere between a girl and a woman, talking freely to her "young man."

But, amidst all this unbounded warmth and hearty display of merriment—of even *this* portion of the swarming masses, there was a wild gaiety, a mirthful levity, which, if anything, is at least unbecoming. And they are surrounded by unfavourable circumstances within and without. They are not only assailed everywhere by strong temptations, but many have left home as supporters of the drinking habits, and not a few are already under the sway of vitiated appetites. And as for the company they are in, what is it? Alas, for the results.

Those to whom I have referred, have been designated the better paid of the working classes, but I do not mean to say that they are better behaved than their less favoured brethren. Pay has more to do with comfort than with morality, though it may, and does effect both. A poor man may be honest, and a rich man may be a rogue. The company to which I particularly refer as unfavourable, is chiefly that of those who live upon their wits at the expense of those who follow an honourable course of life; and let it not be forgotten that St Monday, and every "*Saint*" day that is thus rendered "*holy*" by unreserved homage, sends forth, in large numbers, the fearful proofs of sad depravity as well as of deplorable wretchedness, vice, and crime, as well as filth and squalor, of the deepest dye, swell the rolling mass wherever stopped or wherever bound. In their place, or on their way to play their parts in the midst of coarse sport and uproarious noise, are the smirking clown, the poor columbine, and the faded harlequin—the bull-dog pugilist, the dark gipsy, and the talkative quack—the card-sharper, thimble-rigger, and the pickpocket; but more dangerous than all this is the demon, strong drink. It is this monster, with the help of his agents, that leads the greater number of holiday-makers to prefer the poisonous to the refreshing, the debasing to the elevating. One would readily suppose that London might well prove to be a noble exception to this sad rule; but such is not the case, and this blackens the blackest aspect of a metropolitan holiday.

None require the benefit of a well-spent holiday more than any Londoner, and none have a better chance. Not to speak of the country spots, which cheap trains bring so near to him, there are the parks and gardens which encompass the metropolis, and which draw upon our national exchequer to the amount of not much under a hundred thousand pounds a-year. And there are the exhibitions, museums, picture galleries, and other great and worthy sources of entertainment and instruction for holiday-makers; but here, as elsewhere, there are other sources of "amusement," falsely so called; other "gardens" beside Kew Gardens; but too many reject the pleasing and useful means of improvement provided by the nation and good friends; too many foolishly seek enjoyment in beer shops, gin palaces, and other strong drink rookeries, falsely called pleasure-grounds. Hence, though in the morning there is politeness, in the evening there is rudeness; many who in the morning seem "merry as a marriage bell," are in the evening like furies from the depths of hell. A few hours, where strong drink and its drinkers make up the leading features of the scene, and the "nods and becks and wreathed smiles" are changed for rough jests, blustering threats, and hard blows; and as the curtains of night make dark the holiday sky, the scenes also darken. Within and without the metropolis are sad proofs that the so-called enjoyment of the so-called holiday turns out to be—in the sad experience of both sexes—what so-called enjoyments too often are.

> " Such violent delights have violent ends,
>   And in their triumph die; like fire and powder,
>   Which, as they kiss, consume."

III. SUNDAY IN LONDON.

Another of the characteristic features which greatly helped to confirm my first impressions, so far as the black side of London is concerned, were the scenes, what is to be seen and heard, in this metropolis on Sunday.

This is an interesting theme. It involves a variety of subjects; but it is not my purpose to discuss them here. At present, it would be out of place to review the various ideas entertained and expressed in regard to Sunday in London. I mean merely to refer to it as leaving an impression on my mind, yet, I may, in passing, say that my convictions, and hence my sympathies, are with those who regard that day as holy unto the Lord, as sacred as well as dear to every Christian, as instituted by God in mercy to man, as divinely blessed to those who set it apart for special communion, prayer, praise, and edification, as bearing the special seal of heaven, and standing out, in Providence, as an emblem of the rest to come, as " the day the Lord hath made," as " the torch of time," as " the light of the week," as " the working man's true charter."

Apart from the various statements made for and against the Sabbath as a sacred day of holy rest, it is well-known that there is more than one idea extant respecting Sunday as seen in London. The French have one, the Scotch have another, and perhaps the English regard both as somewhat extreme. For instance, M. Assolant, of the *Courrier du Dimanche*, says that the passing of a Sunday in London is the " summit of all miseries ;" and for this reason, " the inhabitants," he says, " are not allowed to walk about, to eat and sing as they please." Perhaps, feeling that this statement is rather strong, he qualifies it by saying, " You may talk or walk, so says the law, but you can do so only at hours previously fixed, and not at the hours you wish, for this would be indecent, improper, and quite shocking. You may eat, but you must do so before or after divine service. You may drink, but it must be in your own home, and not in a public place; and if you want to sing, you must not sing anything but psalms."

Now, my impression was, and is, quite the opposite of this. I can assure him that on the morning of my first Sunday in London, I could not exclaim with the poet—

" How *still* the morning of the hallowed day !"

and, I may add, that my after experience can best be expressed in the old ballad phraseology thus :—

> " Go where you will, up and down every street,
> Some sort of cry you are sure for to meet ;
> In winter or summer, as the time of year flies,
> You will find in London the *melody* of cries."

Most sincerely do I wish that my first impressions might have been worn off, that better ones had taken their place, but, alas, such is not the case. That impression was deeply fixed, and because of this amongst other scenes which passed before me. Betwixt ten and eleven of the morning of the first day I heard the Sabbath bells in London, I was threading my way to Cheapside when two men attracted my attention. One was very rough in dress, manners, and speech ; it appeared as if he had been born and bred in the sphere in which he was evidently moving. But his companion was not of the same stamp of character, though now his equal in social and moral debasement. He had a very shabby hat, set slantingly upon his head; his shaggy hair had once been black, but the rich gloss had given way to the dry gray. His face was dirty, and the beard did not seem to have been cut for a fortnight or three weeks. His coat had once been good, but now it was besmeared with that slimy stuff which generally covers the rags of the smoking drunkard. No fault could be found with his vest, for he had none; and as for his trousers, " Clo' ol' clo " would scarcely have accepted of them as a gift. His shoes had plenty of air-holes, but no laces ; evidently they had not been brushed since they had been gathered from some dunghill. But such men were not neglected even in the street. Some good friends had just passed and given each one a tract. This had given a turn to the conversation, and the last described man would be a preacher in his way; and, in mock solemnity, he uncovered his head, revealing a large and lofty brow. He read part of the tract, as if reading a sermon, speaking in a voice that would have done honour to Exeter Hall, and indicating no small share of previous training. All of a sudden he stopped; the reason was soon evident. Not far distant, and approaching, is a woman—such as is to be seen in those drunkaries next to the lowest. Her face, blue-red, was set with a firm determination; her dress, gaudy and flounced to the waist, was crushed as if she had slept in it all night. Before her dangled a bunch of small keys, and in her hand was a large one. She made for one of the corner dens of iniquity, and no sooner did she open the door than the two men and others rush in, as if drawn by some cord, or driven because of some wild beast following. A few minutes more and the door is again opened, and as quickly shut. Again, the mock preacher is in the street, with a bottle in one hand and the tract in the other. Holding the bottle as high as he could reach, he called out to those around him, "This, this is my religion; gin is my god," and off he went, followed by his companion and the loud laugh of those now gathering round this corner of corruption.

But shocking as such scenes are, I found that the morning was nothing compared with the evening. To me the blazing and blasting traffic in strong drink on Sunday and night was something new and horrifying. "What a sight!—a London gin palace, and open on Sunday!" said I to myself, as I looked upon one of those brilliant and fearful avenues to hell. What a horrid sepulchre! True, it is grand and gaudy. With putty and paint, pewter and crystal, ivory and glass, brass and mahogany, all polished and burnished, and in the glare of gas—what an effort to make the black demon take the shape of an angel of light! How vain! Bedeck a grave with roses, and it is a grave still.

Yes; and after observation proved that the morning is nothing compared to the evening. One illustrative case in point. On one occasion, by invitation, I had gone to the Sunday evening meeting of that useful branch of the Young Men's Christian Association, meeting in the Priory, Islington. About nine o'clock

·I left for home by Upper Street, entering Highbury Gate, passing through Highbury Vale, round by the New River, and on to the Railway Arch, Seven Sisters' Road.

Upper Street, from the Priory to Highbury Gate, was thronged with all classes. The public houses, as elsewhere, were all open, and the gas lights were flaming as brilliantly as on other nights. Within these strong drink dens, glasses and pots were being filled and emptied, and precious hours wasted in uproarious discussions on trifling subjects. And near to the mouths of these places is much unpleasant noise. From the demeanour of the larger number there, it is too evident that the sanctification of the Sabbath is not in their hearts. Many are almost " tight," as they would say. Disgusting and sad were the scenes.

Passing on, I found, to my surprise, the quiet of Highbury Place was being much disturbed, its semi-rural aspect greatly disfigured by a variety of groups of people more or less advanced in the various stages of intoxication. From the moving crowd arose roars and laughter, mingled with curses. A young woman, crinolined to the waist, is " the observed of all observers." From the crown to the heel, she is " The Woman in White,"— white bonnet, white feather, white fall, white dress, white cloak, and white boots. This whiteness was not an emblem of purity certainly ; for that which proceeded out of her mouth told the nature of her character. She had been " indulging *rather* freely," and hence missed the mark of the so-called "moderation," and her manner, as well as her dress, had become such as to invite marked attention. She says she is bound for " the Barn," and that is enough to tell what she is. All this hubbub has been caused by an unknown young rogue purposely trampling upon her skirt of extra great dimensions. But she is off, and shouts of laughter follow her.

On a little further is another crowd, in the centre of which are a husband, his wife, and their children. One child is in his arms, another is fastened into the tucked-up skirt of the mother's gown, whilst two more children are at their feet, looking up and around most pitifully. Both parents are intoxicated. The father can scarcely speak, though he had stopped short to scold the mother, who is so far gone in drink that she seems to be utterly oblivious as to the kind of treatment she is receiving at his hand. Their mutual and silly recrimination is affording no small share of deplorable amusement to the by-standers, who continue to send forth shouts of laughter at every fresh sally.

Not much further on is another crowd. The special objects of attention are a mother and her two children, one an infant in her arms, the other is by her side, evidently an intelligent and a reflecting child. She, with her husband, had been drinking at the "Tea Gardens," doubtless something stronger than tea. One of those who go there to make a conquest had succeeded. With this one the poor woman's husband had absconded. "He has gone with that strumpet again," was the sorrowing mother's reply to the question put as to the cause of her excessive grief. Still crying with rage, and denouncing her husband in no measured terms, she, after a pause, added, "It's not the first time; but I'll find her out, and pull the heart out of her."

And not far distant is a band of young men, varying from fifteen to thirty years of age. They are arm in arm, occupying the entire breadth of the road. Each one is more or less intoxicated, so much so, that it requires the combined efforts of the whole to keep some of them from measuring their length upon the ground. Their conversation is of the rudest kind, and spoken in the most boisterous manner. Utterly regardless of the effects of a gross outrage on the most common sense of propriety, not to mention the higher claims of the Lord's-day, they sing. "The Strand, the Strand," is the song in which they all join as they *marched* along.

Shortly after this I found myself pressed much by the moving mass. Side by side with the jaunty young man and his reckless female companion, is the citizen of the better paid class, with his wife and child, and in many cases by his side are the boy and girl, not yet let loose from paternal restraint, but able to observe and to reflect. This strange concourse of people and their surroundings give the scene the aspect of a rough fair, with all its noise and vice. The weighing machine is in full operation, at a penny a-head. The owner, anxious to gratify his female customers, while filling up the card, and giving it to the girl, takes care to assure her that she is precisely the weight of the Princess Royal previous to her marriage. This is done in such a manner as to give an opportunity for some lewd remark and a roar of laughter. There, too, were the vendors of moustaches and paste-board noses, of all shapes and colours, " for the small charge of one penny." The moustache and the nose serving as a kind of mask, to give a striking appearance on entering the pleasure grounds, and to disguise the wearers so as to allow more license in their speaking and acting while there.

All this, and much more of the same kind, I saw that Sunday evening in the neighbourhood of *licensed* " Pleasure Grounds," where strong drink may be had. And notice these facts :—1. That this was not an extra occasion. 2. That each of these so-called " Pleasure Grounds," or " Tea Gardens," or " Dairy Farms," are representative places in their way, neither better nor worse than any of the rest of their kind. 3. That there are many such places and such scenes in this great and professedly Christian London. And, with these facts before your mind, ask yourself, When such are the scenes, such the life in London *outside* of these *licensed* places, what must that be *within?* (See Chapter IV.)

But shocking as such scenes are, they only make various hideous items of a horrid whole, as is evident to all who leave these " retreats " and return to the main thoroughfares. There, on Sunday evening, we meet the crowds returning from the fields or the country, to the streets, in almost every one of which public houses of all kinds exist; where drinkers clamour for more of that liquid fire which burns up character, health, happiness, and life. So much so, that the scenes completely represent the picture painted by Him who knows the habits and the hearts of those who have " erred through wine, and through strong drink are out of the way ; " of those who " are swallowed up of wine," and " are out of the way through strong drink."

Here I do not merely refer to those who generally figure in what are called the more disgusting scenes of " low life ;" those whose faces have been made hideous, whose bodies are bloated by disease, those who scream, and swear, and fight, so as to shock the more *refined* feelings of others who—in the *morning* at least—had some idea of public decency. I mean those scenes in which figure the better-to-do, who would not *willingly* scandalise their names by such exhibitions as are so often made on their return from their pleasure-seeking on Sunday ; but drink and excitement have done their work.

Without going any deeper into this fearful pit of iniquity— drinking and drunkenness on Sunday—without leading the reader into the squalid localities where the more " repulsive creatures " prefer to lounge within, or stand around, what are regarded as " inferior " drunkaries—only inferior in grandeur and dimensions —not inferior or less powerful in the work of destruction. Without bringing up pictures from such places, and putting them side by side with those just faintly indicated, can any one be surprised that I should have a not very favourable impression of Sunday in London, with all this, and much more of the same kind—more or less black and disgraceful—before my mind ?

And yet this is only one feature of the black side. Apart from this—and certainly it is bad enough—there is the immense traffic in things in general ; and there is the work done, and the pleasure-seeking, on Sunday.

The immense traffic. Who can cast up its amount ? Imagine my astonishment when I was assured, that if the shops open on Sunday in London were placed along side of each other, they would extend beyond *sixty miles !* And yet this conveys nothing of the idea realised by actual observation. It is a fact, that many of the bakers, butchers, fishmongers, grocers, confectioners, tobacconists, news-venders, barbers, and others, openly confess that they take more on Sunday than on the other six days put together. The "tradesmen" study to meet the demands of their classes of customers. As is well known, the lower paid, and many of the less provident of the people, "go to market"—yes, to the market, and on Sunday. A glance at the Borough, Lambeth, Claremarket, the Brill, and other general marts, weekly prove the melancholy fact, that with the great mass of the people, Sunday is the market-day. Nor is this buying and selling confined to these crowded and noisy and dirty marts, it is carried on in many of the streets ; and besides, there are stall-keepers at almost every corner, and itinerant vendors everywhere from morning till night.

And as to *the work done* on Sunday—apart from the supply of this and other demands—it, too, is beyond calculation.

I refer not now to the excessive cooking, to the washing, the ironing, the sewing, the cleaning, and other matters which fill up the time at the disposal of the females ; nor do I specially allude to the preparations necessary for presenting that mighty meal—the weightiest of all considerations—the "Sunday dinner ; " nor do I refer to the special decking of Katy or Sally that she may visit the sweet shop, or traverse the street or square, showing herself off in stiff short crinolined dress and petticoats, that the neighbours might see and envy the " pretty dear ducky ; " neither do I allude to that large portion of the people who consider themselves higher in the social scale, and who, on Sunday, work " for pleasure " in their plots of garden-ground, and with not a few of whom the forenoon of that day is the time for digging, sowing, weeding, transplanting, building, fencing, constructing, and re-constructing. I refer to those who work for gain. One Sunday, I entered the main-door of a house, in which about

six families lived, and just as a rumour was going from room to
room that a child had fallen into a water-butt behind the house.
This alarm stirred the people, and of the five men who came out,
three had every appearance of having just left their work.
This practice is not confined to any particular branch of trade,
such as shoemakers, tailors, and so forth. How many carpenters,
painters, paper-hangers, and others, go out a jobbing! And in
some large shops, I am told, men are allowed, and in some cases
even asked, to work on Sunday. Not only so, when this is not
the case, the men and lads are often taken in on Sunday by the
masters of the smaller establishment where the work is noiseless.

Adding those who work, as they say from necessity—as the
servants of the public—the immensity of such employed, not
only in the general Sunday traffic, but in connexion with the
railways, steamboats, cabs, omnibuses, hotels, taverns, gin
palaces, beer shops, pleasure grounds, *tea* gardens, and all such
places—I say, add these to such as I have named, who work for
pleasure and for gain, and what a mass! Yet, after all, those
who are so employed, willingly or unwillingly, on Sunday, form
a mere fraction of such as make the Sabbath a working, a feast-
ing, a pleasure-seeking, a rioting, a fighting day.

But it is only justice to name two facts here in relation to
Sunday in London. Let it not be supposed that only the real
Londoners are to blame for this sad state of things. On Sunday,
as on other days, there are a great many strangers in London,
and on all the seven days of the week, not a few of these strangers take a prominent part in the follies and vices of London.
It must be evident to the careful observer that some of the vilest
of our places of so-called amusement are supported chiefly by
strangers and foreigners—visitors for the night, the week, and
so forth. Such are afloat on Sunday. As is well known, there
are hotels frequented by those from the same town, or country.
On Saturday and Sunday nights, these places are largely attended.
" It is astonishing how few of these strangers remain indoors on

Sunday," said a gentleman to me lately. He then named a hotel at which he frequently put up, and added that, " when taking dinner there on Sunday, not above two or three from amongst thirty or forty lodgers, sat down to dinner—all save these were out." And what astonished me still more, was hearing from the same lips, the fact that the most of these lodgers were Scotchmen. What of other hotels? And where have these strangers spent their Sundays? How many of them are free from those dark elements which make up the black side of Sunday in London? were questions which at once suggested themselves to my mind.

Again, I must be careful not to convey the idea that all those who may properly be called Londoners, and who do not attend divine service, are avowed enemies to the Sunday. " To give you an instance of this," said one to whom I was speaking on this point, and who knew London life—" two young men lodged for seven years in the house adjoining the one in which I lived, and for all that time they had neither been in church nor chapel, and yet they only went out once on Sunday, and that together, for about an hour, to smoke their pipe."

Doubtless there are not a few such in London, not so steady perhaps, but as quiet, and I mention this not to put the saddle on the wrong horse, not to make blacker those who are already black enough. Yet, the sad facts named stand out in all their blackness at all the seasons of the year. In winter, there is the ice and skating, the shooting and the fishing, for the brave marksmen must fire off on Sunday even at sparrows, because it is fashionable. And in summer, even as early as six A.M., large crowds of pleasure-seekers may be seen hurrying along with large bundles and crammed baskets of provisions, bound for the steamboat, wharfs, and railway stations. After nine or ten o'clock there seems to be something like a calm, at least the bustle is not so great till dinner is over. But then—the bakers having done their part—the bakings being under the roofs of their respective owners, and being duly despatched and washed down by what the pot-boy and the bar-maid have lately supplied,—then it is the sallying forth begins; rather, renewed in earnest. True, the provision bundles and baskets are neither so large nor so crammed as were those carried off in the morning; but as then, so now, the necks of the bottles are frequently as visible. And, to all appearance, there is something of that strong delight which is often associated with pleasing anticipations. But the realisation!—the less said about it the better, for those who uphold such a course of life on Sunday. Leaving the joking, the laughing, and drinking, which soon become the order of the afternoon, evening, and night; leaving out of count the crowded taverns in the surrounding villages, the drunken brawlers in green lanes, and the boisterous mirth everywhere; leaving all that out—for of course the London pleasure-seekers must be " free " to do as they like—and we must keep to *London* on Sunday, and really there is no need to go out of London — the picture is certainly black enough; it is black enough even were we able to forget all this, and merely name the progress of the drink and excitement which has been going on since morning.

Such are some of the facts of the case as they have from time to time presented themselves to me. There are other features—such as the fighting feature—man-fighting, boy-fighting, dog-fighting, and so forth. Upon these and other features of the more disgusting and disgraceful kind I need not enlarge, preferring rather to ask, If M. Assolant had room for complaint? If he was correct when he said, " The inhabitants of London are not allowed to walk about, to drink, to eat, and sing as they please"? Surely he is wrong in this at least. Alas, that such an array of visible proofs should, Sunday after Sunday, stand out against such a statement as that he has made.

One other question—Was I correct in my conjecture when I said that my impression of Sunday in London was (and is) quite ópposite to this Frenchman's? Could I be blamed for saying that my impression was (and is) far from being favourable? The truth is, for one who regards the Sabbath as a sacred day for holy rest; for one who values the means of grace, who is interested in the welfare of man—his temporal and spiritual welfare—to spend his Sundays in London, with his eyes and mind bent upon its black side, as has been slightly indicated, is to suffer the " summit of all miseries;" but there is also a bright side of Sunday in London; yes, thanks be to God, there is a bright side! Though the many are thus passing the Sunday, a few are waiting on the means of grace and being blessed. The faithful are endeavouring to promote and enforce "the truth as it is in Jesus;" but what is all this effort, earnest and energetic as it is, compared with vicious and fruitful tares that are every Sunday sown broad cast? And yet the Frenchman named, and others of like notions respecting Sunday, and all that is precious in Christianity, complain that there is no liberty in England on that day; yes, and they, our " *liberators*," utter their indignant protest in the name and for the sake of " the poor people!" They—the generous fellows—hurl their stock of set, cant phrases against the law which they say forbids the *poor* " to eat and drink on Sunday." How this class *loves* " the people," and yet, if they had their way, this same *beloved* people would have to work *seven days every week* that such *friends* might have the opportunity of " enjoying" themselves, of walking or riding, eating or drinking, singing or dancing, " as they *pleased*," any hour of the twenty-four belonging to Sunday! Really this is very kind. How often are the *poor* people made the horse upon which these *benevolent* social *reformers* ride to their dearly-beloved object, " liberty," to gratify *their* desires at any sacrifice. I hope the time will soon come when the people thus " so *cared for*," will be able to see that two and two do not make five; to know that cant is cant, whether from the lips of a Gaul or those of a Briton. Let the working classes, so often appealed

D

to in this respect, remember that to encourage this state of society—this working on Sunday—is to fetter and fix the chains of slavery about their necks.   It assuredly would be to the loss and suffering of the toiling masses if the enemies to the Lord's day, the Christian Sabbath, had their hearts' desires.   Knowing, as I do, the facts of the case, having had many of them from workmen's own lips, I would tremble for the sons and daughters of toil if I felt compelled to believe that the Sunday traffic is on the increase.   Let the working man join in the efforts to destroy the Christian Sabbath and weaken the restraining and constraining influence of Christianity, and in proportion as he does this, he is forging new fetters, not only to enslave himself, but his children.

CHAPTER III.

I. THE QUESTION.

SUCH is that which helped to form and to fix my first and present impressions of London; and now I hasten to return to the narrative, simply adding, that as an observer, I have kept, and mean to keep, my eyes and ears open, not as a captious fault-finder, but as one anxious to turn knowledge into a means of usefulness, desirous to know the leading causes of the disease, in order to help to apply the proper remedy in the proper manner.

I have said, that when on my way between Edinburgh and London, my chief employment was reflection—not only thinking of the past, but also occupying my mind with the probabilities of the future. No sooner did the "iron horse" begin its fiery race over English ground, than I felt the force of the ideas suggested by the words, "Going to London." How many, I asked myself, have gone to the great metropolis to push their way in that world? How many to sink? How many to rise? How many to leave the paths of righteousness? How many to walk closer with God? What shall be my lot? I had known that some had gone to London, not only to observe and to inquire, but also to wait the proper time, to enter at the proper place into the mighty whirlpool of life, to become useful and respected, favourable circumstances — coupled with sagacity, industry, and perseverance—bringing pecuniary resources and well-bought honours. But I had also known of some who had gone there to endure drudgery, to live in poverty, and die in obscurity, regretting that they had left home ; after, perhaps, showing a courage which only patience can give, they yield in despair, and die unknown and unlamented. Hence, I again asked the question, What shall be my lot ?—and that just before I left the London train at King's Cross Station on the morning of Saturday, December 15, 1860.

Why this question should have moved me to sadness and to tears, I cannot tell, past events, and the preserving care of God had enabled me to say—

> "He will sustain my weakest powers
> With His almighty arm,
> And watch my most unguarded hours
> Against surprising harm."

I felt convinced that I had left my native land not merely because I was in need of employment, but also because I was anxious to be engaged in the work for which a kind Providence had been preparing me. And yet, such is the weakness of human nature, when severely tested, that I felt misgivings—perhaps this can only be accounted for by the fact that past experience had also proved to me that there is many a slip between the cup and the lip ; and that I was feeling the severe tugs at the heart-strings, invisible but more sensitive even than the telegraph cord extending from Edinburgh to London.

II. THE DISAPPOINTMENT.

Scarcely had I left the train when I found myself enveloped in a London fog, which darted through me like an electric shock. It struck my brow as if my head had come suddenly in contact with a body of icy water, and glad was I when the cab drove up to No. 4 Bloomfield Street, Finsbury, the Home Missionary Society's office.

The Rev. James H. Wilson received me kindly, and amongst the first words he said to me were, " You are not able for work to-morrow. You must rest."

He judged correctly; I was weakly and sickly. But though I had been able, the intended place was supplied. Let me explain myself. The friend to whom Mr Wilson's letter containing the invitation was addressed, sent it to me as early as possible; but he seeing something of the express about the paragraph, (" *this* week,") wrote at the same time to Mr Wilson to say he did not think I could be in London that week, especially to speak on the next Sunday. He did so that there might be no disappointment; and he based his supposition on these two facts— 1. That I was yet very weak, and might not be able to stand the fatigue of such a long journey; 2. That I might not be able to command the necessary means so quickly.

But when I read the invitation, I was so overcome with joy, that I forgot my bodily weakness, and wrote at once to say, if possible, I would be in London on the Saturday. This letter arrived, but too late; for, on receipt of our mutual friend's letter, Mr Wilson wrote for a preacher, to prevent any disappointment at the preaching station referred to, there being no time left to write to either of us before we left home. The result was, this preacher arrived from Wales, and had gone to Kent just half an hour before I arrived from Scotland.

Though no blame could be attached to any of the three concerned—to Mr Wilson, his friend, or myself—yet the disappointment gave me a shock of no ordinary nature. Here I was in London, and my family in Edinburgh. It was difficult to tell my helpmate by letter what had happened, but it was well I did so. The letter which I received by return of post was short, but to the point; the theme was, " Trust in the Lord—for ever trust;" and so appropriate was this, our favourite maxim, that I was enabled again to carry it into practice; but only as an almost hopeless and nearly helpless creature could, feeling, as perhaps many others have felt, that there are times when it is not easy to trust in Providence so implicitly as is necessary to enable us manfully to fight the battle of life ; yet I was enabled, even here, again to realise what the persevering always find—that a difficulty is not necessarily an impossibility. As already said, I felt keenly, and at first all but despairingly, in relation to the sad intelligence, as I then regarded it.

III. What Helped to take the Keen Edge off the Disappointment.

One of the means of reviving my hopes was the fact that *my coming to London, and its object, formed a subject for the consideration of the Board of the Home Missionary Society.* I was ultimately invited to meet a committee appointed by these friends to consider the matter and to report thereon. Their opinion was everything I could wish. It resulted in the declaration, made in my presence, that the sooner I entered on my probation the better.

On this resolution, however, I ventured to offer two remarks. One was to the effect that, in the course of time, I might be so placed as to enable me to acquire more of that educational training so essential to the better performance of the duties which such a position would involve. The committee did not slight the idea, but they kept to their former decision, stating that my experience in life amongst the people, and other qualifications, which they were pleased to name, would help me greatly, at least till I entered more fully upon my duties, at which time I might resume self-education.

The other remark I offered also received their attention. I expressed a wish to become an evangelist for a year or so, that I might thereby become better acquainted with the habits of the English people. Though the broad features of the virtues and the failings of mankind may be about the same in Scotland as in England, still I could by this time perceive that there was a difference in details at least, and I had ever thought that a preacher of the gospel ought to know human nature as well as theology—the life that *now is* as well as the life *to come*. To this they agreed; the matter was settled accordingly; and my name appeared amongst the evangelists of the Home Missionary Society.

But that which helped the most effectually, at least the most practically, to take away the keen edge of the disappointment, was a *temporary engagement*, which brought in so much weekly. I once heard a friend say that an author and his publisher were nearly as closely allied as husband and wife. There is something in this. The interest of the one should be the interest of the other; the fortune of the one should affect the fortune of the other. Shortly before the incident to which I now allude, Mr Tweedie had become my publisher in a more comprehensive form than before; that is, than when his name, along with others, was only attached to my books, as agents through whom they might pass to the booksellers. The first edition of "Life Story" having gone off in a few weeks, and the cry being for more copies, I was advised to sell the copyright, and had resolved to do so, and accordingly prepared a new edition. Having faith in Mr Tweedie's wisdom as a publisher, and his character as a man of business, I forwarded to him what became the second edition. His reply was prompt and cheering, as a few sentences from it will show :—

"My DEAR MR HILLOCKS,—I am in receipt of your interesting letters, and also your wonderful autobiography. . . . . You wish to dispose of the copyright. I think you should not. I think it may be a source of profit to you for some time to come. I will do all I can to keep it in your own hands. Indeed, so anxious am I to do so, that I would willingly risk a large edition."

The necessary arrangements were immediately entered into. By invitation, I had the pleasure of an interview with him at his house at Brompton. Amongst the several topics which occupied our attention, was (to me) the all-important one—how I might best wait the time when I could enter upon the duties for the performance of which I had come to England. Being then in want of a person who could make himself generally useful in his firm, he asked if I would undertake such duties as he named. I replied in the affirmative, and in a few days thereafter I was seated at a desk in 337 Strand.

Now it was that I might have been called a business-man; now at the desk registering orders, now at the parcel table supplying the world with literature, now arranging books, now taking a hasty glance at some review of the new edition of my book—(about this time the notices from all parts were pouring in)—now extending my neck and putting my ears on edge when some one had something to say about its author, not knowing he was so close at hand, now assisting in putting to rights the figures of the " A B C Railway Guide," and then writing paragraphs, and doing a host of other things, too numerous to mention, till " meeting time," that is, the hour for the opening of the teetotal meetings. Then I washed, and brushed, and made myself as fresh as possible, that I might appear, as near as I could, a gentleman, because I often ascended the platform as an honorary deputation from the National Temperance League.

My first address in London, as a temperance advocate, was delivered in a hall near Waterloo Bridge. A newspaper, referring to this meeting, among other remarks favourable to me, stated that " one of the features of the evening was a speech from James Inches Hillocks, late of Edinburgh, author of 'Life Story.' G. C. Campbell, Esq., treasurer of the National Temperance League, introduced him, reading the letter addressed to him by her Majesty the Queen, through Sir Charles B. Phipps, in acknowledgment of receiving a copy of that book."

After this, what between appointments and invitations, my hands were full. I have been at as many as three meetings in one night, and was well received in every place, from Surrey Chapel (Rev. Newman Hall's) in the south, to the Cabinet Theatre in the north—from Paddington to Whitechapel.

But amid all this business and speechifying, I thought of those nearest and dearest to me yet across the Tweed; and having made up my mind, God willing, to struggle for bread and usefulness in London, I resolved to bring my family from Edinburgh.

This was not an easy task, but it was an important step, and the difficulty was considerably lessened by the generous and thoughtful " expression of sympathy " and " admiration " with which the Right Hon. W. E. Gladstone favoured me after reading " Life Story." How thankful we were for this timely help. " A friend in need is a friend indeed." So we felt as our hearts filled with those emotions which rush in when new causes of gratitude spring up. It was such a *lift*, to bring a dear family from Edinburgh to London, that we might the better help, cheer, and comfort each other as before.

I need not say I was at King's Cross Station anxiously waiting the arrival of the mother, yet as strong in mind and tender in heart as ever, and the children as lovely and affectionate as when I left them. The husband whose love and devotion have been returned with large interest, the father whose care and affection have been reflected in sweet smiles and entire confidence, knows how the hearts of all concerned must have beat; and those who know what it is to see the hand and kindness of Providence in such an event, are aware of the kind of gratitude which filled our hearts to overflowing, and lifted our souls heavenward.

The day was cold, and, as on the occasion of my arrival, London saw and felt one of her dense and searching fogs. It even entered our cab, and there affected the powers of breathing so much as to make the mother—mother like—exclaim, " Mercy on my *bairnies !* how can they live in this *awfu'* place !" But I had been fortunate in procuring lodgings with a congenial friend

at Kennington, and shortly after we crossed the Thames we left
the most depressing portion of the fog behind, so that she became
more reconciled to remain in the "awfu' place." A few days'
rest and other comforts enabled her again to take her place as
the mother at home—as queen of the hearth; to relieve me of
the responsibilities and troubles of the married bachelor; to enable me to feel at home again.

But she was not long set down when she gave renewed proofs
of her care, not only in seeing to my comfort as much as possible, but also in giving gentle words of needful warning.

"What is it that has made that tear start, Maggie?" was a
question I put not many weeks after her arrival.

"That Aggie (our niece referred to in 'Life Story') writes
so affectionately," was the reply; and a smile shone through the
tear, as the bright sun shines through the soft rain when the
beautiful bow spans the watery sky.

Aggie had written to her "dear Auntie Maggie," and after
some kind inquiries about her "dear uncle," had urged that he
be so watched that he may "not overwork himself *as before*."
And this letter had come in the morning after one of the nights
in which I had been speaking long and late. I had risen as pale
and exhausted as if I had not been to bed; but it was the hour
to leave for the Strand, so off I went, convinced she was right,
and that I had frequently "overworked" myself.

Like the most of really useful and endearing wives, Maggie
has veneration somewhat large, and no small share of it comes
my way. If even a hundred people thought half as much of me,
and I knew it, I am afraid it would turn my mind, or at least I
might rise two feet higher, and so overtop even an American
giant. And as for real worth, in her way of thinking, even
Garibaldi cannot stand or bear a comparison. And then how
the results of those efforts which God is pleased to bless grow
and expand in her mind. A mother is brought to see the error
of her way, and to walk in those paths which lead to peace and

WHAT HELPED TO TAKE THE EDGE OFF DISAPPOINTMENT. 59

joy. "That is not the only good," says Maggie; and then she expands on the happy husband and children, the joy and rejoicing amongst the angels in heaven because souls have been saved. She sees these children become useful men and women, Christian fathers and mothers, whose children in turn become the same. She it is who can see the beauty and feel the force of the comparison of the little stone cast into the water, sending circle after circle to the very verge, at least so far as her husband's efforts are concerned.

Doubtless, it is the force of all this, together with an influence rising out of past experience, that keeps her on the outlook and causes her now and then to endeavour to exercise a generous restraint. Her remonstrances do not often lead to an argument, but when they do, I must give in, for she has always the best of it, not only in real argument, but in telling eloquence.

"When are you to spare as much time as to spend a *forenicht wi'* (an evening with) me?" was the question she put the next morning, for the thought, and how to reveal it, had been working up her mind for sixteen or eighteen hours.

" Wi' *me*," meant nothing selfish, for her good advices were suggested by noble motives. Next to, if not equal, to her veneration, was her self-sacrifice. It was right, we must admit it, that she should look for a few of my spare moments. I never yet was able to grant this natural request without being the better for it and the abler for my duties ; but what she meant to ask was, when was I to take an evening's rest? True, she, then as before, appealed to my tenderest feelings by saying, "What would I be were you taken from me?" and the eloquence was all the more touching because of the quivering lip and the struggling tear; but she wished my preservation also that I might the *longer* continue in usefulness.

"You are *fallin'* into your *auld ways*, working all day and speaking all night," she continued ; "you'll see what will come of it as before. That terrible fever has not made you more cautious. You are just doing in London as you did in Edinburgh when last you were knocked up." And on she went till I made some kind of an attempt to hold my own by saying something about " business first, then pleasure." But she had the best of it, of course, and what really good and wise woman has not?

I met her thus, and pressed on for various reasons, to neither of which she was in any degree insensible. I was convinced that Mr Tweedie's motive in giving me the temporary situation was to help me to tide over a month or two, and hence, for that reason, and from a sense of justice, I strove hard that he might not lose by this act of kindness, so that, when the time was come, we might part as friendly towards each other as when we first met—this we did. And as to the other work, the labours of love, there were the promptings of a conviction that I was being useful. Indeed, my new and closer connexion with Mr Tweedie, so strangely brought about, and hence my introduction to many of the temperance people of London was being blessed; and I felt that I would like to work on and on, so that the blessing might be more and more enlarged. Indeed, this, together with the other turning points, formed an important link in the chain of events. Whilst the reception and excitement at the various places of meeting were very pleasing, yet the pleasure thus derived, and the luxury which springs from the thought of doing good, were not the only advantages gained by this frequent public speaking. It also introduced me to a great many of the very class of people whose wants and wishes it was necessary I should know, in order that I might thereby be the better prepared for the duties I have had to perform.

IV. ENGLISH SCENERY AND ENGLISH PEASANTRY.

Just at the time when the state of my health most required the benefit of a run into the country I began my visits to the provinces.

Sometimes I went as a preacher, " to supply," as it is called, and to preach for others by invitation ; sometimes as a lecturer on social and religious subjects; sometimes as a missionary to visit the homes ; but frequently my duties included those belonging to these three offices, as has generally been the case ever since I commenced my labours amongst the masses, for I believe in their social elevation as a means which may help towards their evangelisation. Indeed, it seems evident to me that God means both to go hand in hand.

I was always a lover of rural life. I frankly confess that it is some time since I looked upon city life as I did in my juvenile days, when I could not believe there was poetry in anything save in flowers, and streams, and stars ; but I have not lost, and never can lose my sympathy with the poet who speaks " of sermons in stones," and of the healthful emotions called forth by the running brook. I feel my heart fill with love, my soul rise in delight when seated " where the bursting prospect spreads immense around." I am aware that there is more poetic matter for healthy contemplation in the structure of a young child, but I know, too, that there is " not a flower but shows some touch, in freckle, streak, or strain, of God's unerring pencil." In city life, amongst the masses, I have learned much that is well calculated to urge one on to obtain a more profound, a more earnest view of life, its aims and purposes ; but where is the lover of nature's beauty and grandeur, who has not found that

> " 'Tis very sweet to walk into the fair
>   And open face of heaven—to breathe a prayer
>   Full in the smile of the blue firmament ?"

The poet has it, " God made the country, and man made the town;" but let us not forget that it requires town and country to make the man wiser and better, to stimulate and develop his nature—to fill his soul with noble and lofty aspirations.

In this respect my expectations rose high when I was about

to visit the English provinces; nor was I disappointed so far as God's works were concerned.

I did *not* expect to find that rugged grandeur which Scotland presents, and the lovers of the sublime enjoy; but the pleasure I derived from beholding the almost ever-beautiful, and now and then somewhat bold, yet retiring outlines of the English land-scape, has added considerably to the delightful associations which the thought of England will ever bring before my mind.   I have been from town when the grass was green, and the buds were fair; when the rich bloom qualified the emerald hue; when the falling leaf called forth varied emotions; and when almost all the flowers were gone, and nearly all the trees were bare; and this I can say, that wherever I went, in whatever time of the year, I felt convinced that if ever there was a spot on earth on which we might look for " free, fair homes," it was in England. It were easy to find fault, not with nature, the climate, nor all which combine to make a lovely picture, but with what belongs to man.   The roads, the fences, and even the hedges might be improved greatly.   With these there seems to be something slovenly; but whether the fault rests with the country squire, the farmer, or the farm-servant, I know not; yet, when feeling invigorated by the freshness, and enraptured by the loveliness, of her vernal beauty—when her summer's zephyrs were softly bathing the velvet cheeks of the country child, and the morning dew was gently expanding the tiny buds into sweet blossoms— when the waving of golden crops bespoke an abundant harvest, and called forth songs of real gratitude; when winter, even in its nakedness, presented a landscape striking and vigorous, the question—*not*, " Wherefore do the poor complain? "—but why so many miserable and helpless poor are crushed into such wretched, life-destroying hovels, forced itself upon me, and that always with a double power when I left the landscape and mixed with the people.   That there are splendid mansions, neat cot-tages, and tidy rooms, beautiful gardens, lovely flower-plots, and pleasant hedgerows in our English counties was soon evident to me, and must be so to all who look about them; but this is only the half of the truth, if indeed it be the half.

In the agricultural districts, as in the metropolis—indeed all over the United Kingdom—there are two classes, the rich and the poor. In the country, as in the town, these extremes meet; but there is a twofold aspect of industrial poverty. To the honour of Britain, there are many who are still listening to, and acting upon, the injunction—

> "Be not like dumb, driven cattle—
> Be a hero in the strife;"

but there are also many—are they not a majority?—who seek not to strive, or who have given way beneath the crushing pressure of poverty and its surroundings. It is true this may not be observable to the passers-by—those who form their ideas of the greatness of England and the beauty of the country by glancing at the surrounding stately mansions, and passing quickly the best streets,—but there are facts of which I am aware, and alas! which the poor know to exist; facts which, to a feeling heart, must at least mar the pleasing delight which the poetic soul feels when beholding the beauties of nature as seen in England. Surely Mrs Hemans had not entered the hovels of the poor when she sang about the

> "*Free, fair* homes of England."

I have read agricultural dinner speeches, and addresses delivered at " harvest homes," both before and since my visits to the provinces; yet my conviction is, that a large proportion of those in the country, especially those engaged in agricultural pursuits, are very poor and very wretched, forming the lowest grade of English humanity, lying at the lowest strata of intellectual status, utterly dependent, and frequently driven as if they were without the faculty of guiding themselves. In many cases I found poverty so ghastly, that I could not help shuddering at the miserable and helpless aspect. The coarse filthy rags which are used to robe the thin and often bent forms, and the languishing look which comes from the downcast eye, and tells of the utter want of self-reliance, make the victim an object of pity, and cause the observer to ask, " Is it possible I am in England —'glorious England,' 'prosperous England,' 'wealthy England,' '*happy* England,' '*Christian* England?'"

We hear much about the delights of agricultural life, about the enjoyment to be felt at beholding the "dawn and sunset," and there is something in this; but how many, reduced to the position of the country labouring classes, to all but imbecility, can enjoy such sights? In the poet's imagination there is something inexpressibly delightful in the words "country cottage," and there are some such very beautiful and really comfortable; but, taking things as they are in the majority of cases, how different is the experience of the poor suffering and toiling people! My journeys were frequent, and to various places; the time devoted to each place varying from three days to as many weeks; and during the time I spared no trouble that I might know, or at least have some idea of the normal condition of the people. So far as I could thus hear and see for myself, I was led to regard that condition as truly deplorable, and enough to make any Briton hide his head in shame. And what is still worse, the moral feeling and spiritual destitution seemed to be equal to the physical degradation and mental stupidity. Who is to blame for all this? It is true that those who are responsible for the present may have had but little control over the past; it is true it is very difficult to crush bad influences, the seeds of which may have been scattered long since, but what is being done now? Some there are who, to their credit, are manifesting a noble desire to see to the comfort of the toilers on their estates, who are spending large sums of money on cottage improvements; but the present state of house accommodation proves that there is much room for this worthy example being followed by others.

It is also true that evangelistic efforts are being put forth by almost every Christian denomination; and yet here we are, in the nineteenth century, worse than in heathen darkness. Cases are not wanting to prove this. Think of the murderer of the blind woman near Bristol only being three times within the church walls during his long life! How many such would there not be if circumstances rose to lead to the sad revelation? Who are to blame? God knows there is blame somewhere. We hear much of the unwieldy nature of the metropolitan parishes, but can the same be said of country districts? What an idea it is to think that so many are living in ignorance and misery, and dying in sin without hope! Surely it is time to think of the country as well as the metropolis, and of the latter as well as the former!

V. County Fairs.

Being sadly depressed because of this state of things, I remained only a short time by the running brook, and on the green grass where life is fresh and fair. How to help my fellow-creatures to a higher and better position? was with me an absorbing question.

And besides visiting the provinces for these general purposes, I have also gone to them on special occasions, such as to the county fair and to the race course, with the view of helping in efforts to rescue the benighted and the thoughtless from the snares of the wicked one, and the grasp of his wretched agents.

I have heard it said that English fairs are improving, but this only makes me ask, What must they have been before undergoing this alleged improvement? It may be true what an aged woman once said to me, " They ain't *all* extra bad as comes to fairs." I have met with the well-intended, and I believe this same sweet-stuff seller was one of them, but it must be evident to the careful observer that many, too many, belong to the

E

" extra bad." Whilst freely admitting this exception, one is compelled to regard the character of the majority of those who are said to provide the so-called " amusements," and what are as falsely designated the " refreshments," as far from being what it ought to be. By spending an hour, even in the morning of the fair, with the former, when erecting their stalls or booths or shows, one learns what is within from what comes out. I have done so, and found that it is then that they manifest their real character, especially if pressed for time, as they generally are ;—the curser is sure to curse, the passionate to be enraged, and the violent to give the cruel blow. I pitied the wives and children, and yet I was struck with the hardness of feeling evinced by these wives, in their utter indifference to the coarsest of abuse. This mode of giving and receiving went down from the *heads* to the youngest members of the family, those of them who are able to prove practically that " as the old cock crows, the young one learns." And as for the day and the night, what pen can describe them? It may be possible to give some idea of the outward appearance. Attempts have been made again and again, and as often have the lovers of the descriptive felt interested in the descriptions. One has descanted upon the fun and jollity, another on the wild beasts and outrageous pictures, a third on the *music* and the musicians, a fourth on the dances and dancers, a fifth on the acting and actors, a sixth on the sellers and the ubyers, a seventh on the jostling and bandying, an eighth on the noisy cries and various lights, a ninth on the wise pigs and biped asses, and so on till the " *awful* phenomena" of the fair has been laid before us with amazing minuteness. But the inward effects, the influence of the fair upon the mind and peace of the masses, who can imagine, far less describe? I have looked upon these saddening scenes from early morn till early morn again, and I am convinced that they are eating out what good is in society. This is not to be wondered at. It is to be expected,—not only because of the vicious cunning of those who live and fatten on the errors and miseries of the people, but because of the condition of those thus brought in direct contact with vice in its various, and to them attractive, aspects. Alas! it seems that the greater number of the swarms who rush to see the fair, and take a part in it, are by social wrongs prepared for being the more readily victimised. I have seen these people before and after the fair, and both aspects were depressing. In the morning the main avenues to the town or village are thronged. In clusters and rows the people hurry and hop along, having one object,—to get to the fair. And amongst them are not a few already flushed with beer and fierce with gin; but even those who have not yet been tempted by the demon Alcohol, bespeak something which one would not expect to find in British society,—an almost universal absence of the least indication of moral intelligence and moral government. This is evident in the looks and words of the fat farmer in his car, and the lean ploughman on his feet, (nearly all the English ploughmen I have seen are *very* lean;) in the boys and girls, who trip with light foot, if not with light heart, as well as in the toothless men and women, supporting their tremulous limbs by unpolished staves. It is truly deplorable to see our fellow-creatures so reduced,—socially, intellectually, and morally; and then to think they are hurrying on to mix with the vicious and the cunning, who live on the follies and vices of the people!

VI. The Race Course—Epsom Downs.

The same remarks apply to the Race Course, especially to the Epsom Downs on the " Derby Day." It is possible that some of the lovers of such sport would readily point to Ascot Heath as an exception, at least so far as the visible aspect is concerned. I hear that the Ascot is to the " upper ten thousand" what the Derby is to the " million." This I can believe, and suppose the presence of a fashionable decorum and a refined quietness in the former that are not found in the latter; but in both there is the waste of time and money, of character and peace; in both fortunes and happiness are gambled away, proving that many of Her Majesty's subjects, from the peer to the peasant, yet seek to obtain money otherwise than by honest effort.

But it is of the Epsom Downs I can best speak, because I have been there, and on the Derby Day. That is *the* day, the great day in England, to England's disgrace. It is said, and it really seems to be the case, that this "*holy*" day possesses a national as well as metropolitan importance. I have seen it in London in rainy and sunny days, in the evening and the morning, on the road and the rail. So far as the metropolis is concerned, the morning and the evening of the Derby day surpasses any of the other holidays, even Easter Monday. Especially on the evening of the former occasion, there is even more of the exuberant and disgusting signs of vagabond and depraved life, with very little of the modifying and redeeming elements here and there observable on the latter occasion. On the Derby evening in London the aspect is darker, the sights and sounds are more debased and debasing even than on Easter Monday. There are not so many women and children on Saint Derby as there are on Saint Monday, nor so many of the really honourable portion of the people, whose desire is *to work* for their bread, but more, much more, of the real roughs, and those who make out to live at others' expense.

It was on the bright morning of a sunny day when I arrived at Epsom Downs. Already large numbers had passed through the town on to the Downs. That which first struck me forcibly was the large numbers of ragged and wretched creatures sleeping by the road sides, in the corners of the fields, and even on the course. Poor and miserable outcasts! And about half a step higher in the social scale were those who had also rested all night on the turf, but who had already begun to vend their wares, or beg for a copper. And a step higher still, were those who were young and strong, but rough and ready, making every effort to gain a penny by *any* means. The sable minstrels (some in petticoats) shouted out their unmusical sounds, accompanying them with disgusting antics. The would-be-comic music hall *Irishmen* roared out their "whack falderals," as if they had just come from the "Coal-hole" Company. The Cheap Jacks had also mounted their yoked cars, ready to start at a moment's notice, after they had made lighter the pockets of the foolish. These and many more means of extracting money were in active operation, while the Downs were being covered with all classes of people arriving by every possible mode of conveyance. Besides the thousands on foot, vehicles of every description, from the stylish chariot to the wheelbarrow, were unloading their strange-looking parcels of humanity, which I need not here describe. Soon the crowd was dense everywhere, and those who expect to make by such gatherings were in their glory. But it was in the drunkaries where the greatest ruin was being accomplished. There many who, because they were from home, and therefore could act without restraint, and many more, under the mask of "jolly noses" and green veils, were saying and doing that of which, under healthful influences, they would be thoroughly ashamed. But in addition to all this, there was the business of the day, the betting, —and that amongst nearly all in these hell-holes, from the stout *gentleman* to the ragged beggar. But time advances, and hearts palpitate. Excitement rises, and birds of a feather flock together. In this compact mass of humanity, the brilliant now outnumber the deplorable. The gay seem to have crushed out of sight those of humble garb, and cheerfulness, real or assumed, is the feature of the Downs. An hour more, and the scene resembles an orchard in rich blossom of white, red, and every shade between, when a thin white cloud passes over the face of the bright sun at noon, and is immediately followed by another cloud, thicker and less fleecy. Then it is that the "Paddock," the spot set apart for saddling and parading the horses, presents a scene made up of anxiety, hopes, and fears. The bell rings, the police shout, " Clear the course! clear the course!" The officials become churlish, and the underlings insolent. The sleek and handsome formations of horse flesh enter the course, mounted by ornamented creatures called riders, and how eager the examinations of the passing " beauties," what a clamour (yet) within the course, upon the stands, and far distant upon the hills. " Of great power," " In amiable temper," " Good God, I am done for," and so forth, were some of the expressions I heard as the racers passed ; and the man who used the last one, what a countenance was his! His limbs seemed unable to support him, he was so intensely excited ; but, the police suiting the action to the words, " Clear the course," drove him from my view. Poor fellow, I wonder what has become of him. A few more minutes, and the intense excitement of the tremendous panorama is perfectly wild, which wildness becomes the more intensified as every false start is made. At last the swift creatures sweep the course, and in less than three minutes the tantalising uncertainty has given way to the delirious reality.

The people move away. The event of the day has passed, but what of the tremendous results, the maddening ruin, the awful misery it has brought about? I saw smiles play upon the faces of a few of the winners and those who were connected with them ; but on the frowning brows of the many who lost, were imprinted the signs of sad hearts and evil passions. Often and graphically has the Derby *day* been described, but " who can, who dare, depict the features and incidents of the Derby *night ?* " was a question lately asked in a popular newspaper,— and well may it be put.

But, apart from those more immediately concerned in the eventful few minutes—I mean the increasing betting class,— what has been done by way of spreading immorality, of adding to the awful wickedness, the debasing depravity, and social corruption of England ? Who that has carefully reviewed these scenes, and has had an opportunity of knowing somewhat of the fearful results, is not driven to the conclusion, that races, like fairs, are the devil's instruments for ruining bodies and souls.

What says the Christian to all this ?   Is it not time that those who seek the glory of God, and the happiness of man, should stand forward and dispute these fields of wickedness with the wicked one ?   Surely it is time for the intelligent Christian to be up and doing something at the fairs and races, where great masses of the people from all parts, (I had almost said, and in some cases, it is, of the world,) gather, each one leaving " footprints on the sands of time."   Yes, " footprints," but of what kind ? that is the question with those who believe that

> " Life is real, life is earnest,
>   And the grave is not its goal ;
> Dust thou art, to dust returnest,
>   Was not spoken of the soul."

It is true that some of the messengers of mercy have gone to tell of God's love and the means of salvation.   Though they have not all been " wise as serpents," they *have* been useful ; and more good will yet be done when those who are thus working study more carefully the ground upon which they have to meet the enemy of souls.   But oh, what is the supply when compared with the demand.   I speak so because I know what I say to be true to fact, having, as I have said, gone there to take a part in the good work.

CHAPTER IV.

REMOVAL TO NORTH LONDON, AND SOME OF MY EFFORTS THERE.

I. THE REMOVAL.

AS was usual on my return from my short engagements in the provinces, I called at the office of the Home Missionary Society; and on one occasion, when there, Mr Wilson introduced me to two gentlemen, who, through the press, had heard of my success in the country. Each of these gentlemen asked if I would talk with him for a few minutes. I did so, and the subject of conversation was how best to reach and improve the people.

One of the gentlemen was a clergyman of the Church of England, labouring in Islington as one of the Diocesan Home Missionaries, under the presidency of the Bishop of London.

At that time the friends of missionary labour in this district thought of making an extra effort on behalf of those who stood in need of more favourable influences. The clergyman who conversed with me consulted his fellow-workers, and those who supported such labours; and, after reading my " Life Story," one of the friends offered a donation of £40 to help to bring me into the neighbourhood,—others having also signified their wish to contribute towards my salary. Mr Wilson received a letter containing this question—" Could not Mr Hillocks's labours be retained for North London ? " This letter being put into my hand, I called upon the writer, who introduced me to some of the friends. I consented to undertake the proposed duties, believing that the work, such as was expected from me, was that for which Providence had been marvellously preparing me. In a few days thereafter, we removed from Hanover Square, Kennington, S., to Burnard Terrace, Holloway, N.

II. Visiting at the Homes of the People.

Being desirous to rise to the height of my new responsibilities, I began, perhaps more anxiously than ever, to renew my study of life as seen in London, and that with the view of suggesting such plans as might aid me in my future efforts. I did so by mentally connecting the past with the present, which mode I found very profitable. Next to the wish to become acquainted with those with whom I expected to co-operate in all good works, was the desire to know those amongst whom I had to labour. This inquiry led me to become acquainted with the nature of the many hindrances which stood in the way of improvement and happiness, and to know what was being done to remove such formidable obstacles. Without this essential knowledge, neither man nor woman need expect to be able to help the people to help themselves.

As was said in a pamphlet noticing, or rather calling attention to my entering the neighbourhood, the object of my mission was to help to open the minds and enlighten the consciences of the neglected classes, to draw and wean them from degrading habits ; and this I was to do, as " Missionary and Lecturer," by personal intercourse with them " at their homes ;" at their " places of work during meal hours ; " also, by " cottage meetings," " public lectures," and so forth ; and hence I commenced my inquiry as to the condition of the people at their firesides, which is unquestionably the very best plan for the purpose, if we can once get there ; but I had previously discovered that the great secret of success in mission work of this kind is to feel at home in the

homes of the people, and to make the families feel at home in
the presence of the visitor. Without this, visiting is not only
useless but positively injurious.

Though, when previously lecturing throughout the metropolis,
I tried, if possible, to spend half an hour or so in the district
where I had to speak; though, during that time, I looked and
listened, and this helped me the better to apply my remarks;
yet, I had not before this gone to the hearths of the people to
learn from their lips the nature of the various hindrances which
stood in the way of their improvement and happiness. But
from the first day I sat down north of the Thames, I began my
study at the firesides of those regarded as most in want of the
good influences which my mission was intended to bring about.
But my readers will misunderstand me, if they think that, by
virtue of my situation, I intruded myself, and what I had to say,
upon the people. By no means. I knew human nature too well
to give those whom I met an opportunity of saying—"He is
another *arful* bore." Alas, this is the light in which a large
body of the people look upon many of the visitors, whether
known as Scripture readers, missionaries, or evangelists, ministers or clergymen. That such is the case it were folly to deny.
"Of all the *hocracies* in the world, I hates that *borehocracies*
found among them fellers called missioniers," said a man to me
on my first introduction to him; and he went on to point out
what he called "impositions," but what I regarded certainly as
errors on the part of some—the leading objection being their
intruding themselves into the homes of people *because they are poor*
—the poverty of the people being made the only passport of the
missionary; so he said.

The question, Why has this been brought about? is a very
important one, yet I cannot at present enter upon it. This, however, I would say, I hope that the time will soon come when every
such visitor will, as far as possible, study *not* to intrude into the
poor man's privacy, but rather regard his home, be it ever so

humble, as his castle; that he will only enter such homes—or *any* home *not* his own—as on sufferance. That he will treat those to whom he carries " the good news " as fellow-creatures who have bodies as well as souls—virtues as well as failings. It is true that Christianity must be aggressive, but there is a proper as well as an improper way of attack; true, the motive which leads to battle is good, but that has *first* to be proved *to those visited*, and after this is done they will welcome the messenger for the sake of the message. I confess the difficulty of proper approach is great, yet we must not *intrude*. We must carefully and prayerfully use the means by which the people might not only make us welcome, but invite us to come again.

III. Cottage Meetings.

Having, by visiting, become somewhat more intimate with those in need of counsel and encouragement, I next thought of cottage meetings, which soon became a means of usefulness. I love such gatherings, there is so much that is domestic about them. Those who come can be free and friendly, and hence the more readily reach and improve each other's hearts. But they press heavily upon the time and mind of the leader. To him the earnest and anxious look for something fresh and stirring every meeting, and this tests his originality and powers of reflection, when this is only one of his many efforts. Such was my position; I could rarely find a substitute of whom the people heartily approved; and certainly this difficulty does not tell against the *benefit* of cottage meetings as a useful means of promoting a good cause, especially that of evangelisation.

The first cottage meeting at which I presided at North London was held in the room of one who had been lately " rescued " from drink, and brought to Christ. By request, my subject was the Bible aspect of Total Abstinence from strong drink. We met in God's name, and He blessed our meeting. Hearts were touched and souls moved heavenward. The prayers which followed my half-hour's address were earnest, being the heart's desires expressed in simple and direct language. Amongst the utterances in prayer was this, " Lord, thou knowest I·have been a great drunkard, a mighty sinner; forgive the sin, and help me to keep from the drink that cursed me." This is a representative sentence, and nearly every one prayed, each confessing sin and crying for help. It was at one of our cottage meetings, held in this room, that we formed the "Christian Temperance Society;" and this is one of the spots in North London, which to me will ever be surrounded with those hallowed associations which are connected with blessing, arising from the efforts to do good.

IV. With Workmen During their Meal Hours.

But though I found that visiting and cottage meetings were being blessed, yet I know there were some in need of a like blessing whom I did not thereby reach, and hence I went to some of the public works during meal hours, chiefly at dinner time. There I have read and spoken to nearly a hundred working men at once, and to as few as three. It was at what was called Pocock's Brickfield where I first tried this mode of personal intercourse with the workmen. At that time, a large number of those connected with brickmaking, building, draining, and so forth, were congregated. At first I found the men very unwilling to give attention. It appeared, as some of them really said, they thought I should pay them for the measure of attention reluctantly given. Beer was the payment they asked. There were very few who were not beerized, affording another sad proof that beer is the god, the ruin, the curse of the British workman. But after some attempts, I found the men were not all alike; that one or two here and there in the field were sober, (as they would call themselves,) and inclined to listen, though

they had not the courage to show the example. It is a difficult
thing to get that courage to stand out for good, and it is strange
to watch the movements of Providence in this respect. But
many were the hours I spent in this field, and not a few of them
were ultimately pleasant and profitable.

I found another opening of this kind of usefulness at the New
River Company's works. There too, at first, the men looked
upon me with a kind of suspicion, and some even seemed determined to oppose every word I said, but we became so friendly
that I was made heartily welcome. " We look for you, governor,
and are out of sorts when you miss," said one of the attentive
listeners on one occasion when I had been detained. "That's
right, mate," chimed another. " Hear, hear," said a third, and
so on all round. This hearty welcome served as a restorative
charm, and was bestowed when I was much in want of it.

At the same time, quite a town of villas were being built at
Highbury New Park, and there I also went during the dinner
hour. And though the battle there, for and against temperance
and righteousness, was not so severely tested, yet I had not a few
hand-to-hand conflicts. " Come at twelve, sir, we shall eat our
dinner all the better that you are speaking to us," is only one of
the many expressions which served to encourage me from time
to time; but such invitations were uttered after I had been often
with them and had gained their confidence. Of course, they
were not all alike, nor always alike, but before I left, I was
favoured with an almost universal respect.

I also visited the men, the artizan class, working at the General
Omnibus Company's works, Highbury, during the dinner hour.
Here I frequently had large audiences and always attentive. The
tendency there was more to refute than to disturb. As a rule,
the opposition was less manifest, but was more intelligent. I
only remember one occasion on which I felt uneasy, and even
then there was not any rudeness. The men had been enraged
the week before by the manner in which they had been addressed

severely on what the speakers were pleased to designate " the impropriety of working-men's wives wearing silk gowns." This they regarded as an insult, but having asked and received my opinion on that point—to the effect that the working-man's wife had as good a right to a silk gown as any other woman, *if he was able and willing to work for it*—I was again received as heartily as before. In honesty to this class,—indeed, to the working classes as a whole—I must say that, generally speaking, earnestness and intelligence is almost sure, ultimately, to gain attention and respect.

V. THE DROVERS.

The Drovers or " Forces," as they sometimes call themselves, formed another class to which I paid attention at their *waiting times*. I met them shortly after I went to North London, and soon found that as a class—with few, but worthy exceptions, —they were very ignorant, some of them not knowing the letters of the alphabet, and but very few could read. What little knowledge they once possessed had been almost forgotten. " It's no use, master, I can't read," is the general reply, when offered a tract *without pictures*. And even those who can read, say it is impossible to do so to any extent, that the whole system is against improvement of mind and heart.

Whilst waiting, and with them there is much waiting, time hangs on their hand, and the public-house, which is never far distant, offers facilities for loitering about. Indeed, the men and lads are often drawn to these poison-venders in the hope of meeting those from whom they expect a job. While there, and idle, the cards are resorted to, partly with the view of having a little amusement, but chiefly for the purpose of winning to have some drink at the loser's expense. This is one of the causes of two of their leading habits, drinking and gambling, and these in their turn become causes of other evils. I have met with some of the more intelligent and less degraded who knew better, and at times wished to do better, but who had not the moral courage to stand out and show a good example.

Surely it is time to ask, What can be done to let such oppressed ones go free, to give them a chance to be sober and intelligent, to give them an opportunity of knowing Christ and following Him? Certain am I, from what I see and know, that if more effectual means are not soon applied, the *possibility* of improvement may be destroyed; and that, if the proper means were rightly applied, good would follow.

VI. LAUNDRESSES.

Nor were the wives and daughters, as such, considered as beyond the influence of my labours. To neglect them would be to weaken efforts put forth in behalf of husbands and sons. The great influence of women for good or evil has been long since admitted; and hence that which stands in the way of her improvement and usefulness demands attention.

Alas! how many of the wives of the London workmen are from home; and often the daughters, as they grow up, follow the mother's example, and hence the miserable, as well as sorry homes. They are employed in various ways, some of which are very unbecoming a woman, but a large number take to themselves the name of laundresses.

Not to speak about the children being left, and its results, nor about the waste of food and money, nor of the discomfort to the husband and all concerned, when the wife is " out from eight to eight," may I not ask how many have thereby become drunkards? and my experience has taught me how difficult it is—if not altogether impossible—to reform such *whilst they go to the laundry.* Doubtless, there are some of these establishments well conducted, and some who go to them spend what they earn to good purpose; but it is a sad fact, known to those who know life amongst this class, that there are many laundries which, for strong drink, are complete sandbeds, the chief object seeming to be to make drunken wives and drunken mothers. Let me here give one illustration of the mother *from home:*—" The husband is a 'labourer.' He is very sober, very industrious, and a Christian into the bargain. The wife was once clean and tidy, once industrious and anxious for the comfort of the family; but these days have passed away; all her good qualities have now, alas, become absorbed in the cup—she is a drunkard, cunning and deceitful. He is very much troubled; she is very careless. He wishes to manifest his love for the young ones by feeding and clothing them; she invariably gratifies her desire for strong drink at the cost of everything, and at all hazards. He sighs over the looped and windowed raggedness of his children, and brings clothes with which to cover their nakedness; she sells them off their backs. He pities their cold bare feet, and brings shoes to cover them; she, utterly regardless of frost or snow, or pain, sells their shoes for drink. He is anxious to furnish his home comfortably, but she disposes of everything that a publican will take for the price of a half pint of beer or a drop of gin. He leaves the house in the morning to enter upon the toils of the day; she has just made fair promises of amendment, yet scarcely has his footfall echo died away in the distance, than she commences her accustomed work. A little sugar is in the house, and it goes the old road, the poor children being left to drink the insipid infusion of a few bleached tea leaves. The half-quartern loaf must also go, and that on the merciless and unmotherly assumption that the children may get a little bread in their begging rounds. Everything is gone, and for drink. In the evening, the children are crying, for scarcely have they tasted bread during the day. The father makes his way homeward, fatigued with labour, harassed with care, and afraid lest what has been before may have occurred again. He reaches the hovel which he must call his home; but ah, the state of matters there!

Does he find the frugal meal prepared and sweetened by the smile of conjugal affection? Does the fire blaze brightly on the hearth, suggesting an evening of comfort? Do happy juvenile faces greet his approach, eagerly expectant of the paternal cares, striving the "envied kiss to share?" Does the smile, flitting across the face of innocence in the cradle, soften the asperities and soothe the ruggedness which the rough contact with the world without has occasioned? Alas! how wide the contrast! How truly deplorable the aspect before him! No mother is there. The neglected fire has long since ceased to burn. No evening meal has been prepared. The children, huddled in a corner, are crying as if their little hearts would break. The dear infant, that should have been nestled on its mother's breast, has cried itself into a fever, and is now utterly prostrate with sheer exhaustion. The match is struck, and the short piece of candle is lighted, and, alas! what a miserable group its feeble glimmering reveals! Who could picture the father's sorrowful face, and the pitiful looks of his helpless children! In that corner, crimped up and on a heap of dirty rags, lies the infant. The light and the motion have caused it to move its tiny hand. It makes an effort to raise its small voice, but that has become softer now than the softest sound of the lute. The poor thing moves the parched lips, but no mother's breast, responsive, is near. No, no! that breast has lost all feeling, all sense of duty. Love—the purest and most intense—has been quenched in the poisonous cup; the mother is a drunkard, a drunken laundress.

VII. What some Laundresses come to.

But I found two kinds of laundries,—those which employed elderly and married women, and those at which only single and young women are engaged. Amongst this latter class of *laundresses*, as in the former, there are not a few who date their ruin from being *employed* in such places. If mothers go wrong, what

F

can we expect of the daughters, especially of those who have grown up amidst vice, and without the benefit of happy home influences? If thus mothers fall before temptation, and so forget themselves and their responsibilities, what can we look for from daughters, who, in many cases, have to pass through a more severe test, not only of sobriety but of purity. To the credit of our young women be it said, that many of them as soon as they are able go to work, from the good motive of supporting themselves; and I have known not a few who have gone to help aged or sickly relatives. Some of these do well, and others fall; but most of those who sink have not evinced the same purity of motives. Some of the more thoughtful and sternly virtuous have preferred service, believing that they might thereby know more and more of household management, and so become useful wives when wedded to those they loved. On the other hand, some there are who, having heard of over-work, patience tested, and temper ruffled, at some places where service is irksome, have preferred to work where the wages might afford a better chance of richer dress, or where they might have more "liberty" in the evenings to go where they please. How frequently the latter supposed advantages are misapplied! and as often do they bring about new evils, and feed those already in existence. No place of work brings these sad effects upon society more frequently, certainly, and sometimes purposely, than establishments called laundries. Here one such, and how it was brought about.

E—— loved a "leetle amusement of a night," and therefore preferred the laundry. She dressed well, and thought herself "good-looking." At last she was married; but though her husband could command steady work and good pay, yet she returned to the laundry after the first week or so of their married life. They returned home in the evening about the same time, and as soon as a cup of tea could be made (oftener procured at the coffee-shop) and swallowed, they dressed in their best and

made off for some of the " pleasure-grounds," "music-halls," or
" public dancings."   Thus they continued, till she was compelled
for a time to relinquish washing and ironing, which loss was so
regretted by both, that as soon as possible the baby was given
out to nurse, and again she went to the laundry.   For some
time the first flush of maternal love so restrained her, that
he went often alone to his "leetle amusements; " and on those
nights she remained at home the fires of jealousy consumed her
heart and racked her mind, for well she knew the character of
those with whom he nightly associated.   As might be looked
for, they lived more and more in strife, till, notwithstanding his
high wages and her extra earnings, they had to remove to an
inferior house in a dingy locality, and poverty was added to their
want of peace, till they separated—he absconding, leaving her
to provide for herself and the child.

Soon after this she was known as Mrs ——, the laundress.
She *did take* in some washings and *hire* some girls; but as is
the case in too many such laundries, it was soon perceived that
she hired the girls for a twofold purpose; for her house became
the resort of those rakes, old and young, who frequent such dens
of iniquity as were the means of ruining her and her husband
—those fellows who hire carriages to drive those they fancy to
the country, to get " a day's pleasure."

Deplorable as this is, it is nothing rare; and the ruin brought
about thereby cannot be conceived, it is so general and so wide-
spread.   And what adds to this is the fact, that worthy parents,
not aware of such a fearful state of matters, send their daughters,
pure and well-disposed, to such places, to learn washing and
ironing, that they may be the more useful.   But, alas! being
ensnared, how many give way!   And what a change a few years
bring about when every day leads nearer and nearer to destruction!

VIII. OUR LICENSED "PLEASURE"-GROUNDS.

The facts connected with this kind of life, and revealed to me by the lips of some of the victims, led me to watch more closely those places which afforded opportunities to the vicious, and those who lived by vice, for carrying out their base purposes. I found that the traffic in strong drink, as a rule, rendered them much service in this way; but that which most directly and much more successfully accomplishes corrupting purposes are the *tea* garden or *pleasure*-ground, the public dancings and music halls. Because of what I had heard and seen, I consented, at the request of some of the friends interested in the temporal and spiritual well-being of the people, to visit these places and see for myself. This I did, and took notes on the spot; but many of them are such as cannot be recorded without shocking the feelings of those who hate vice in all its manifestations. However, from these notes I extracted matter and facts for three popular lectures, which I have given at various places. They have proved interesting, and I trust useful. A newspaper critic referring to them, says, " The descriptions are given most faithfully, and in such an impressive manner as to excite a sense of shame that such sinks of iniquity should exist in, and be so extensively patronised by the inhabitants of the metropolis of a Christian nation." Another, also noticing the same, says, " The publication of this ' Peep at London Life, as seen in the Licensed Pleasure-Grounds, Music Halls, and Public Dancings,' in a cheap form, for circulation amongst the young of both sexes, might be rendered an unspeakable benefit to them."

But still I cannot here enter into details regarding the sights and sounds to be seen and heard within the fences of these the devil's gardens of iniquity, corruption, and ruin. I may, however, give a passing glance at one of such—one regarded as neither the highest nor lowest in the social scale, but standing midway, and yet including the three modes of attraction.

We enter the "pay here" passage, and that which is at once evident is the fact that the proprietor has spared no expense in order that a striking effect may be produced. Great care and some skill has been employed to arrange a brilliant arch of light, which spans the threshold, so that, by variegated coloured glass, the light gives a pleasant roseate tinge to the most haggard and debauched face in the crowd below. This space is called the Foreground, but if every thing or place had its proper name, it would be called the Mart of Vice. It is surrounded by a large number of gas-lights, and high up, at the further end, is a large star of gas-light. In the centre of this star are the letters V. R., doubtless intended to convey the idea that the revels below are under the patronage of the Queen. What an idea! What an insult to the virtue and purity of womanhood, as happily exemplified in the true and blameless life of our sovereign Lady! What an insult to her womanly virtues, to suppose, even for a moment, that our mother Queen ever set her foot within this den of vice! What, then, must be the rendering of the letters V. R.? What is their legitimate and appropriate meaning? Laying aside the idea of royal recognition as absurd—at least, so far as the inclination and example of the Queen go—I am disposed to regard the V. R. here as contractions for "Vice Reigns." Thus they tell their own true tale, speaking of what they nightly behold. This is not an imaginary explanation, for underneath the glaring eye of this star are avowed and open harlots, and those who associate with them. The former are there, seeking and finding the simple ones; the latter are there, catching fresh prey. Both classes are lying in wait, both are parading their fading attractions and plying their horrid art, more or less successfully.

There is that old lady, dressed in silks of the finest quality, a feather of spotless white in her fashionable hat. She is talking to that overgrown disgrace to his class, his tastes extending not beyond the precincts of the brothel.

There, too, is that younger *lady*, much younger, but as gay in dress. She is in earnest conversation with that miserable counterfeit of a man known as "a gent "—a self-conceited fop, his white hat set jauntily on his highly-perfumed head, his "superior" cigar in his vile mouth, his short cane in his useless hand, and his gold-*like* rings upon his tapering fingers.

And, as if to give variety to this variegated scene, there, too, amongst the fast youths, is the sprightly sailor, flush with the money for which he has laboured long and hard during many a stormy day and dreary night. Young as he is, he is an apt scholar in this school of vice; but he is being taught and caught, whilst it may be that his kind old mother is earnestly praying for him in the dear old home far away.

But here there is no end of character. I shall only add, before proceeding further, that whilst the spectacle, viewed as a whole, is one of amazement and of dazzling brilliancy, so gay is the glittering throng, yet the whole scene is as vile as it is gay, as corrupting as it is brilliant, as ruinous as it is enticing. True, at this time, about the commencement, that woman in silken attire smiles pleasantly, and goes about her business in a manner partaking of the would-be dignified; but she is rather "free," evidently purposely free. And that man of the same class is anxious, at this stage of the proceedings, to be polite, and to earn the title of being "quite the ladies' man;" yet, even here, at this early hour, vice, in some of its grosser forms, begins to manifest itself.

Leaving this mart, we pass on to what may be called the chief or common bar. There, almost all present are drinking one or other of the various intoxicating liquors. They are being served by good-looking, clean, and tidy females, upon whose countenances flit that conventional smile so common amongst all engaged at that work. As circumstances will permit, these barmaids lend all the ear possible to the discussions of all sorts of subjects having reference to that profligate villainy which has made miserable, and engulfed so many victims. Yes, and listening is not all; these girls frequently exchange oblique glances with the better-known of the male customers.

Here the scene is ever shifting; and yet the leading features of this strange, corrupt, and corrupting assembly remain about the same, week after week, night after night. In conversation with the unabashed profligate is that young girl, yet beautiful, and upon whose fair cheeks are now and then suffused the blushes of shame; giving some, though fading, indications, that from her the lingering traces of virtue and modesty are unwilling to part. But, alas! she is there, amidst the seething mass, nearly all of whom are more or less advanced scholars in this vice-training institution.

Passing through what are called the "spacious halls,"—"inviting drunkaries" is the more appropriate name,—we come out close to the Platform, on which a great concourse of people are whirling round and round. They are said to be dancing, but nearly every dance is of the most repulsive kind. The music, to which the so-called dancers are keeping time, is certainly superior, but dance after dance is repugnant to all that is pure, disgusting to all who have the least respect for morality.

We pass on again and enter the Promenade, which we find also thronged, and in which the fruits of strong drink and vicious habits are beginning to develop and manifest themselves in a variety of ways. One is loudly laughing, another is fearfully cursing—but I dare not particularise further.

At the extreme end of this Promenade, as well as the shed-like erections that surround them, things present a very gloomy aspect. This gloom increases as we turn round by the lower corner of the other side than that at which we entered from the Platform. So dark and dull is this side of the Promenade, that a tiny rushlight, placed on a table in the centre of the hut or bower, serves the purpose of making the darkness visible, and many of these erections have not this slight advantage.

We enter the Music Hall—large, gorgeous, brilliant, and in

some places elegant. The sentimental singing, doubtless, may be regarded as " superior," but much of it is sound without sense, notes not words. The comic department is merely outspoken and coarse rubbish. When any meaning is conveyed, it is such as to please the gross taste of most of the audience—the vilest of women and the basest of men—nearly all of whom are either drinking or smoking; some both.

After thus making the round, we come again to the foreground, the mart of vice. It is still thronged. It is late, and this seems to be the time for a certain class. The males are of two extremes in the social scale, the richer being the majority. The females may be also divided into the oldest and the ugliest of those who have as yet failed to get a chance. Strong drink has put many of them off their guard, to the commercial disadvantage of the owners of the bloated and uninviting countenances, which even the artistic roseate tinge produced by the surrounding lights cannot make pleasant to look upon.

Another glance, obtained by a quick walk round the grounds, shows that drink, temptation, and excitement have done their work. Both the sexes, now more than ever, display their wanton depravity and wretched modes of life. Now debased humanity revels in licentious and unbridled riot. But it is morning, and large numbers are pairing off, and cabs are in demand. Truly, it is a relief to get out of this, as it is to get out of many other so-called pleasure-grounds. These are the places which rob our sons and ruin our daughters, which work hand in hand not only with the brothels, but also with such laundries as those which I have already described. Truly, such places of " amusement " are the great curses of London.

In Chapter Second I have referred to Sunday in London, but, as I said, only by a passing glance at what was most visible. I did not even attempt to describe such places as Petticoat Lane, where there may be more furniture, tools, and stolen goods than at other such Sunday marts, but where there are less groceries, toys, and those other articles of commerce more generally suited to the larger masses of Sunday purchasers, such as meat and vegetables, fruits and sweet-stuffs, drapery, hardware, &c. Nor did I enter the so-called pleasure-grounds on that day. But we may here take a passing glance at that one just referred to. We need not, we dare not, for the reason already given, stop to describe minutely what goes on here on Sunday evening, and on other evenings. That which is particularly noticeable within on Sunday is the number of children accompanied by their parents, especially between six and nine o'clock in the summer time. A stranger might suppose, or rather wish, that this gathering of parents and their offspring, in such a den of pollution, is something rare; but this cramming of the young into such places, full as they are with moral corruption, is nothing new. The truth is, that every convenience is provided for "families,"—perambulators for infants, and swings for children of larger growth; the latter of whom are quite familiar with every corner, whilst the parents themselves are on the most intimate terms with the waiters, whom they frequently address by name. And let it be remembered that this moving mass, and those yet seated, are not of what are called "the lower orders." It is far otherwise, especially from about eight o'clock till midnight. Truly, one may exclaim, What an atmosphere is here for any, but especially children and youths, who have to inhale moral poison at every breath!

Scarcely have we passed the "pay here" box, until we hear the sound of whistling and singing, not of sacred music, certainly, but snatches of profane and ribald song, frequently followed by language revolting to all having the least respect for purity of morals. And not unfrequently a kind of coarse merriment is brought about by the would-be witty remarks upon the couplets of obscene songs, half said and half sung by somewhat tipsy men and women, whose language and gestures are truly disgusting.

But these filthy allusions are not confined to the more youthful portion of the assembly. There, too, are the "regulars," as well as the "irregulars"—the two classes into which all pleasure seekers in such places may be divided—that is, those who attend occasionally, and those who would as readily think of being absent from dinner as not be present on the proper nights. In many cases the *regulars* will not mix with the *irregulars;* and even when they do happen to meet under one roof, or within one place, there is little or no association, seldom a mutual greeting. Indeed, so strong is this caste or class idea amongst these people, that they will not recognise an equality even on their march to the City of Destruction. Sunday evening is the chief occasion on which there is anything like a blending of these classes. And if we accept the version of those who must know best, as a true one, this Sunday mixture would not be but for the horrid fact, known to many a woman now astray, that many of the "regulars" go in search of fresh prey from amongst the sons and daughters of those of the better-to-do and better paid of our tradespeople and mechanics, who have been drawn there, it may be for the first time. These rakes having there fixed their base eyes upon the object of their choice, they follow up, or, as is often the case, employ those wretched women who make it a business to entrap the thoughtless of their own sex. How many are thus ruined and made wretched! How many who, perhaps, had lately left a virtuous home, but have been thus drawn away, are now walking our streets! One instance out of thousands may serve to illustrate my meaning.

"You feel very uneasy to-day. I hope you are trusting in God. He is the same yesterday, to-day, and for ever."

Such were the words addressed by a Christian visitor on approaching the death-bed of a suffering woman, who, though poor in regard to this world's means, was rich in grace.

"Blessed be God, I know that my Redeemer liveth, and is waiting for me;" and a gleam of joy suddenly flashed across her pale face; but it was only for a moment. "My daughter is lost, lost!" she added, and wrung her hands in agony.

"Is she dead?" said the visitor.

"Worse than dead; she has fallen," was the reply. And after going into details, naming the licensed "*pleasure*-ground" to which the daughter regularly went, she added, "I am told a young woman may be innocently led to such places; but if she continues to go of her own accord, it is from a bad motive. I have advised her, and pleaded with her; set heaven and hell before her, and then she declared I might say what I pleased, she *should* go, adding, she saw ' no harm in a little amusement of an evening.' She leaves this about eight at night, and returns about four next morning; sometimes not till noon next day. Have I not room for fears?"

The visitor could not reply, knowing the poor mother had room for fears. After an oppressive silence, the sorrowing mother added, as her emotion increased—

"I go to God and the saints above, but have to leave my poor daughter here, in the hands of the devil and his agents. Good friend, bear with me. *My* daughter is not the only one. I did not think of all this till it was brought to my door. Pray for me. You have influence, and as a dying mother, I plead that it may be used to help to shut these places. Already you have prayed for me, and God has answered us, blessed be His name! Now, help my dear child and such poor pitiable creatures as go to these horrid dens. It was on a Sunday she first went, and now she is there every night. How can a mother die and leave her daughter living such a life! Oh, can nothing be done? Will Christians not inquire and do their duty? Will they not plead in behalf of even their *own* daughters? Two years ago, my dear child was as fair, as virtuous, and as promising as any; but what is she *now?* Can nothing be done? Forgive me, my daughter's soul is precious; her present, and perhaps her future misery, what a thought! and must it be the last on my mind?   A few days, and I am in Paradise—glory to God, my Redeemer!   But my daughter!   How can I die?   Can nothing be done?"

IX. Out-door Efforts.

But I stop not to comment, preferring rather simply to say, Let us not forget the dying mother's question—"*Can nothing be done?*"   These and other awful facts touching the state of society, induced me not only to labour the harder in the way I had already walked, but to try wherein it was possible to open other avenues to useful means by which I might more effectually reach the falling, as well as the fallen; and, in out-door efforts, I was successful.

By this I was brought into contact with many I could not have seen by other means.   The first of these efforts, in the highways and byways, as well as in the courts and alleys, was preaching the gospel, and that on a Sunday morning.   I had been invited by a few friends to meet them in a school-room previous to their going out to the corner of one of the neighbouring streets, there to hold "a service."   Our leader was a clergyman.   He dressed in gown and bands, and marched to the street in this attire, we following behind.   I thought more than I said, but believing, in my simplicity, that all this parade might prove to be useful, I did not even smile at the scene—at least if I did, I checked myself.   The first part of the "service" being over, the preaching came, and with that, opposition in the shape of clamour, random wit—everything but attention.   Six or seven minutes and the preacher gives in, to the joy of those for whom he had held the service.   Whether fired by this opposition triumph, so roughly expressed, I cannot say, but the clergyman again tried to address the audience.   Again he failed to gain attention, but this time he, speaking in another tone, informed them that there was present a "little Scotchman" who would perhaps address them.   Of course, I knew this referred to me, but how was I to meet such an audience? Yet speak I must, for in a moment every eye was upon me. And speak I did, but not before I lifted up my soul and said, "God help me." He did help me. The people listened attentively. What I said seemed to go home. At the close some of the roughest of them asked when I would come again? Of course, I went again and again, not only there, but round about to every available street and square and court ranging from Upper Street to Upper Holloway.

And *North* London has not been the only scene of these efforts in aid of the glorious work of evangelisation ; but I know not how I then succeeded. Surely it was, as it has been, by help from above in answer to the prayer, " God help me," offered on the spur of the moment, but in faith. I knew He had been my help long before, and that He would continue to help. He has done so from time to time; but had any one said to me, before I left Scotland, " To preach in the open air will be a portion of your duty," I fear I should have remained north of the Tweed. Previous to my coming to England, all my addresses and lectures partook much of the style of an essay or " composition," and almost all written out——the very opposite of what was essential to success as an open-air preacher.

Awkward as I must have been, because of my previous training and practice, I made out at once to arrest the attention by telling a Scotch anecdote, which, in its application, led to the consideration of the propriety of asking the three questions,—— What is God? What is man? In what relationship do they stand to each other? (See " Open-Air Preaching," Chap. VII.)

X. IN-DOOR MEETINGS.

But my open-air efforts were not confined to preaching; I delivered addresses on various subjects, such as temperance. Yet, useful as I found this mode of reaching the people to be, in-door meetings were not only necessary but useful. There are various reasons why in-door and out-door efforts should be combined, especially in the promotion of the principles and practice of Christianity. Useful as the latter are, there are some people who *cannot*, and some who *will not*, stand outside, but who may be led to a meeting held in a room. And then, though some, in very crowded places and market streets, continue their open-air services throughout the year, still there is an understood season for out-door preaching.

One of the in-door meetings may be, as ours were, called mutual improvement meetings, in which I so far put use and wont aside as to try (and I think I succeeded) to lead those who came to interest each other in this way: I read an essay or delivered a short speech, never occupying longer than fifteen minutes in the delivery, and then invited all present briefly to offer any remarks upon the subject. This proved that good comes of earnestly and honestly believing in man, and treating him as a fellow-creature. I am aware that it is said that familiarity breeds contempt; but earnestness and prudence help to counteract this tendency. I know from experience that there is a danger of the selfish and the ambitious taking advantage of such an effort to induce them to rise and to co-operate; but the good that may be done by trusting those we wish to benefit became so manifest to me, that I now make it a rule to " run the risk," as a brother was pleased to call this mode of treating those in need of encouragement. The subjects to which I called their attention were such as directly affected those likely to assemble, such as " Self-help." We took it up in its several divisions, and spent one evening considering " The necessity of self-help;" another, on " The obstacles to self-help;" a third, on " The means of self-help;" a fourth, on "The past and present examples of self-help;" and a fifth, on " The advantages and importance of individual and national self-help." This and such subjects answered nicely where those assembled wished to consider general subjects; but we had meetings for the promotion of special objects, such as teetotalism, and there I selected such subjects as "Strong drink : its nature and tendency." And again, "Water;" one evening being devoted to its " elements," another to its " properties," another to its " uses—general, dietetic, and curative." This is a quiet work, but it generally becomes interesting and instructive to all present. The number may not be more than a dozen, but these go into their homes and workshops so much more enlightened on the given theme than they were only a few hours before. Mark me, this is no mere " debating club," speaking for speaking's sake, but an earnest and honest inquiry after truth, with the noble motive of knowing the right in order to practise it. In proportion as such an exercise falls short of this, the element of improvement vanishes.

And to such duties I added that of lecturing on various subjects, studying to render them as popular and instructive as I could. This, I saw, was necessary. It was evident that for one who would seek to be improved by the means just named, there are hundreds who would not; hence other meetings are necessary to bring out such, to speak to them, to gain their confidence, and perhaps lead them also to be anxious to learn and to rise. Public meetings, if truly popular, are useful for this purpose, whether to lead to social elevation or religious improvement. There is no end of suitable subjects for such occasions, but I always select those most suitable to popular treatment, and which admit of something relating to the social and religious elevation of the audience. But I may here observe that there are two errors which public speakers ought to guard against :—1. That of "rising," as it is called, above the supposed mental strength and culture of an audience. 2. And that of making an effort to come "down" to those listening to them. These are sad mistakes. Supposing that there are present some who may be favoured with an advanced degree of intelligence, is the speaker there for their benefit alone, or for the general benefit? or would the so-called intelligent thank the speaker for going out of his element for their sakes, even were he thereby to please their ears, which at best is very doubtful? But even supposing that all attending were the work-a-day people who may not have had intellectual advantages, is it fair to infer that they are dunderheads, that nothing but coarse language and vulgar illustrations are suitable? Those who do so are mistaken, and those whom they address are the first to see as well as feel the insult. Let every speaker consider the responsibilities he has to sustain in the sight of God, and there will be fewer attempts at flourishing, and far more benefit for those called together with the view to their improvement. Another tendency I endeavoured to avoid was that of speaking *at* the people. This is not desirable, as it causes those who are listening to ask, "Are *we* worse than others? Is the *speaker* a perfect man? If he was surrounded as we are, what would he be?" And the worst of it is, such questions are not often asked aloud, so that some explanations might be given, for it might be that the speaking which calls forth such questions is only the result of following a bad example; but they lodge in the heart, and operate there very injuriously against the speaker's usefulness and the hearer's benefit. I am glad to say that, by the blessing of God, and my desire to avoid what might be useless or offensive, the meetings at which I spoke were numerously attended; and years after, words which I had spoken have been referred to and repeated by the listeners as having proved useful for *their encouragement and guidance.*

XI. Formation of Societies.

The power that lies in co-operation, who can define it? When that power is wisely wielded for good, who can count its happy results? Hence we have the motto, "Union is strength." But this is not only applicable to what are called the things of time.

There may be, and there ought to be, the united action of all who are anxious to share the happiness of being the means of promoting the interest of the Redeemer's kingdom. Convinced of this, I began as soon as possible to form societies having kindred though distinct objects.

As might be expected, and as everywhere, even amongst good workers—that is, workers for good objects—I found here some such with one idea and that a very small one; but my heart was also gladdened to find some with wide hearts and elevated souls. I listened to all, and thought more than I said; but when the time came, I endeavoured to give some idea of my plans, namely, that those who were brought under their operation and influence might, by self and mutual help, aid in the advancement of *everything* calculated to cause and enhance their own and others' happiness, and thereby be the more likely to become better neighbours, truer friends, and more devoted servants of the living God. These Christian friends and fellow-workers severely criticised the ideas I sought to develop there, not only at the commencement but even after the societies began to tell for good. Some said the idea was "too large for a *district*," that it was big enough for all London; yet good came out of these friendly discussions. To me they served the more to give increased confidence in the plans proposed for consideration. Again we met, and again we parted, without seeing eye to eye; but I went on holding meeting after meeting, forming society after society, till at last the friends saw it proper to co-operate; and then, with greater speed we went on doing our best to help to open the minds and enlighten the consciences of those with whom we came in contact.

Almost immediately after the formation of this union of action, the Ragged School, Hornsey Road, became the centre of operations. Referring to this favour so kindly and freely bestowed, and to the results of our operations—so far as they knew of them—the directors of that useful institution, in their report for 1861, say, "The use of one room is permitted every evening, Sundays included, to a committee of gentlemen, who have for some time been endeavouring in various ways to reach labouring men. . . . . They have rejoiced to see the rooms (thus) freely used for the general good of the neighbourhood. One spirit has animated these different agencies; one object has been kept in view, viz., to offer Christian education to the children of the poorest, and at the same time to extend to their parents the warm hand of charity in its best practical manifestation, by assisting them in every way to improve their own moral and physical condition."

There we had popular lectures, total abstinence meetings, religious meetings; a free library, a reading-room, evening classes, a Bible class, a singing class, and provident and other societies. At all these gatherings, as has just been indicated, the future as well as the present happiness of all was kept in view, and as was intended, each society helped the other. This was readily admitted by all who knew anything of the results. This applied to all the societies—the total abstinence society providing members for the provident society, both helping to improve the homes, whilst the three easily and naturally united in behalf of the educational efforts, and so on, not only making homes happier, but leading souls to Christ.

CHAPTER V.

ANOTHER CHANGE, BUT FOR THE BETTER—FROM THE NORTH TO THE NORTH-WEST OF LONDON.

I. INVITATION TO BECOME A PASTOR.

ALL these operations were very cheering, and I was truly thankful for their results, especially as the success manifested itself even in the midst of obstacles not a few, and led to an event which proved that those amongst whom I laboured appreciated my efforts. It took the shape of a short but expressive memorial, of which the following is a copy :—

"DEAR SIR,—Being now acquainted with you for some time, and during that period having seen the amount of good you have done amongst the working classes, and felt the good each of us individually have received from you, we, the undersigned working men of this neighbourhood, have met to take into our most earnest consideration how we can most effectually gain the object next our hearts, viz., the well-being of our fellow men.

"After due consideration, we have come to the conclusion that it is absolutely necessary to have a Working Man's Chapel, with you for our pastor.

"Should we succeed in getting a suitable place of meeting, would you be so kind as to accept of the pastorship?

"Your kind attention to this our wish will greatly oblige."

In reply I wrote :—

"Your acquaintance with me has not been of very long duration, but I rejoice that my humble efforts amongst you have been such as to lead you to find out the aim of my life—to do good as I have opportunity—to endeavour to help the people to help themselves—to do my best to induce them to become careful and anxious concerning their spiritual as well as their temporal welfare—to bring poor dying sinners to Jesus that He might heal them and save them.

"Your efforts and their object do honour to your head and heart; and the conclusion to which you have come—to make an effort to form a congregation and erect a chapel—is a proof that you have a knowledge of the wants of our neighbourhood. It must be admitted the people have not the opportunity of assembling themselves together on Sunday and other occasions. The present provision is made in kindness, but alas! time has proved that it is not the kind required.

"Believe me, I think the more of your effort inasmuch as it is also for the good of others. All of you would now be made welcome by any religious denomination, and might—health and employment granted—fulfil the other duties connected with the maintaining of a place of worship. To find men who have baffled temptation, and so far risen above the frailties of humanity, is a feature in human progress of which London may well be proud, and this of itself is enough to gain for your aim the favourable ear of those who not only have the will, but also the means to forward your grand and good object.

"I now come to that part which refers more closely to myself. You ask, If I would accept the pastorship of the congregation referred to. I answer, Yes. I need say no more, inasmuch as you know my heart is with you and those among whom Providence has placed me."

Perhaps I should here notice three of the more prominent points contained in their appeal to the public for assistance in their project.

1. To show that it was not meant that my labours were to be merely those of the pastor, they said, "we have no idea of laying aside the means which have been so successfully applied in bringing about the happy results referred to. It is our wish, and Mr Hillocks's desire, to keep in motion the present machinery which God has so blessed."

2. And lest a mistake might have arisen as to the nature and purpose of the proposed scheme, they added, "Though our efforts must, of necessity as well as choice, be brought to bear

more particularly upon our fellow working men, because we best know the wants and wishes of those with whom we daily come in contact, yet we, from principle, have no notion of encouraging the idea of dividing the people into classes, especially in relation to moral and spiritual matters. In common with every true Christian we deplore the evident existence of such distinctions, but we must take things as we find them, or leave them alone."

3. Again, knowing what had been, they honestly spoke out as to the proposed congregation. They said, "While it is our wish and Mr Hillocks's wish to know nothing save the glory of God and the good of man, yet we think it proper to state that he being an Independent, we have resolved to be recognised as belonging to the denomination known as Congregationalists."

The memorialists proved their earnestness by doing their best. For instance, one of their number gave £5 to help to meet the preliminary expenses, and promised another sum equal to it to help towards the building of the proposed chapel. Yet this effort was crushed, and the people were disappointed.

But though they failed in this plan they tried another. Connected with the efforts named at the close of last chapter, there were Sunday evening services, but because of the previous arrangements, the people were not certain when I would be there. Some of those interested in the success of these services wished to see them otherwise conducted, and now they made their request known. A number of those working men who desired this change, united together and offered to visit the homes of their neighbours—to urge them to come out to the Sunday evening meetings—if they were able to say that I was the preacher. But this was objected to. Those who took upon themselves the power of saying "no," agreed that I should come now and then as before; but this did not please the people.

Another effort was made, and this time I was under the painful necessity of appearing to stand in the way of its success. In the neighbourhood there was a meeting place to which some of the more anxious friends had frequently gone. On the same condition they made the same offer to the conductors of this place. These friends applied to me, through their superintendent, and offered to give the conducting of the Sunday services into my hands. Now came my greatest difficulty. I knew my friends had made the request from the best of motives. I was also aware that the friends who supported this place had complied with that request for the sake of the good which they thought would thereby follow. But there was also this fact before me—the meeting-place belonged to that portion of Christ's church which I had refused to abandon. I say, *refused to abandon*, because I had not been long in North London before I was asked to bring my influence with the people to bear more directly in favour of the Church of England. This request was made by one person three times, and in three different forms, but I refused to yield. As is known to the reader, and as was known to those who engaged me, I had come to North London, as I had gone elsewhere, a Dissenter. I could not have gone under false colours; my connexion with the Home Missionary Society told what I was in this respect; but let me add that, in my labours, I knew nothing save Christ for the Christless. And this was not only in accordance with arrangements entered into on my going there, for I acted so as a matter of choice. If ever the minor ought to give way to the major, surely it is in this respect. The question of Church and State is an important one, but surely to the people, the subject—a Saviour for the unsaved—is much more important; and certain am I, with the evangelist, it is the all important. And besides feeling the force of this conviction— a theory which has ever agreed with my practice—I knew that my salary was paid, partly by those who belonged to the Church of England, and partly by those known as Dissenters, and I felt convinced that both classes contributed from this noble motive— that the neglected and outcast might be brought to Christ, and hence, as arranged, I entered upon my duties neither as the servant of the Church nor as the servant of Dissent; hence I refused either to turn to the left or the right; hence I not only refused to yield to the desire that I should bring my influence to bear more directly in favour of the English Church, but I was under the necessity of rejecting the offer thus made by those who belonged to that portion of Christ's vineyard of which I was a member, even though in the offer I saw a chance of increased usefulness. It was with reluctance that I came to this resolution, because of the disinterested manner in which this offer of an opportunity of holding regular Sunday services was made; but knowing that this mission station was avowedly denominational, I was bound, in faithfulness to my engagement, to come to this decision—to hold on my way, striving for the glory of God in the good of man—working hand to hand, and heartily, with any Christian, whatever the denomination that Christ-like one belonged, but at the same time retaining my previous views on the matters referred to; and surely the real, intelligent, and liberal Christian would neither blame me for having an opinion, nor for having respect to it. In regard to opinions, I never was dogmatical towards those who differ from me, I never was a sycophant, I blame none for adhering to a principle so long as they are convinced that it is true and useful, and this is all I claim from others; but I suffered for the exercise of the right of thinking for myself; I endured—but not for the first time—the penalties of having a mind of my own.

II. The Sudden Decision.

But it is only justice to state that this threefold attempt to induce me to change my church fellowship was only made by one person; and, though he said he acted for others, I never met with another there who was foolish enough to press me on that point; yet my "stubbornness," as my refusal was called,

became, and continued to the end to be, a festering sore, easily
inflamed; and what added to this sad feature of the case, was
the fact that he had influence with others interested in my
mission. So much so, that my remaining much longer in the
neighbourhood became a doubtful question, in which not only
the poor but some of the rich manifested a deep interest.

"Do not think of leaving. It would be a pity. Things may
yet take a better turn." So said one of the good ladies in the
presence of others, who also gave assent to the same idea.

"Is it true you are to leave us? Who, in God's name, will
help us after you are gone? Do remain, if it is possible." So
said one of the "rescued," as he incidentally met me on my
way home one afternoon.

With such friendly advices, and such earnest appeals ringing
in my ears, I stated that I was willing to remain, and try to
overcome whatever obstacles might have arisen in the way of
my usefulness, because I believed I had secured the affections of
the people. For a time my mission work went on as before,
with the exception of some hindrances, and it became generally
believed that I was to continue in the district. Indeed, so confidently was I led to feel on this point, that I had refused offers
of such work; preferring to remain with those whose confidence
I had already won. But the sore referred to was still open,
and I still inclined to think for myself, and to act as conscience
dictated; so this opponent, although he had left the district,
called a meeting of some of those who were likely to take his
advice. I cannot say what passed in my absence, but on being
called in I was told that another year's salary would not be
forthcoming. On hearing this decision I distinctly asked, if
they had any fault to find with my character or work? This
was answered by the emphatic negative, "no, no, no," right
round the table. When in company with this leading person
after the rest had gone, he put this question to me—"Whom
do you blame for all this?" My answer was—"I blame you."

III. A Working Man's Testimony.

I had reason for saying so, being by this time aware of what he had done, not only whilst in the district, but after his removal. One of his efforts proved to be in my favour. I refer to it here because it is one of the many proofs which can be given, that whatever people may be whilst under the influence of strong drink and in the service of the devil, there are amongst the " rescued " many who are noble and honest, who can, and do, prove themselves to be superior to every inducement to become the creatures or tools of others. This " *leader* " applied to one of the " rescued " for information respecting me and my work, and positively assured him that *whatever* he said would not come *against* him. But this working man was more honourable than was supposed. He could not be induced to turn against me. But he wrote, as he said, "after thinking the matter over," and his first sentence bespeaks the motives which suggested the inquiry. This son of toil bluntly writes, " You were asking me if I thought our esteemed friend Mr Hillocks was doing any good in his mission."

Now though this " *earnest* inquirer," as I have said, had left the district, yet he had visited it frequently, and knew all about my mission—that it was no hole-and-corner effort, as even the letter indicates. The workman goes on. " I give you a few of my own observations. Our own (cottage) meeting is carrying on exceedingly well. In fact, those of our neighbours who have hitherto done all they could to stop our efforts are now coming in amongst us, and we have the signs of a glorious and prosperous year. At Albany Square, too, the work is going on well. From time to time cases come to my ears of some of the *worst* of all *worst* coming and joining them there. Mr H. still continues his Friday lectures at Highbury Works with great success. I believe at many other places also. I have great reason to believe he is received not only with pleasure but with cordiality.

Our Christmas entertainments came off with great success. At Mr H.'s lecture on the 2d of January, I may say we took fourteen fresh members, which I think is a fair start for the new year. I may also mention before I conclude, that men are not only joining our pledge-book, but, through the blessing of God on Mr H.'s efforts, are earnestly seeking for that comfort which cometh from above. I *do* believe that God is in the camp, and we shall prevail." Such was the news, signed not by one man only, but by three working men. Whatever the letter proved, it indicated a sturdy independence not yet driven out of British hearts when possessed by good and bent on good.

IV. The Valedictory Address.

But this was not the only proof of appreciation from those amongst whom I laboured. Though this Inquirer could not bring up any mud by such underhand currents, yet he succeeded some way or other. Victory was his, sorrow the people's, suffering mine. Those amongst whom I had laboured had not been slow to perceive the disagreeable position into which the envy of such a man is sure to place another. Indeed, they saw the gathering clouds sooner than I did, because I deal with every man to be truthful, till he proves himself to be the opposite.

When the time came for my departure, a meeting was called in the hall of the Holloway Institute, where the people proved that *their* affection towards me had not lessened. I need not characterise that meeting and the speeches, but I may give the following extract from the valedictory address then presented to me :—

" We take this opportunity of expressing our sincere gratitude to you for the invaluable services rendered to us and to the public generally, since you were providentially placed amongst us as missionary and lecturer. At that time we were glad to hear from various sources of your character and ability as a Christian teacher and a zealous advocate of temperance, and we now rejoice to know that your energetic and unwearied perseverance has far exceeded our expectations. It is not necessary to enumerate the various ways by which you have gained the affections of the people; these efforts are well known; but be assured of this, that you carry with you the warm affections of every heart."

But though I am under the painful necessity of placing the conduct of one man in opposition to that of others, yet I would not be doing justice to those who did their best for the welfare of the people in that district did I convey the idea that he was a representative man. True, he led some; but there were others who continued from the beginning to the end to take an interest in my mission—some whose friendship was true, whose countenance was cheering, whose counsel was profitable. Though I can only call occasionally, because of the pressing nature of my duties, where I am now congenially yoked, yet there are some of the workers, the noble workers, in the former scenes of my London labours, towards whom I feel the warmest affection, to whom I will ever be grateful, and the chief of whom is a gentle lady. The deep interest she took in this work, her tender and practical sympathy for the poor, her Christian charity towards all, and her carefully gathered wisdom, fit her well for the place of usefulness she takes in all efforts to help the bodies and instruct the souls of those in need of comfort and counsel. She is one of those ladies who will be ever respected by me. May her useful life be long spared.

V. ADVERSITY ONCE MORE.

I need not stop here to describe our trials and sorrows, during the months that followed in which I was without a salary. Though sorrowful we were not miserable, in the common sense of that term. Touching the incidents referred to, I felt sure, after a close self-examination, that I had entered upon my labours, and continued at them to the last, with a single and sincere purpose. Never had I faltered before difficulties, nor shunned duties however arduous. I had struggled to be faithful to God and to the people, zealous for His glory and their happiness, and hence I had a clear conscience. It was true, the question, " How best to keep the hoarse cry of the wolf, starvation, from being heard by those who were dear to me as life," stirred in my breast some of those cares which at times gnaw at the heart of those who are anxious honestly to provide for the household; and these pangs were all the more severely felt because poverty and want would not have come so quickly had I received what I considered to be morally, if not legally, due to me. But, as before, I had the sympathetic encouragement of my heroic helpmate, who as ever enhances my joys and shares my sorrows. And the very sight and thought of our young ones—even when we had but little, and sometimes not anything to give them—were enough at least to modify our grief. And to this may be named another, and the chief means of keeping us from sinking. Alas! we had had much cause to doubt the word of some of our fellow-creatures with whom we had met; so much so, that were it possible in relation to such of them, to crush everything like trust out of our hearts, it would have been done; but with God our experience had happily proved the very reverse, so that we could take Him at His word. The previous wonderful proofs we had had of His kind and constant upholding enabled us implicitly and lovingly to trust in Him; hence we could not be utterly miserable, though often very sad.

I admit we were often sad; not only because we were without the means of comfort and usefulness, but because of the variety of darkening elements which made up this cloud of adversity. One of these elements was this: previous to the hurried decision referred to, I was so confidently induced to believe that all was right in relation to my salary, for at least another year, that I had stated so in answer to questions put to me where I might have been congenially and usefully engaged, and as all generally find, when once *out* it is not so easily to get *in*.

But another drawback lay in the fact, that from the beginning to the end of my labours in North London, I had not had a single holiday. This hard and constant pressure on mind and body had, previous to this, been telling upon my frame, but now it was that I felt it most. This can be easily understood, especially by those who have gone through a like ordeal; and many are the zealous and noble workers for Christ who have felt themselves to be at the whim and *mercy* of one man who, *for the time*, had influence enough to gain *his* object.

VI. GRATIS WORK.—A HINT.

But though without pay, I was not long without work. Almost before I had time to rest, so as to regain some strength, I was induced to give *gratis* lectures, addresses, and readings at religious, temperance, and other meetings. This is a kind of work that is very abundant in London and elsewhere, and hence I shall offer a passing remark touching it. Certainly I am not inclined here to open the question, Whether or not this kind of wholesale *gratis speaking* is the most favourable for the good object sought? But it is worth the consideration of committees and others, and so is the following hint.

I am free to admit, and glad am I to have it to record, that there are men who ever manifest a willingness to give their spare evenings for such purposes, and so to render a service, the value of which cannot be named. And amongst such are friends not so light in purse as to mind whether or not their travelling expenses are paid; but there are others, equally well intended, to whom this is not such a trifle. If the committee "forget," as is too often the case, the speaker of the latter class has either to draw on himself, at the expense of his family, or add to his fatigue by travelling on foot. I speak from experience, and that in Scotland as well as England. I believe, with the doctors, that the all but fatal fever,—the sad results of which are referred to at the close of my Prize Autobiography,—was brought about partly because of such. I was (and ever have been) so bent upon doing all the good I could accomplish in this way, that I consented to speak wherever I was asked. So keenly do I feel on this point, that when I read a report of so many meetings, and of so much good being done, I ask, "What of the *gratis* speakers? Have they not suffered? How stand matters with their families?" A good rule would be, for the secretary to post to the speakers, with the bill announcing the meeting, the expenses to be incurred in going and returning. This would be beforehand, but all that the better. I have myself, even since I came to London, travelled a long way to deliver a *gratis* lecture, *because* I had not at the time any spare pence ; yes, and when the committee "forgot," I have had to get home the same way. Surely such mistakes arise from the want of thought more than from the want of heart ; but *why* do good people "forget?" If a speaker is worthy of the name, and is willing, for the sake of good, to forego the rights involved in the declaration, "the workman is worthy of his hire," certainly his travelling expenses ought to be paid.

And whilst I am on this point, I may mention another, that of the correspondence connected with this gratis work. This increases in proportion to the popularity of the speaker. It is a heavy tax upon him. I refer not now to the time employed in writing replies, which is considerable in many cases, but to the amount of stationery and stamps required. Let committees but think of all this, and not forget that some of the gratis speakers, indeed many of them, are far from rich in a pecuniary sense. I speak out thus honestly and openly, because every society who have done me the honour to ask my humble services in that way know that when it was at all possible I ever have complied with their request; nor do I regret having so laboured, even at this time, when I was without salary.

VII. A Few Links in the Brighter Chain.

But I pass on to name a few of those links in the chain which ultimately connected me with my present sphere of labour.

."I have just bought your ' Inner Life.' I have been so anxious to see the whole work in a complete form," said a smart gentleman to me, and to whom I had just been incidentally introduced in Mr Tweedie's book shop. "I have often *heard* of you," he continued, "but now I shall have to say I have *seen* you. Let me congratulate you on the interest many whom I know have felt in your ' Inner Life.' I have read the most of it, but I wish to have it in my library."

My new acquaintance was so earnest that I could scarcely get a word in edgeways, to tell him of his mistake. It was true he had met with the author, but the work he referred to is not yet published. Should it take the shape of a volume, the title most likely will be, " Struggles for the Mastery in the Growth of Inner Life." This work was thus suggested. Soon after my " Life Story" became popular, several friends expressed their regret that I had not in detail recorded my religious experiences in so severe and protracted conflicts with adverse circumstances. This regret was frequently accompanied by a request that I should, as early as possible, narrate these " Struggles for the Mastery." And as if in sympathy with this, one of the reviewers wrote :—" Though we agree with a former critic, that the author evinces a spirit of piety truly refreshing, and his path, though thickly strewn with thorns and briars, which might have made many a stout heart quail and give way to despair, has been nobly trodden hitherto, as it should be by every honest working man, with temperance, charity, and integrity, yet we should have liked more of his experiences as to his spiritual condition while under his pressing difficulties. They must have been peculiar, and would have been instructive to the tried Christian."

As was stated in the commencement of the chapters which appeared in the *Christian Cabinet*, and to which my new acquaintance referred, one object is to illustrate the spiritual aspect of life as experienced in the struggles between the lower and the higher powers of our nature, under the various influences which generally surround those who have to work their way through great difficulties; another is to encourage those who have to encounter similar obstacles; and a third is to shew from real life the necessity of exercising Christian charity towards the poor. The matter consists of two parts. The first contains some of those incidents connected with my early life, and which were the means of preparing the way for the dawn of truth upon the soul; also those circumstances which so operated as to threaten to overturn religious belief. The second takes up my spiritual history from this point, traces it on through the critical period, until peace is found; and, subsequently, through the various vicissitudes of a somewhat eventful career. The work was thus suggested.

But, as I have said, the work is not yet published. My friend had only bought " Life Story," which he took home; and after having read it, a pleasing correspondence was commenced. This led to an invitation to speak at Kentish Town, both outdoors and indoors, to the old and to the young.

And this led to another incident, an introduction to the Rev. James Fleming of the Kentish Town Congregational Church, an earnest, ardent, warm-hearted gentleman, popular and useful as a pastor. I felt comfortable and at home in his company, and he was pleased to say he would remember me whenever he heard of a suitable opening. At a second meeting with him he learned of my connexion with the office at 4 Bloomfield Street, but suggested that I should continue to labour in London, rather than go to the provinces, naming a society which had not been long in existence, but which proposed to do for London what the Home Missionary Society was successfully doing for the country, namely, the London Congregational Association, the objects of which are "the evangelisation of London, the promotion of fraternal fellowship among the associated churches, the calling forth of their separate and united efforts for the diffusion of Christian truth, and the establishment of worship in connexion with congregational principles among the neglected portions of the population."

This was another link in the chain; but though this association is ready to grant pecuniary aid, "with a view to originate or extend the aggressive efforts of churches which are zealously engaged in diffusing the gospel in their own localities," yet it was necessary for some church so engaged, and in need of an evangelist, to make the application. Nor was this latter link wanting—years before, it was being formed.

Shortly after my "Thoughts in Rhyme," with Gilfillan's Introductory Sketch, appeared, I was at Glasgow, and there met with the dear friend named at the commencement of chapter first. When speaking of the literary notices of that book, I mentioned one, and expressed a wish to know the name of the critic. "Professor Guthrie," was the ready reply. Previous to this I had heard of this gifted scholar, but ever after his name to me was associated with a rich imagination, a wide sympathy, a tender affection, and a mental capacity of no ordinary nature. He, too, ultimately came to London, and settled down as pastor in the north-western district. We met one afternoon at his residence, and a happy meeting it was. I soon perceived that my estimate of him, high as it was, was not too high, and our connexion since has only proved, in addition to what I had conceived, that he is "a Christian in the highest style of man," hearty and congenial, liberal and loving.

Shortly after this conversation, I was honoured with a request to take a service for him in his chapel, on Sunday, August

H

25, 1862. As will be remembered, this was about the time of the Sunday-School Union Conference, and there was on this day a series of composite meetings in many of the churches and chapels,—his being one of those selected for the assembling of the Sunday schools and others in that neighbourhood. This not only gave me an opportunity of speaking to the children from the words of the " Children's Friend," " my Father's business," but it served as my first introduction to the teachers and other Christian workers belonging to Mr Guthrie's church and congregation. And some of those I met then and there are now amongst my best friends and co-workers.

Again, I visited him by invitation, and this time our conversation was almost entirely confined to the various means employed for the work of evangelisation. After giving some idea of the mode I had endeavoured to act upon, he said, " I wish I had your assistance in *our* neighbourhood." And no sooner had he said so, than I thought, " How glad would I be, if associated with such a noble friend." I am happy to add, to our mutual joy, it was God's will so to unite us. On the 1st of December 1862, Mr Guthrie wrote, " Good news at last! The Committee of the London Congregational Association have agreed that you commence your labours in our district at once."

VIII. MY NEW SPHERE OF LABOUR.

As events have since proved, this was good news.

Tolmers Square is the centre of the district referred to. The spot now known by that name, was once called the " Old Reservoir," but the changes that have taken place there are so manifest, that those who have not been in the neighbourhood for ten years, would not know it to be the same. In the midst of this new square of large buildings, is a handsome church of which Mr Guthrie is the pastor, and in connexion with which I have the pleasure of labouring as an evangelist.

This centre of my labours is near to the junction of the Euston and Hampstead Roads. From each of these great trunks, a variety of streets, passages, and so-forth, meet and cross each other, in such a manner as to shew that every available spot is built upon and inhabited. At first sight, especially when passing through the leading thoroughfares, the general aspect seems somewhat favourable, but to find that things are *not* what they seem, one has only to get a peep behind these streets. George Street has its Little George Street; Albany Street, its Little Albany Street; and so on. The leading streets are comparatively wide and clean, but the most of the second class, and all the third class, are narrow and filthy; and these qualities greatly increase in the many densely-peopled parts, such as the courts and alleys which fill up the back ground of the black spots of the parish of St Pancras.

Here the population is much more densely packed than in Islington, but I found all the variety, perhaps a greater variety, in St Pancras than I met in Islington. Some of the classes are more numerous in St Pancras. This may specially be said in relation to " costermongers," and " labourers." And alas! the spectacles of guilt and misery are more visible and hideous. In both parishes, I met with many who had been so besmeared in the filthiest mires of the moral marshes, that all traces of manliness were hid—the brand of the devil standing out in bold relief. Hence, as might be supposed, for several months at least, I laboured with downright sadness of heart; but hope began to rise as I began to see proofs of the fact that

" Whilst the lamp holds on to burn,
The greatest sinner may return."

I cannot describe my feelings when I found that here too it was possible, in God's name, and by His help, to do some good even amongst those who were blindly plunging into deep wretchedness, and rushing impetuously to sad destruction.

With congenial workers I endeavoured to bring my past experience and observation to help me, and God blessed my efforts and those of congenial workers.

In the report of the London Congregational Association, dated February 25, 1864, are these words—"The mission in connexion with Tolmers Square Church, in the north-western district, has been abundantly blessed." And quoting from a letter written by Mr Guthrie concerning my labours and their results, the Report adds, "He (Mr Hillocks) has opened both for himself and his gospel message a door into many hearts. He has already secured a firm hold on the neighbourhood, and attracted considerable numbers to the public services. I help him from time to time, and preside or speak as he or his committee express their desire. We find that he is doing much, under God, to link the poor around us to our new sanctuary; and we feel that it would be a calamity to lose his services."

To say how this "door" to the people's hearts and confidence was "opened," would occupy a large portion of a volume; and besides it would suggest the discussion of questions, the full and free treatment of which would not come within the scope of this narrative. But I may, in passing say, that after carefully surveying the district, after ascertaining the condition and disposition of those at whose benefit I aimed—after learning what was being done to help such—I sought to aid those most likely to do good. Amongst such there were some good and earnest workers belonging to that portion of Christ's vineyard with which I was now happily connected. What was going on here I tried as much as possible to develop, endeavouring from time to time to supply what appeared to me to be wanting, in order the more effectively to obtain the desired object. Thus I gained the friendship and co-operation of all whose real object was the glory of God in the happiness of man. And this I must add, that never did I meet with a church in which the workers, in behalf of its surrounding district, were more earnest; and whatever Mr

Guthrie and others may kindly say of me and my humble efforts, not a small share of the happy results referred to, is due to the hearty encouragement and cordial co-operation of the brethren of Tolmers Square Church. These have been accorded to me from the beginning, and by none more sincerely than by Mr Guthrie himself. His large and warm heart, strong and noble mind, have done me much good personally; and our mutual confidence in each other has not only bound us together as pastor and evangelist—co-workers for the Lord, and each in his place—but it has given me that scope and freedom of thought and action which is essential to success in a work so peculiar, so difficult, so trying to the mind and body, and yet so noble and ennobling as being the means in God's providence of lifting a fellow-creature from the lowest position in the social and moral scale, and leading that person to Christ.

X. OUR EFFORTS.

Perhaps I could not do better than give the leading ideas of a circular lately issued in connexion with my work here. As will be seen by it the various societies in working order are united under this name—" The North-West London Evangelistic Association." Its object is " to promote the social, but above all, the religious well-being of the neglected masses of the population." Its sphere is defined as " the north-west division of London, commencing with the densely-peopled district intersected by converging portions of the Hampstead, Euston, and Tottenham Court Roads." It " consists (1.) of distinct societies that variously conspire to promote the common object; (2.) of individuals subscribing not less than 2s. 6d. annually to its funds." The means adopted by the association " are (1.) to encourage and strengthen the several societies in it, by union, counsel, and mutual encouragement; and by harmonious arrangement in regard to social meetings, lectures, and interests common to the whole; (2.) to organise efforts to raise funds from the district it seeks to benefit, and especially to aid in supporting the evangelist, whose entire time is devoted to the promotion of the good work." Its management is intrusted to "a president and vice-presidents, a treasurer, a secretary, a superintendent, and general committee—the latter being composed of the committees of the associated societies, with power to add to its number from among the individual subscribers." The stated meetings "are, (1.) the annual meeting of the members in December, to receive reports in regard to operations and funds; (2.) quarterly meetings of the general committee; and (3.) monthly meetings of the executive—when the general committee finds it needful to appoint an executive." This "association, as such, has no control over the affairs distinctively appertaining to the several societies it embraces—these being under the sole management of their respective committees; and, on the other hand, no member of the association, as such, stands committed to the specific policy of any of its societies in particular, but only to the great object contemplated by them all." And "the principle of the association is to discourage everything of a pauperising tendency, and to encourage and develop self-respect and self-help. Noble and needful though it often is to relieve the wants of the poor, it is still nobler and more needful to help them to do this by their own exertions, and to deepen in them the sentiment, that both for time and eternity, 'God helps those who help themselves.'"

The following are the societies already in working order:—

1. *The Christian Instruction Society*, " which seeks, by religious services, open-air preaching, tract distribution, and domestic visitation, to gain an entrance for the gospel into benighted hearts and homes. In connexion with this is the 'Bud of Promise,' a juvenile meeting, which seeks to bring children to the Children's Friend." 2. *The Total Abstinence Society, and the Band of Hope*, "to promote the cause of abstinence from strong

drink among old and young." 3. *The Mending Home Society*, "to improve home and home-life." Its membership is open to all wives, mothers, and daughters, (the latter from fourteen years of age, and upwards.) Several Christian ladies take a deep and active interest in the furtherance of its objects. And 4. *The Mutual Benefit Society*, "into which the savings of the poor are placed, and the proceeds either put into the Savings' Bank, or devoted to the purchase of coals, articles of clothing, or other necessaries, on advantageous terms."

I may only add here, that I find all these societies necessary and useful. The one helps the other, and all blend together with a pleasing harmony. Nor are they all I need in this good work, and hence others are in course of formation.

CHAPTER VI.

WORK OUTSIDE THE COURSE.

I. " YOU ARE IN MY DISTRICT."

SHORTLY after I had opened a new preaching station, and whilst I was speaking to a large and attentive audience, a man appeared amongst the rest with white neck-tie, and as one having authority. After the service was ended, he came to me and said, " Do you know you are in my district? " I answered in the negative, and asked if he had been in the habit of preaching there on that day, and at that hour? " No, no; but this is *my* district," was his reply. I urged him to come and occupy the place, adding, that if he felt inclined, I would soon find another place equally in want of good influences.

We parted on the best of terms; but finding that he had not thus attended to *his* district, I returned to the place, and have not been so chid since. Yet I am afraid I have often laid myself open to the same charge, and from the same motive that led me to this station—namely, to search out, and if possible to occupy, places that are *unoccupied*. As has been said, one of the objects of the London Congregational Association is to send its evangelists " amongst the *neglected* portions of the population." And the same desire prevails amongst those with whom I am associated. Our object is to supplement, not to supersede, any of the good workers. We have resolved—and as far as possible have carried out the resolution—to go where and when others are *not* found; and hence, though I endeavour to make Tolmers Square the centre of operation, yet necessity—the claims of the poor and needy—even of those who come to our various meetings—demands that the circle be somewhat extended. And whilst it is my wish to concentrate my efforts so that they may tell more effectively towards this centre, I have frequently had to step even beyond the bounds I have attempted to mark out for myself. By special invitation from those most deeply concerned, as well as by providential promptings, I have often been induced to go " outside the course."

II. EXCHANGE OF LECTURES.

If anything will test the most prolific mind, and lay the most active thinker under severe obligations to those who attach themselves to him, it is appearing before them, as a speaker, five or six times in the course of the six week-days, and twice or thrice, and oftener, on Sunday. It is true, if the evangelist or missionary keep before his mind the social and spiritual well-being of those brought under his influence, he has plenty of subject-matter; but he must think, and that carefully, if he means to be useful and worthy of his "high vocation." It is also true, without the good Spirit to help the thinking and bless the speaking, the fruit will be small; but then God has asked *us* to use the means, and promised the blessing, so that not a little depends on the thinking and speaking—on the matter and the manner—even the look and the tone. And besides the position and disposition, the virtues as well as the vices of those to whom he speaks, call for his exertion and care. Those who best know such as are most in need of his efforts are aware that in the same assembly, even on the same form, or in the same pew, are those who know not the first three letters of that amazing alphabet which makes up the gracious plan of salvation; and others, who, though now reduced to the lowest social scale of being, have, in better days, been able in their own way at least to analyse and readjust the various elements of learned theology.   Surely this even of itself is sufficient to suggest careful and prayerful preparation.   But one way to help one's-self in this case is to court a suitable exchange of labour with a Christian brother; and this, if not too frequent, is generally appreciated by the people.   Believing in this, I endeavour to get and to give help; and this is one of the means of occasionally leading me to lecture to others whom I could not in the narrow sense call " *my* people."

And I have had cause to rejoice that I have done so.   For instance, one day a brother called and named a person whom he wished me to visit.   " You do not know me personally," I said, whilst introducing myself to the person referred to.   "We do, and we make you welcome; please be seated," said the wife of the person whom I wished to see.   After a pause she added, " I bless God I have seen you before and heard you too," and on she went to name and describe the lecture, and its happy effects on her mind.

And having renewed my visit, and seen the husband, he, too, soon changed for the better; but my influence arose in no small degree from what I had said in an " outside " lecture delivered six months before this.   Doubtless great good would come of an increase of the occasional and judicious exchanging of labour between Christian workers in the home-missionary field.

III. At the Police Court.

An important place is the police court, and an important personage is the police magistrate.   There, and before him, crime and misfortune appear.   What an amount of work is done there! What a variety of character and of deeds pass in review in that strange little room !

" Oh, sir, I am sad to-day—my boy is in trouble," said

a mother to me one day, and in such a way as led me to make inquiry, and to induce me to see what could be done to help to get him out of trouble.

This I endeavoured to accomplish, and that was the first time I saw a police court in London. But the appeal has been made since, but with this slight alteration—instead of the words, " my boy," they are sometimes " my husband," " my son-in-law," " my wife," or " my daughter," who, of course, is innocent, or has " been led by that base *fellar*." I am the readier to go *if* it so be that I have known the person in trouble, and may have had hopes of him or her.

From the first I have regarded the London police court with peculiar interest. It is truly interesting to listen to the surroundings of all classes and degrees of offence, as they centre round the stories of the offended and offending—from the complaint which is merely the result of spleen to the weightier charges rising from crimes of the deepest dye. The poor and the destitute, the low and the vicious, the larking and the lurching, the quaint and repulsive, the lout and the lost, the stupid ignoramus and the forlorn wretch, the betrayed girl and the unsexed woman, the cruel parent and the ungrateful child, the fast man and the ragged rough, the timid pilferer and the incorrigible thief, the cunning swindler and the fraudulent clerk, the vulgar garrotter and the horrid murderer, in all the varieties of their odd types and diversity of strange peculiarities, pass and repass day after day to be dismissed, censured, handed over to be punished, or sent to the higher courts. Truly it is a sight and a study to be there; and I have found it to be a place where good may be done even to the roguish and the ridiculous, the daring and the dashing, but especially to the sorrowful and repentant.

IV. AT THE HOSPITAL.

Another means of usefulness I find to be visiting the hospitals occasionally. Besides the pleasure which one derives from the conviction that he has done some one good, visiting the hospital serves as a study which may be attended with profit. The "visiting day" is one on which much may be learned from the look, the word, and the tones which are interchanged. Husbands and brothers, wives and daughters,—in short, all kinds of relatives, friends, and acquaintances, flock in and seat themselves, each cluster round the bed of the patient, and tell all sorts of news which call forth the soft smile or trembling tear, in either of which there is a thrilling eloquence. If one is intimate with the patient and relatives, and knows when to put in a suitable word, then it is that the manifestation of tender affection may be improved. I have known of much good been done thereby. The watchful and experienced eye and ear may soon find a sufferer jubilant, even in the midst of pain, and the visited are grateful because the pain may not be so severe as it was; then it is that the hearts are likely to become one and melted in love, and then it is that the name of Jesus may be mentioned and blessed to all present. Yet the visiting day is not the most suitable time to try to lead the minds of the afflicted ones heavenward. It must be in the quiet hours—when there is the absence of excitement as well as bustle—that the messenger of mercy may expect more successfully to direct the sinner to the sinner's Friend, the diseased to the Physician of souls.

So I have found it; but nowhere have I felt more at home amongst the sick and the suffering in hospitals than in that very valuable institution at Soho Square. Every time I have visited that institution I have felt as in the presence of those who have the Spirit with them. Those who see to the sufferers are not "sisters," severe and cold, but "mothers," gentle and warm, practical Christian women, who do not only try to relieve the body from pain, but who carefully, prayerfully, and effectively use such means as are blessed to the peace and joy of the soul. Of adversity God makes many uses, and out of affliction He brings many blessings. One is to render the bed—even of sickness and pain—as a looking-glass in which to see one's-self, and then to see God as merciful and forgiving, as ready to help, and anxious to save. What a blessing it is when such are helped on their way rejoicing by those around them, as is the case especially in this hospital.

V. At the Workhouse.

The visitor who makes it his duty to give ear to the cries of the deserving poor cannot but deeply deplore the sadness and suffering which almost everywhere encircle honest poverty. The more attentive he is, their dreadful wants become the more obvious, and the oftener he calls, their various maladies become the more apparent. The wretched agony—whether concealed as much as possible, or permitted to manifest itself in sighs and groans, in words or tears—is likely to cause him to make inquiries, and what a revelation is that which the answers generally call forth ! What can be done? is the next question he puts, but this time he puts it to himself. Money he seldom has, and though he had a large fortune he would soon find room for it. He then calls to mind the fact that London is the metropolis of what is regarded as a great Christian nation listening to the voice of God, obeying Him as the all-wise Instructor, the Giver of every good and perfect gift. He remembers, too, that in the blessed gospel God has "spoken unto us by His Son;" that the all-loving Saviour said, " It is more blessed to give than to receive; " that Jesus, when He saw the people, and knew their condition—as sheep not having a shepherd—" was moved with compassion towards them." Hence he reasons—*if he knows no better*—that relief *without delay* may be obtained, and that of the best that Christian charity and human art can procure. He names that place called the "workhouse," where the "guardians of the poor" are said to represent the benevolent and the charitable; and then he hears a tale—what a tale! His heart filled with grief, and yet trying to suppose the best, he makes for "the house," expecting that their tales of want and woe will be attended to. With difficulty he passes the beadle, who is *not* the herald of charity. The relieving officer—who is seldom the messenger of mercy—listens to him with a cold indifference, as if he were saying nothing new. "I'll call," is the promise, and the amount of success; but these words are accompanied by many more, the purport of which is to blacken the character of the poor. He returns to the poverty-stricken abodes, reports progress in a tone approaching hope, and yet near to despair. His own pockets are light, but he has left all he had to save life, or, as he thinks, to keep the gloomy lamp flickering till the officer "visit the case." He returns shortly after the time that the officer named, but only to find that in "the house" promises are made to be broken, that, as he had been told, "it is all a pretence." Again he applies, and after hearing many excuses and more abuse of the poor, the promise is renewed, but only to be broken as before, only to compel him to regard the whole as a mockery, and cause him to make inquiry as to the principles and administration of the poor law, —only to find that whatever the theory may be, the practice is a disgrace to London. I say London, because I am at present speaking of its workhouse—*so-called*—"relief," and in these sentences I have simply given my own experience before I really knew how matters stood. I had expected that if indigence, caused by misfortune or old age, sickness or incapacity, could find comfortable asylums anywhere, it would be in the great metropolis; but I was mistaken, especially as regards the workhouse, and the poor who have a right, an *understood* right, to protection when unable to protect themselves.

"Why, sir, let them come to me and speak for themselves.

You will have plenty to do if you listen to all you hear from those who live in these localities," said a relieving officer to me when I pressed for an explanation as to why he had not called to see a case I had brought under his notice. The case was this :—

A " gentleman's servant " was out of place, and had been so for some time. Everything had been sold that would sell *to get food*—not beer nor gin. His character was unimpeached, but he had great difficulty in getting another place. His wife had done her best to help to bring in something to support the large family, but she was ultimately confined to bed. In this state two of the members of our Christian Institution Society found the family—starving, and without hope of any relief. They rendered immediate help, and told me what they had seen. As was my duty, I went to " the house," and at last the question just given was asked ; but what was the fact? This poor man had been there before this, and had been so " abused and threatened," that he left, resolved that, sooner than be so " insulted by a fellow," he would die in the streets.

It was only after I threatened a public exposure in the newspapers that this family's wants were attended to—and then to what an extent ? An answer would lead to the exclamation— " Niggard cruelty !"

And mark these two facts :—1. This is not a rare case. 2. It did not happen at Bethnal Green. I know, and others know, there is more than one Bethnal Green—I mean, more than one parish—where the poor are robbed of their rights ; where the victims, even of honest poverty, are insulted ; where the helpless are neglected ; where the abuses of the workhouse (did that occur which would bring some of them to light) are such as to haunt London with remorse.

This poor man got work at last, but not for long. Not that he was dishonest, not that he was unworthy of his place ; he became ill, broke down, came home, and was shortly carried to an untimely grave. He did not die the profligate's nor the drunkard's, but the Christian's death; he was not poisoned, but *he was murdered.* Who were the guilty parties? Not his dear wife—for she waited upon him with all the care and tenderness of a worthy wife. Nay, though very ill, she sat by his bedside almost night and day. Though almost blind—an infirmity brought on by the weakness of want, and the baby tugging in vain at her breast for milk—though thereby almost blind, she affectionately attended him to the last. It is possible that it could be stated that he caught cold, that it set down upon his chest, and that he died of what is called consumption. This might have been the more immediate cause, but what of the more remote cause, that which so weakened him and racked his frame—without food for days, and when it came his way, insufficient, and this for months? Like many of the honest poor, he and his wife were averse to parading their sufferings, and horrified at the idea of asking for parochial relief, but necessity compelled them to apply, and the result was as I have stated.

Was he killed? Who killed him? Are not many sharing the same fate to-day? are questions I leave the reader to answer. I have my own opinion, and that is borne out by what I see and hear every day. It was only the day before I penned these lines that I called upon a poor woman, whose tale made the tears come to my eyes. She had lost her husband twelve years ago, and since his death had tried to " keep the life in " by sewing, when she could get it; but now that she was nearly seventy years old, she could neither see well nor walk far, therefore she sat a helpless creature in her wretched hovel, with little food and less fire—in short, being slowly but effectually killed, inch by inch, and day by day. An answer to the question, Do you get any help from the house? brings forth such a revelation as makes one tremble. The sum is, application has been made, abuse has been received; the " test "—you must come in, or let us hear no more of you—has been applied in her case, as in many others, with effect.

"I'd rather live on a penny a day, I'd rather die in this sorry place, than go to the house," she said, and then went on to give the stereotyped reasons—reasons which call for a great change in our poor law administration.

In speaking thus of the poor in relation to the poors'-house, I do not attribute individual culpability to any one. I know not why it is that the beadle snaps the poor, nor why the *relieving* officer is so unlike the first portion of his official name; but I know, because I have seen, the results of a system which calls for improvement. I do not here intend to enter into the personal merits or demerits of any individual connected with these places, which are regarded as prisons, and something worse, by those who know them best; but I know this, that many of the industrious and struggling poor—those who in their better days had paid poor-rates—those who for long had been next door to pauperism—would suffer much before they would endure the abuse and insult which they dread; and as for going into the "house," they would rather die, as not a few do. Is this the spirit of the poor law? Who could say that those who framed it meant such? Is this the wish of those who pay the rates? Surely it is not. And yet, here we are in London, the capital of Christian Britain, in the nineteenth Christian century, the poor neglected, the helpless suffering, the sickly dying, because of workhouse abuses! Are we in this respect listening to the voice of Heaven?

But I have just made use of the word *merit* as well as the word *demerit*, and I mean both as applicable here. However black the aspect may be that surrounds, and enters into, the best of our London workhouses, I can believe there is connected with them not a little of personal merit. I have been received courteously, as well as insolently. I have seen the poor treated with compassion, as well as with harshness. I know of officials who are worthy of the trust they have, who feel for those they have the care of. It is but lately that one instance of this kindly

I

feeling, tender compassion, and careful attention became conspicuous, because of the absence of the ready hand and the cheering voice of one of the medical staff connected with the parish of St Pancras. "We have lost our doctor. I hope he is in heaven. He was our friend," said a poor woman to me, referring to this poor man's friend; and she only said what she and others felt, what I knew. Yet such *personal merit* will never be able to counteract the *collective demerit*. It is evident there is something radically wrong somewhere, and the voices of justice and of mercy join in the cry for redress.

But I have gone to the workhouse not only to plead the cause of the poor and the needy, the sick and the dying; I have also gone within its walls, and into its wards, to tell the inmates of the Father's "house" above, of Him of whom they might say, " I am poor and needy, yet the Lord thinketh of me." In going from bed to bed and from ward to ward, I have been listened to with attention and gladness, not only at the regular place of meeting for praise and prayer and the proclamation of the gospel from the pulpit, but also at other gatherings, some of which to me have been very striking. Every class and division has its peculiar characteristics, though over the whole there seems to be a sepulchre aspect; the gloom of the tomb seems to press in before time, as if some cruel worm were gnawing at the sunken heart. The children, poor creatures, how dull and sad! The aged seem as if all hope had fled from their being. The able-bodied look, as if looked upon as worse than a felon either are utterly indifferent, or as if anxious to escape if they but knew how. What can be more distressing and sickening than the afflicted pauperism of London as seen in the workhouse? But the most harrowing sights are to be seen in the infirmary and insane ward. Here meet the worst of human ills, the accumulation of all those fearful, sad, and degrading forces which weaken and crush those who have—in grim and dirty localities—huddled together and struggled with adversity in the absence of proper food and pure

air. Here may be seen the most distressing marks of want
upon the frame, and of woe in the countenance, the racking pain
of " the rheumatiz," the torture of festering sores, the faint-weak-
ness of sickness, and the infirmities of old age; these are only a
few of the items of the bill of torture which constitute the gloomy
agony of the poor wretches of the infirmary. And then, the
insane ward! There, to all this, may be added the aspect which the
various degrees of sheer ignorance, idiotic stupidity, and positive
insanity, ranging from the momentary fit to the continuous
raving or sullen silence. Surely if ever a place of suffering and
of woe required a Nightingale for matron, and a Howard for
master, the noblest of men for doctors, the tenderest of women
for nurses, and the best amongst their number as attendants, it
is a London workhouse. And what of the spiritual advisers,
those who go to tell the good news,—salvation for the sinner,
and joy for the sorrowful? Surely *he* ought to be imbued with
the spirit of the Master, of Him who had compassion on the
people, who prayed for the people, who wept with the weeping.
Certainly, neither the proud Pharisee nor the formal priest, who
looks on and passes by " on the other side," is the man. What
a mistake to think that *any* man may speak to the inmates of a
workhouse! They have hearts, and they rejoice when they meet
with hearty sympathy. I speak from experience, for many are
the evidently sincere expressions of thanks from their lips which
have met my ears, with the request, " Let us see you soon again."

I refer now especially to St Pancras Workhouse, because
there I am best known; and I am glad to add that there the
officials, from the master down, have ever evinced a readiness
to enable me to comply with the oft-repeated request, " Let us
see you soon again."

If space permitted, I might here refer to a variety of incidents in the workhouse which have come under my notice. I
shall only name one, which must be interesting to all who love
home and the ties of home. One day, when passing from the

infirmary to the insane ward, I observed a man hastily making his way across towards a low wall upon which was a large iron railing, and on the other side of which were a woman and child. They were looking towards him.   It was mother and child; and the object of their attraction was the husband and father.   Who could depict the manifestations of emotion which were deeply impressed on each face, as he—*between the railings*—snatched a kiss from baby's cheek !   The oakum test gives bleeding fingers, but the separation test causes bleeding hearts.   God help the poor !

CHAPTER VII.

SOME INCIDENTS AND RESULTS ILLUSTRATING THE NATURE OF MY LABOURS.

I. THREE ERRORS.

REFERENCE to my notes remind me of the maxim "to err is human," and I should not be true to facts did I not here notice three errors by way of specimen.

1. All who have heard me speak—especially without preparation—are aware that not a few Scotticisms fall from my lips. This arises from the fact—a fact which I do not hesitate to admit—that my form of speech was all but fixed, whilst I was in the midst of those who had not even any pretensions to education; of those who are in the habit of not only using Scottish words, but, as one has properly phrazed it, "using English words in a Scottish use, or construction." Hence it is, that the more earnest and natural I am, the more Scotticisms come from my lips. But this error illustrates the truth of Cicero's statement—"The manner in which an individual expresses himself, is a matter of the greatest importance."

In the course of my calls one day, I observed that an aged and ailing woman seemed worse than I had ever seen her. Feeling most intensely for her, I said, "Poor creature, you are very *sober* to-day." She made no reply, and I inferred that her weakness prevented her from entering into conversation as before. It so happened that it was some time before I had an opportunity of renewing my visit, and this added fuel to the fire. When I next called, she was very reserved, till at last she mustered as much courage as to tell me what was troubling her; how the word *sober* had operated upon her mind, depriving her of peace, and rest, and sleep. She thought I meant to convey the idea that it was something rare to find her *not over-powered by drink*. Nothing could have been further from my thoughts; and so, after explaining my meaning, we became as friendly as before. But, curious enough, the very next person I visited was an elderly Scotchwoman, the daughter of a late minister; and on my inquiry as to her health, she replied, "Very sober, sober indeed." I understood her, but I thought of *my* error.

2. One dear lady called to inform me of a woman who was anxious to see me. I was preparing for Sunday—one of the very few in which I had consented to preach in the country. I had been up very early in the morning, but was not satisfied with the preparation I had made, so I halted between two courses—to complete the sermon I was preparing, or to visit and not finish the preparation. Time, and the train, shut me up to one or other, for I could not think of travelling on Sunday, even to do good, if I could possibly avoid what at best would be a disagreeable, because a questionable course. Though I felt the impulse to visit, yet I continued my study till I had just as many minutes left as enabled me to enter the railway station in time. All that night I was uncomfortable. I felt sure that the ailing woman knew of Christ as her Redeemer; but she wished to see me. And what to me was remarkable, I did not use that portion of the discourse which I finished after I knew of her wish. The occasion suggested the propriety of introducing other thoughts essential to the purpose for which the sermon was preached, and to put aside the portion referred to. But imagine my sorrow when, on my return, I found I was "too late." When on my way to the address given, I met the same

lady who called on me. "She is gone—she breathed her last about ten minutes ago—and she did want so much to see you." So said the lady, scarcely able to speak. Words cannot tell how I felt, because I had not obeyed the first impulse to "go at once."

3. The only other error I shall mention, was also somewhat serious in its nature. On one occasion I left London by train on a Saturday afternoon. My object was to preach three times on the morrow. It was winter, but I never saw a more bright and beautiful day. The frost was keen and the snow was fair. How I did enjoy the magnificent and picturesque scenery around and above me, especially when at the station, waiting the conveyance to take me to the place appointed; for then the silvery sky gave way to the variegated colours which make up that gorgeous display seen in England on a frosty evening, when the red sun sinks in the west. But I paid dearly for my too great devotion to the beauties of nature. Though I had the sermons which I intended to preach all sketched in my mind, yet I foolishly thought of changing the subjects, and that because of what I had seen, and the thoughts thereby suggested. I fear I had thought of being grand, without thinking that the grand might come in the way of the useful. By some mistake, the conveyance which I expected to find when I arrived at the station was not there. Night came on, and a beautiful starry night it was; but I became concerned because I did not know my way. Being cold, and out of sorts, I began to travel, expecting to meet the car. Not being so fortunate, at last I spoke to a man, who happened to know the farmer with whom I was to stay on the Sunday. I took his advice—which was to hire a conveyance—and arrived on Sunday morning, my blood almost congealed to ice. The friends were kind and attentive; but sleep I could not, I was so cold and so troubled. In this state of mind and body, I endeavoured to do my best; but oh! it was sorry—so *I* thought, for I felt that I could not

keep the mind fixed on any one point, neither on the subjects I had before contemplated upon, nor those thus suggested.

I record these errors because they taught me lessons which I never shall forget.

II. Providential Promptings.

At the close of the second of the errors just referred to, I made use of this sentence—"words cannot tell how I felt because I had not obeyed the *first* impulse, to *go at once*."

This *impulse* I believe to be a providential prompting to duty. In my time, I have had many such, often leading me to act when I scarcely knew wherefore, and at other times when at a loss to know what to do, because of surrounding difficulties, the suggested thought would flash across my mind like lightning in a dark room. But let it be kept in mind that there is nothing in what I have designated "Providential Promptings," akin to that diabolical legerdemain falsely called "spiritual agency." As far as the east is distant from the west, so far is the one distant from the other. The second is held forth by the pretender, and admitted by the credulous; but the first is realised only by those who believe in the special providence of God, who willingly give up their hearts to His will and influence. And there is also a wide difference between these promptings, and what may not improperly be termed a mere sentimental impulse, such as that referred to in error third. Though the ideas then suggested—and which induced me to change my subject—have again and again come rushing to my mind, not only to be acceptable, but to be useful in the country and in the metropolis; yet I scarcely ever see the heavens flush without remembering that failure, and the remembrance is all the more disagreeable, because I cannot persuade myself that the impulse rose more from a desire to tell for the good of souls than from a wish to please those who might listen to me. This is an awkward confession, but I cannot well avoid it; for, although the latter idea did not exactly form itself into as many words, yet I cannot say that the former idea was prominent. What a difference between the result of that impulse, and the following instances of providential promptings—a few out of many!

1. Last summer, I opened some new open-air preaching stations round the centre of my present sphere of labours. At one of these newly-opened places, I observed an old man as if half-inclined to go away, and yet half-inclined to remain. He was evidently uneasy, but he came again, this time for about twenty minutes, and listened more attentively. All of a sudden, he left and again returned as restless as ever. It was then I felt and obeyed the impulse to repeat as nearly as possible all I had said in his absence. It seemed to be laid on my mind to preach to that man as if he was the only person before me. That was on a Sunday evening, and at the end of that same week a friend came to me, and in an earnest tone said, "Oh, sir, do continue the preaching at the station we were at on Sunday evening. Blessings are sure to follow; they have, I hope, already followed. You saw that restless old man; he has only heard two sermons for years, and they were at that place. You saw him concerned on Sunday evening; well, he was dead by Wednesday morning. I hope the truths you laid before him and us are blessed. Continue to speak there if your strength and time permit."

How glad I was that I obeyed the prompting to repeat for *his* sake what I had previously spoken, for that which I had said was such as is likely to be blessed to those around me, but especially to one in his condition—a condition of which I knew not, never having seen him till he became a listener.

2. "They are plotting against your life, sir. For our sake, and the sake of your family, do not go." So said a number of men and women who were waiting my arrival at a preaching station to tell me of the danger I was in. It was a place

infested by many calling themselves Papists; but not a few of them were fearful drunkards and base sceptics. These three classes had frequently combined to oppose the preaching at that station; and some who had gone before me had given way to them. This gave them some hope of driving me off the field by fierce and rough opposition.

I was alone, for the friend who generally accompanies me had gone to enjoy his holidays. I saw the group to which these warning friends alluded. I listened to their advice, and thought of usefulness and of my family. In this plight I carefully reflected, prayed in secret, and at last resolved to face the foes. How to meet them, and what good I might do, I knew not; but I believed He who was with Daniel in the lions' den was with me. Listening to the promptings to go, I left the terror-stricken friends and passed on towards the plotting group. Soon one of the number approached me, but I soon found that though a Papist, *he* was not so much set against me as the ringleader. There had been a sudden death in the place, and this man incidentally referred to it.

" I shall go to see the bereaved friends," I said, and passed by the group as if it had not been there.

What had happened before I returned I know not, but the group was dispersed, and this same man now assured me, that none dare lift a hand to injure me whilst there was Irish blood in his veins and he was able to use his strong arm. I commenced my service as usual, shaping my discourse to suit the incidents known to the people; was listened to with marked attention, and I know good was done. I saw tears in the eyes of many as we affectionately parted, and never since have I been opposed there.

3. But these promptings have also been of good service to me in visiting as well as in preaching. At the close of one of our meetings, some of those who had been lately brought to see the error of their way, named a man who was yet on the

broad road to destruction, and added, "He would be worth bringing in about, were that possible." I listened to all they said, and inwardly resolved to do my best to meet with him, assuring them, by the way, that *every* one was *worth* "bringing in about," because every one had a soul. Three weeks passed and I had failed to obtain a suitable approach to him, and scarcely had he ever been out of my mind. True, I might have gone and told him who I was, and that I knew what *he* was; but that would have most likely shut out the only chance left of reaching his heart. I have waited as long as four weeks before obtaining the first and longed-for interview, and that sometimes only a few words, perhaps about the weather, or the children; but I would wait and watch four months before I would destroy an opportunity by intruding myself and what I had to say in such a manner as to lessen my chances of success. In this instance the third week had almost passed, for its last night and almost its last hour had come, when I had gone home and pulled off my boots, with the view of resting my weary limbs. I did rest for about an hour, when I felt I must go, though I could not say why, again in the streets; but though I found plenty of work to do, yet there was nothing new for the first half-hour—just what may be found in any such place on a Saturday evening about eleven o'clock. But, when on my way home, I saw a man whom I believed to be one of those I had been in search of, and I found—after I had introduced myself to him—that he was the man I had sought for during the previous twenty-one days. For nearly an hour we walked and talked together and then parted, promising to meet at a given time and place. Every meeting increased my hopes of his improvement. He became a reformed man. Not only was he soon seen at our temperance meetings, but also at the gatherings called specially for praise, prayer, and edification. I did not regret having acted upon the inward prompting which said, "go."

4. And at other times I have felt, as it were, impelled to go

to a particular place, though I felt almost sure all was right. This was the case on one of the festival occasions. I had some months previously been introduced to one of the finest specimens of the sons of toil I ever met with—a good workman, and he had been manly in his bearing, and womanly in his affections, noble in mind and tender in heart; but he had given way to drink and lost sight of God. Ill treatment at the hands of some who professed to believe in Christianity had caused him to forget principles and look to men. He said he believed in a god, but not the God of the Bible. Many had called to reason with him upon these points, but he only respected them in proportion as their lives corresponded with their statements. If he did not oppose their assertions and arguments, " it was," he said, " out of respect to their feelings ; " but all they said only served to confirm him the more in the opinions he held—so he declared to me again and again. We met often, but not so often as he wished, owing to the pressure of my other duties upon my time. " Sit down and tell me the story of your experience when a *doubter*, and how you was led to see the light," he would at times say to me, " and make way to dust a plank ; " and after I had told him he would add, " What I'd give to feel as you feel ! " I have seen him moved to tears, for he was in earnest. He lived a considerable distance from the centre of my field of labour ; but I sometimes visited him at his home. It was on the occasion named that I paid one of my visits. As a rule, Christmas and New Year's-day give me cause to feel very anxious respecting the rescued, especially those who have been lately saved from the power of strong drink by abstaining from it. It was so on this occasion, but my fears had not extended to his clean, tidy, and comfortable home, and yet I *must* go. He answered the door, and I soon perceived he had broken his pledge. He had been enabled to withstand the temptations of Christmas-day, and the force of habit, but at last yielded, and then, how the demon dashed him to pieces !

"Oh my friend, God has sent you just in time. The devil has been tempting me to take my life; but God has sent you to help me—I thought He would, I prayed He would." Such was the salutation with which I was met by him.

"Oh, thank God, He hears prayer, my dear. Be seated, be seated," said his good wife, gently leading him to a seat.

They wept, and I could not withhold the tears. My silent but earnest prayer was, that God might direct me, so that my visit might be blessed. This prayer, also, was answered. Once more this brother was rescued; and oh, how thankful I was of the impelling impulse which caused me to visit this man, and in time !

5. These inward promptings have frequently prevented me from returning home at the time I had promised. One day I had continued from morning to go out and in amongst the people till the approach of night. But, though very much exhausted, I thought of one whom I felt bound to visit before I could go home. He was a considerable distance off, but I *must* go. I had called before, but he would not see me. Arrangements, however, had been made by which we would meet, *if he was at home*. His wife answered the door, and her first words were, "You are too late, sir, we have agreed to part, and he has gone for the broker to sell these few things you see." But he returned whilst I was doing my best to encourage and advise her. At first he was very distant; but no sooner had words passed between us than he gave signs of regret, which were soon followed by promises of improvement. He signed the pledge before I left. The broker did not get the "few things." Woman-like, this poor wife forgave the wretched husband for all the nineteen years' ill treatment. A few days after, I called again, and though he was ill because of his past doings, she was filled with hope and joy. Again, I was glad I obeyed this providential prompting.

III. A FRIEND'S TACT AND ITS EFFECT.

On one occasion I went to Hitchen at the invitation of a "Friend." When I say *friend* I mean so in more ways than one,—a friend to the friendless poor, and a friend in relation to his profession in the Church of Christ. Often, in town and country, have I met with the wise and good in all sects and all parties, but never did I meet with kinder and wiser men and women than those known as the "Friends" or Quakers.

This kind gentleman manifested his wisdom, his knowledge of humanity and the feelings of those he thus sought to benefit, in the way he advertised my coming to that town. When I went I was surprised, and yet delighted, to see the words, "Lately a weaver at Dundee," below my name on the bills announcing that I was to speak. Amongst the numerous notices of my autobiography there was not one which sounded more pleasant to me than that in which these words occurred—"He is a native of Dundee, where he first worked as a *weaver*, and then held, with great credit, the position of a *teacher*." The fact of my having laboured hard with my hands I often use as one of the keys by which I am enabled to open the way to the hearts of those with whom I am brought in contact. In Edinburgh and other places in Scotland, I was familiarly known as, and often called, the "young weaver." This perhaps arose from my having written a little book entitled "Passages in the Life of a Young Weaver"—these "passages" touching my juvenile days. Hence it is that Gilfillan, in his sketch of my life, says, "It was to us always truly delightful to see our '*young weaver*' presiding in the school—a child amongst children—*leading* them, even as Una led by a line her milk-white lamb, by the unseen cord of love to the green pastures and still waters of knowledge, and by those ways of spiritual wisdom which are pleasantness and peace." As I was then "a child amongst children," so do I wish now to be amongst the working classes a working man.

This my friend properly anticipated to the enhancing of the efforts there made.

The very first meeting was well attended. People—men, women, and children—who would not come out before, came to the meeting to see the Scotch weaver. And having gained their attention, I managed to keep it. Meeting after meeting— Sunday and week-day—became larger and larger. Our last one during my stay was held in the town-hall, and even that could not contain all who wished to come. The school-room across the way was also opened that night. It is well to get a good start, and my friend, doubtless, helped to accomplish this by inviting the people to come to hear "what the weaver had to say."

IV. The Scoffer in Tears.

On another occasion I went to Windsor as an open-air preacher. One of the places at which I spoke was a lane. Not one of the "*green lanes*" in which the poet walks, and writes of singing birds and primroses. No; this lane had been made into a street, behind which were many of those dwellings and dwellers which often disgrace English towns near to London.

It was on a Sunday evening, but the aspect around did not accord with that hallowed day. Before, behind, on each side, and stretching far on either hand, were the public-houses, within and around which were people neither few in number nor attractive in appearance. If these places of "*refreshment*" were not brothels, they were next door to them, for never—out of Ratcliff Highway—did I see in one street more of the wretched women who tell by their words and ways what they are.

Whilst the friend who preceded me was speaking, a scoffer passed by, and said—

> " 'Tis religion that can give
> Sweetest pleasures while we live;
> 'Tis religion must supply
> Solid comforts when we die."

He then passed on. My friend spoke shortly, and then introduced me. By this time the scoffer was again returning, but without the strumpet that before was dragging him along, and before whom he must be *brave*, if not gallant. I thought it proper to take his words as my text, believing that most of the audience then present heard them thus uttered.

This was successful. All seemed anxious to know what I had to say, and none more so than the scoffer himself. After endeavouring briefly to define what true religion and real pleasure are, I presented, by a series of life-pictures which I had seen, the contrast between those who knew not religion and those who felt its joys. During my discourse I referred to a pious mother's anxiety for those who give proofs of their serving the devil and his agents. This picture met the scoffer's eye.

"It was a photograph duplicate of my mother," he said; for at the close he came forward before the immense crowd, and asked to speak to me. "You were correct when you said I repeated the words as a scoffer, but they were not out of my lips before I felt the force of their truth." He then related his determination and struggles to get away from the woman with whom he had just been associated, and again added—

"My dear, good mother proved the truth of these words in life and at death; but she was sorry for me; she died praying for me; and yet here I am, the devil's servant for forty years."

Here he paused, and wept, and pressed my hand, and then went on narrating the leading features of his wicked and wretched life. It was late and dark, and we were by this time alone, but I did my best before we parted to point him to " the Way, the Truth, and the Life,"—he promising henceforth to walk therein.

V. A Distressed One.

One day, on returning from a visit to Ratcliff, I was making my way to Tower Hill, when a man introduced himself to me by saying, "It is a very cold day, sir." This was a fact which everybody, outside a comfortable parlour, knew—a fact which was telling sadly upon him, for he was trembling very much.

His address was pleasant, but his dress was shabby: hat—old, bruised, and far from being a "good fit;" coat—long, greasy, and out at the elbows; vest—he had none; trousers—short and rent; shoes—without heels, and much in want of toe-bits; shirt—dirty, the wrists invisible, and the breast torn and buttonless; necktie—a piece of a tattered worsted garment. His frame had once been strongly built. He was tall, and the short sleeves of his coat shewed that the bones of the wrists were large, though now fleshless. His face yet retained those marks of intelligent pleasantness which one can only associate with elegance of mind and gentleness of heart.

"You 're a stranger, sir?" he added, and paused for a reply, and then continued—"I am a stranger to you, though not a stranger in London; but I appeal to you as a fellow-creature. A drop of beer would help me; treat me to the share of a pint."

His tone and his look were such that, had I not been an abstainer from strong drink, I might have consented. I told him that I abstained from such drinks on principle, but I would give him a cup of coffee and bread and butter.

"God bless you, sir!" he exclaimed, and led the way to a coffee-house.

Poor fellow! he ate voraciously, and glad was I to be able to appease his hunger. I had a cup of coffee for myself, but was so distressed to see a brother in such a condition that I could not eat.

"God bless you, sir!" he again exclaimed, showing by his movement that he wished to leave; but I urged him to remain a little longer to warm himself by the stove. He did so, but soon after the large tear-drops rolled down his furrowed cheeks.

"I am the hopeless victim of that grinding rapacity which the unprincipled strong bring to bear against the hapless weak. I

K

was commercial—I had a dear wife—once we could look upon sweet children—now you see what I am. God bless you, sir! We may never meet again."

He would have gone after giving utterance to these sentences, there being a pause between each; but I took his half-extended hand, and assured him we might meet again in heaven. To this he emphatically said—

"No; earth is hell begun to me, and I dare not hope for heaven; but the time *was*"—

"The time *is*," I added, and endeavoured to point the way to a free and present salvation, through Christ the Saviour.

"I have known something of the grandeur of humanity and something of its poverty, but humanity without divinity is poor indeed."

Here again he paused, but soon added, "I have in my time, like others, boasted of our national wealth and strength, but I have been led to question our natural wisdom and benevolence; I admit her power, but I question her religion. Like thousands in my time, I was *religious;* but religion never did for me what it has done since I came into this box of a room—it never induced me to do for one what you have done for me. *I* have never fed one with the 'bread of life,' because I have never eaten of it myself; I have helped a little in my time and in my way, but never as a true disciple of Christ—never in the name of Jesus. But in His name I ask God's blessing on you, and pray that for His sake we may meet in heaven. Farewell!" and in a moment he was off sobbing convulsively.

This was my first *sermonette* in London; what may be its effects I know not, but there was room for hope.

What is his history?—how has such a noble specimen of humanity become such a deplorable wreck?—is he more the victim of "man's inhumanity to man" than of his own imprudence, his folly, and wandering from the great Source of light and happiness?—how many such claim the attention of those who feel for others' woes?—were questions to which none but He who ever pities the poor and the needy can furnish replies. Had he not spoken to me I could not have known of such a man, of such a case, of poverty so overwhelming, of misery so intense.

VI. How the Drunkard was Led to Believe in the Power of Prayer.

One afternoon I was making my way home in the company of a clergyman and two ladies. We had been endeavouring to do good amongst the drovers, and were conversing as to the best mode of gaining our object, when a very tall, strong, and rough man stepped up to us, and said, " You belong to those who can heal the sick, make the lame to walk, and the blind to see, can you heal this arm?" and he pulled aside the cut-up sleeve of his coat, and exhibited such a sight as almost sickened the ladies. His arm had been long sore, and that afternoon he had fallen, so as to reopen the wound and cut other places. The clergyman said he could take him to a surgeon, but the man replied, "You have the cure of souls, and cannot heal bodies."

Seeing he was rather witty, I thought it was time to meet him on his own ground, and offered to heal his arm if he would act as directed. This took him by surprise, and he agreed on condition that I should go home with him. I consented, and we left the clergyman to escort the ladies. The task of going home with this poor fellow was somewhat difficult. We had to pass several public-houses, into each of which he wished to go. Though, by reminding him of the conditions, he did not enter, yet he frequently gathered a crowd about us. He would be as witty as ever, and create laughter, as he thought, at my expense; but this gave me an additional opportunity of saying a word or two, which I trust were blessed. However, we at last reached his home,—the drunkard's home. I dressed his arm, and obtained the promise that he would not go out that night.

Feeling the craving for the drink, he began to regret having made such a promise. The thought grew upon him, and off he would go. I pleaded, and appealed to his promise. For a moment he calmed down, and then he became enraged, cursed ministers and missionaries, and declared Christianity to be a humbug. Often did he threaten to put me "into nothing," to prove, though his arm was sore, " it was strong and fit for the prize ring." At last we parted good friends.

I visited him again on Sunday, and found he had kept his word. Having dressed his arm, he renewed his promise, and we entered into conversation, in the course of which he assured me that his bible was a sporting newspaper, a copy of which he had been reading before I entered. When leaving, he invited me back soon, adding, as he gave me a hearty shake of the hand, "They's the best missionaries as can help body and soul, as can employ hands and head."

Thus I continued for weeks till the arm was healed and he had resumed work. The promise to keep from strong drink only extended to the time when " the arm was made whole as the other," as he termed it, with emphasis. Now it was that I urged him to take the pledge to abstain from all intoxicating drinks, pointing to the curative properties of simple water in the cure of his arm. This was a fact he was compelled to admit, as well as another—namely, that his general health had improved greatly whilst acting under his promise; but he had gone "to *work*," and he was now sorely tempted. Yet he listened, and still invited me back.

One Sunday I found him " a little the worse," as he admitted, and reading *his* bible, the sporting newspaper. Feeling himself accused, he began to defend himself by again abusing Christianity, and pointing out the errors of some of its professors. I saw he knew what he was saying, so I accepted his indirect challenge, drew closer to him, and asked him to say all he could against Christianity *itself*. He rambled about and at last objected to prayer. This gave me an opportunity of briefly delineating its nature and tendency. He listened, and then said, "You really believe in the power of prayer? Suppose you try it on me. You wish me to take the pledge,—well, pray for that."

" I have—I did so this morning," was my reply.

"You really thought of me before you came! You not only cured me and healed my arm, but prayed for me! It's you I ought to listen to. And you prayed for me this morning?"

This last sentence brought tears to his eyes.

" I did," was my answer, and we parted.

When I next called, his wife, taking a paper from the mantlepiece, took from its careful folds a card, which she put into my hand, saying, "Look, sir, not a drop has he taken since you last left."

I was overcome, and so were they. We shook hands again. For a time all were silent.

" I now believe in prayer," he said, and then went on to tell how thankful he was, declaring he could not resist the appeals of one who had done so much for him, and who had prayed that God would do more.

VII. How a " Clever Fellow" was " Shut Up."

It is not the best intended who always show the best example, nor is it so frequently the case as we would wish that those who take the lead do so from the best motives, yet good often comes of it. The man who first consented to hear me read during the meal hours, did so, not from a desire to be benefited thereby, but to show he could do what none of his fellows would. He possessed the natural qualifications for what is called an intellectual man. No doubt he thought himself clever, and perhaps he was regarded as such at the " tap." In that jocular manner peculiar to his class, he said, " I will listen to you, governor, if you do my work this afternoon; and I'll give you five shillings into the bargain."

I told him I could not do his work, and that it was perhaps all the better for him, since every working man was in need of every crown he could earn. This went home, and I added, if he would listen to what I had to read (sometimes I read as well as spoke at the meal hours) to him, it might, with God's blessing, save five shillings against Saturday.

"You say so," he added, with a sneer, "but I cannot believe you. You kind of people, as knows nothing o' working men, are all wrong. I'll prove it." He paused, and I waited for the proof, which was not produced. But he continued, and mark his words, "There's a good round hundred of Christianities as preached at King's Cross, where I lives. Now, tell me which is the right one?"

He looked round in triumph upon his fellows, some of whom were in roars of laughter, and others were anxiously waiting for my reply, which was simply this:—"There is but one Christianity—that taught and practised by Christ and His apostles."

This settled the bluster in my favour, and I added, "And allow me to say you are mistaken as to those who seek your good not knowing about the working man's difficulties. They think of you, and wish you well, and try to do you more good than you are aware of or willing to admit."

"That's about it, master, that's about it," chimed one who had been an attentive listener. This afforded me an opportunity of assuring them that I knew something of them and of their many difficulties; and that I was desirous of being able, in some measure, to help to improve the social, the moral, and religious condition of all who stood in need of such.

"How can *you* know about us? Look at your hands. Many is the lady as would give half her fortune for such. They is only fit for kid gloves. Where is the blisters?" and taking my hand into his, he examined it, and compared it with his, to the satisfaction of his companions.

Here, again, he glanced round in triumph. I purposely paused, and then added, "Now, friend, you think you have it all your own way, but, let me tell you, that hand has worked as hard as ever your hand did. With these hands I have laboured not only to support myself and aid a dear father, but also to pay for what education I have had, and which has enabled me to work my way, and come here to help you to help yourself. In the fullest sense I can give you—each one of you—my hand as a fellow working man."

Again the victory was mine, and I told them in as few words as possible the simple story of my life. The man was, as the rest said, "shut up." His hard heart was touched. With tears in his eyes he took my hand and said, "It's you I'll listen to," and down he sat, and I began my reading from that telling narrative in the *British Workman*, entitled, "John Stepping Forth."

VIII. MONDAY SCENES.

Very soon after I came to London, I perceived that with a great number Monday is a holiday, and that with many the chief places of resort are the public-houses; and hence, however much exhausted on Sunday, I try to get out on Monday, and from these two motives—1. To see life as thus developed; 2. To render what help I can, either to man or woman. The incidents to be seen within and round about the public-houses are nearly as various as they are numerous. Indeed, to see life as daily manifested there, especially on Mondays, is to behold a curious development of character and passion. On this day, as on all the other six days of the week,—not even Sunday excepted,—there are sights of a most repulsive kind within and around these strong-drink places, spectacles sad and hideous; but on Monday there is something peculiar. Amongst the more

disgusting forms of drunkenness and wretchedness are not a few
who yet desire to appear to be clean, though not always tidy.
Amongst such are wives, mothers, and daughters; also fathers
and sons. They venture out thus more publicly on Monday,
because they are then "dressed." That is, as is the case with
too many such, even of some who may yet hold their heads
somewhat high, their clothes have only been reclaimed on Saturday, and are most likely to be sent back on Monday night or
Tuesday morning, where they remain till Saturday. And sad as
well as strange to say, on Monday drinking women are more in
number by far than men. Many come out on that day as a
matter of course; but there are others who feel, as they think,
more at liberty then to drink deeper, because of some incident
having happened—some adversity having overtaken them, or
some friend having come up from the country.

On looking about me, and in trying to do good, I sometimes
find myself in rather a dangerous position; whereas at other
times I have been enabled to do good without much risk. One
Monday, when on the outlook, and passing a noted public-
house, I noticed a young soldier and an old man suddenly
emerge from it. Both were the worse for the drink, but they
were also deeply concerned. Words of reproach escaped from
their lips. They were angry, yet affection seemed to claim her
place in their hearts. They parted with something like a wish
to be reconciled, yet could not, because of the rage and the
drink. The soldier went off in haste, and the old man made
his way slowly and sadly in another direction. When about to
enter another public-house, I accosted him. Having soon gained
his confidence, he told me amid his tears the sad tale of his life.
It was the story of sin and misery—of a dear wife gone to the
grave broken-hearted; of an only daughter on the streets; of
an only son enlisted; and of himself, the father, now about to
take as much more drink as to give him hellish nerve to end his
wretched life.

"How thankful I am that you stopped me from entering that public-house," he said, when we were about to part; "had I got the drink, I had done the deed. I am not a stranger to the things you speak of. I was well brought up. The public-house led me from the house of God." Taking advantage of this statement, (one often made by such poor victims of strong drink,) I again entered more deeply into the question of hope even for the backslider.

"Be assured, my mind is not in the same state in which it was two hours ago. I shall go home." I hope he did go home; but "Essex" was all the reply he gave in answer to the question where he lived.

IX. AFTER THE CHRISTENING.

Another day, whilst passing along one of the leading streets, I observed all the children I could see running to a point. Soon shouts are heard, and curses follow. In the centre are two women, and with them is a girl between thirteen and fourteen years of age. She is pleading with one of the women, who, making an effort to strike her, falls heavily on the ground. The children shout, and some of them laugh. This enrages the woman, and she tries to run after them. What a ridiculous sight! The other woman has a baby arrayed in a long and what, some hours before, had been a white dress. She is "protecting" the child, though so tipsy, and can scarcely walk; but, like her companion, she can curse, and that very loud.

"Give me my child, you ——," said the other woman, for she was the mother.

"Never; I 'll see to the child," was the reply, and a struggle followed to the danger of the child's life.

I had been watching them for a time. Having stepped up, and demanded that baby be given to the girl (its sister) they moved on, the crowd following, till they came to the next public-house. In they went, and in I went; and here I was between two fires—the drunken women and the publican, all of whom would rather have seen me far enough off. I resolved on two things—1. That the child should be protected; and 2. That the women should have no more drams. At last the women promised to go home if I would disperse the crowd, which was done by the help of two policemen. The difficulties of my task increased as we passed along, every public-house and every street corner brought round about us others like themselves.

"Come with us; we dare not go home without you speak for us. My master will murder me," said the mother to me, and I consented. But the police would not come further than the entrance to the group of houses in which the women and others of the same social level lived. What a scene was that which followed the shutting of the street door! The stories I listened to, the fury that was evinced, and the cunning attempts to find the depth of my pockets, were—even to me (because of what I had previously known of such heroes in such strife)—surprising; but this mother's "master" (her husband) was as harmless as a dove—he was lying on the hearth "*dead-drunk*."

"I say, friend, I would not have entered that door and had it shut upon me, as you have done, for the best five-pound note in the Bank of England," said one of the policemen who had lingered about the locality. "I expected every moment to see you pitched out at one of the upper windows. Do you know what kind of people they are? That girl who held the child is a street-walker, and she is the chief support of her father and mother, though not yet fifteen years of age."

But those who know life amongst such in London are aware that scenes like these may be daily witnessed by hundreds; that many a child is thereby made a cripple for life; that many more receive such injuries, under like circumstances, as cause them to linger and die. Yet—would my reader believe it?—this child, the mother declared, had just been baptized! She and others had been at church, to which a large number of children had been brought by their parents and "god-parents" to be introduced to the church and congregation. What a change this is—from the baptismal font to these fearful brawls in the lowest drinking-dens! If that child had *god*-parents it had not *good* parents.

X. "KEPT FOR YOU, MOTHER."

Nor have the streets on Saturday evenings proved to be less interesting to me. For various reasons I have thought it my duty to traverse them on that day, especially after pay-time till midnight, and sometimes till Sunday morning. In many places the crowd is almost impassable—quite a fair. One common scene may slightly indicate my meaning.

I stopped for a little where the butchers in blue slops were jabbering, "Buy, buy, buy," under a flood of gas-light which struggled with the wind for existence. A woman stopped, and took up a piece of meat, but before she had time to ask the price, one of the sellers said, "That's the piece—the very thing I have kept for you, mother." And he took up the bloody and black stuff, which any sensible woman would not have taken home to her cat.

The woman was "elevated." Poor creature, she again looked so foolishly at the meat, then at her money, when he added, "Just four shillings, mother; but four and sixpence to any other save yourself. Just four shillings, sold again, buy, buy, buy, buy, buy, buy a-way!"

She staggered in at the door towards the counter to pay for her "bargain,"—to give four shillings for a piece of carrion, disgustingly black.

"What a robbery," said I to myself; "and the drunkard is not the only victim."

She was a wife and a mother, and her husband and children must suffer.

"Is not the husband of such a wife, the children of such a mother, to be pitied?" I again asked myself, and resolved to try what could be done.   I followed her that night as a detective would follow a thief, only I did not follow her into the gin-palace, rather waiting till she came out.   At last she was joined by one of her boys, who urged her to go home, because "father" had came; but by this time she was scarcely able to walk. The boy dragged her on for some time, and at last she became as unwilling as unable to comply with his frequently expressed wish.   That is indeed a sad sight,—to see a sensible and earnest child pleading with a thoughtless and besotted parent to go home.   Now was my time.   The young and the old laughed at her words and ways.

"Do not make light of the scene.   She is a mother, and you hurt the boy's feelings," I said, but only to be laughed at by the crowd, some of whom would most likely become as bad as she was before many hours.

"You shall have enough to do if you interest yourself in that one," said one who knew this wretched drunkard.

"Hear, hear," said others; but I pleaded for some one to help me to see her home.

"Come along, mate; she is a woman; let us help her to her crib," said a fast young man, whose heart was not yet petrified.

We got her home.   I called to see her from time to time. At last she took the pledge, and I had the pleasure of seeing not only a changed woman, but a changed home, and greatly for the better.

XI. OPEN-AIR OPPOSITION TO THE PROCLAMATION OF THE GOSPEL.

Already I have indicated the fact that those who go to the highways and byeways to proclaim the gospel meet with opposition; yet I may here give a few incidents illustrative of this and connected with my own efforts.

Though I have known of good being done in the midst of opposition to open-air preaching, yet experience has taught me that it is better for the preacher of the gospel and his success, as such, not to enter into a discussion with those who oppose his efforts, if it is possible to avoid it honourably. Generally an unconverted person, when brought to see his ignorance, weakness, and vanity, *especially before his companions*, becomes *enraged*, not *convinced*. And, as a rule, it is those who care little about Christ who oppose the preaching of the gospel. Again, many such seek to prime themselves for this opposition by swallowing strong drink, and therefore do not know well what they are saying. As a rule, when opposed, I make these three offers:—1. To visit them at a time they may please to name. 2. To invite them to meet me at my home when most suitable. 3. To wait till they are sober. I never *discuss with a person the worse for the drink.* To do so is to encourage blasphemy, taking the name of God in vain. Often has this determination on my part been tested, but I have never yet yielded, though I have more than once thereby suffered bodily harm.

On one occasion a big, burly, drunken Irishman came up whilst I was speaking, and offered to discuss with me. I made him all the three offers, but in vain,—he must, as he phrased it, "expose the false Protestant Bible." Being so wordy, and so noisy, I thought it better to close my discourse and leave him, but he stopped me, and out of his grasp I could not get. I stood in silence, but with my eye fixed on his. Five or six times he aimed a blow at my breast, but only once succeeded in effecting his purpose. This roused the people against him, many of whom were Papists. Yet I might have fared much worse than I did had not a young man—of "no religion"—been bold enough to come to my rescue. Then it became my turn to save the drunk and cowardly fellow from a good beating. For long

I felt much pain in my chest, and my face was much disfigured for nearly a week after.

"I killed one of your cloth by hunting him down for fourteen years, and I'll send you after him if you come here to disturb our peace of mind," said another infidel drunkard, who called himself a Papist, at another station.

Kindness failed to induce him to cease his opposition. Time after time he appeared, continuing his threats, till one time he had brought some of his " mates " with him, and seemed more determined than ever that he should make a display, as he thought, at my expense. It entered my mind that this time I should accept of his challenge, on these conditions :—1. That he give me the same length of time to reply which he would need to object. 2. That there be no interruption by either of us, nor by any around us. 3. That those hearing us see that these conditions are acted upon.

Accepting these terms, he began and spoke for a considerable time. His chief matter seemed to be made up of efforts to show that the Church of Rome was distinguished by many marks as the true Church, but he lengthened out and laid particular stress upon her unity and her apostolic succession. ' I let him run the full length of his tether, and then followed him,—first proving, to the satisfaction of the crowd, that he was most ignorant of that on which he spoke most positively ; and then I entered into the facts connected with his favourite assertions, proving that the Roman Catholic religion *has changed*—that the *present* creed of the Church of Rome was not the same as the ancient one, having in it many doctrines *now* considered essential, which were not named before. Here he became very enraged, as he observed some even of his own party admit the force of truth. He would have stopped me, but the people reminded him of his promise, so I went on to the other leading point—the apostolic succession charm—the monster delusion—that which leads so many of the ignorant Romanists to oppose the preaching of the gospel by any one not a Papist priest. The people listened attentively, but when I came to that knotty point, the pope's or priest's intention, my opponent could not contain himself. Becoming quite frantic, he made a rush at me, not to meet me by arguments, but to frighten me by curses, and crush me by blows. His friends were wiser. They saw it proper to seize him and carry him off by force to his house. On seeing this, I took occasion to address the people, assuring those Romanists present that I had no intention whatever to wound their feelings, and assuring them, of what the most of them knew, that I did not come out to speak against any religion, but to preach what I conceived to be the gospel of Christ, to teach apostolical Christianity,—that the present debate had only been an exception to the rule, and that had been reluctantly forced upon me. In this all agreed, and I then spoke briefly on the point upon which I had been reflecting previously to my going there that afternoon.

The poor fellow was cured. He has never opposed me since.

"Speak another word and I'll give your friends the privilege of gathering your brains from the pavement," was the fearful threat of a furious fellow who had just rushed out from one of the doors opposite to the place where I was preaching. He appeared as a maniac escaped from the madhouse; and, suiting the action to the word, he seized the chair upon which I was standing and made an attempt to strike me; but I looked calmly and firmly into his face, and he failed in his effort. But what a scene followed! He had a few of the Romanists with him, but now a few of his own class were on my side, and all who were not with the *priest* were in my favour. Again he got out of the grasp of those who had held him from me and came right up, but again I caught his eye, and, without a word, defied him.

This was severe to withstand, even when supported by those who before had evinced no interest in the preaching at that place; but it was cheering to find the hold I had on the public mind, a hold stronger than I expected.

"You shall have my parlour, sir, and you can speak to the people from the window," was an offer kindly, earnestly, and urgently made by one, and repeated by others.

This time my dear friend, Mr Dash,—who has gone with me in storm and calm, through thick and thin,—was present. We consulted, and agreed that to give up the place would be unwise, and yet to continue *at that moment* would not be prudent—the commotion was so great, and some of the Romanists, with this fiend at their head, were so furious. We resolved to accept the offers, and to come again at six o'clock that evening. We left, had a cup of tea, and retired to a room privately, each to thank God for the past, and to ask help for the future. The hour came; and we found the people anxiously waiting. I entered one of the offered parlours. The window was drawn up, but, finding that my voice would not reach all who wished to hear, I spoke shortly from under the threshold of one of the street doors. But, again finding myself confined, I placed my chair on the pavement. On doing so, the same fellow made his appearance, yet without his coat, as if prepared to fight. As he left his door, I looked him in the face, his head drooped, and he passed on without saying a word, nor did he return whilst I was speaking.

This opposition and its results proved two things—1. Greater is He that is for the preacher than all that are against him. 2. The devil, with all his cunning, sometimes proves himself to be a stupid fellow. As with his servants, grasping makes him overshoot the mark. Though, with few exceptions, I have been opposed at the commencement of the opening of new stations for open-air preaching, especially where Papists, sceptics, and drunkards resort, but *more* especially where all three are united under the first named, as is often the case, yet good generally has come of it.

For instance, when speaking amidst strong opposition, I was struck on the brow with a stone from some of the windows. "Curses be upon those who threw that stone," said one aloud, and the opposition gave way to a perfect calm. Though in pain, I spoke for ten or fifteen minutes, and in such a strain as to gain the affection of my hearers; and on my next visit to the same place, I found that doors which before had been shut against me were now open to receive me. I found the people in a sad condition, socially as well as spiritually—all kinds of low and fluctuating fevers, severe and stitching pains, arising from crushing poverty and sanitary derangements.

"It was drink and the devil that *was* in him, sir," said one, referring to a leader of the rough opposition I had endured.

"Sure, sir, the priest would have nothing to do wid 'm," added another.

"Do not be put away, sir, as others have been," pleaded a third one, and so on, till all had said something.

I continued to preach and to visit, and was enabled to do them good in several ways,—one was to bring the Act of Parliament, touching sanitary matters, to bear in their favour. This, in its turn, made me the more welcome. My past training and experience also enabled me to give some simple directions in cases of illness. Water was my medicine, which, being taken inside and applied outside, was blessed to the relief and joy of not a few.

"What's the boy *arter ?*" asked his mother, in a tone evincing a pleasing satisfaction.

"It's a chair for the preacher," was the prompt reply.

"He loves you so much," said his mother.

"The same with us," chimed another mother, who had been telling me how much her child had improved under the water treatment.

Such was the change soon brought about, and doubtless earlier than it would have been had not the devil so overshot the mark.

L

Again, in that case where the man threatened to scatter my brains on the pavement—when I yielded at the moment, but only to conquer two hours after—it did not only give me an opportunity of knowing how much those upon whom I had not calculated really respected me for what I said, it also gave rise to another cheering incident.   It so happened that I was unable to get back to that station at the usual time.   The result was— a deputation waited upon me to express their fears least I might not come there again, and to assure me that the people wished to hear me, and were prepared to protect me. Of course, I went again as before, and the attention has since been very marked.

But sometimes opposition has been blessed to my hearers, by suggesting to me what is profitable.   For instance, whilst preaching, a man, with the pipe in his cheek, came forward and would stop me unless I spoke about Garibaldi.   I had either to comply or suffer those disagreeable feelings which are sure to rise when a row is created on Sunday.

"You speak about a Redeemer we know not; speak of a liberator we all know, Garibaldi, the best friend of mankind," continued the man, making way to stop me by force.

I obeyed him, knowing that the Italian hero was at that time occupying the minds of Europe, for he had just returned to Caprera after his late visit to England.   After not only admitting but admiring what the hero was as a man and a liberator, I then turned to *the* Liberator, Jesus, and went on with the contrast till I had to leave Garibaldi behind, showing that Christ was Lord of all, higher than the highest, greater than the greatest, better than the best, *the* loving Saviour, the mighty Counsellor, the Prince of Peace.   This was a happy hit.   The infidel was satisfied, the people drank in the discourse, and I know God blessed it.

And, besides, I am happy to add, it is not always opposition. No, no; I can count on earnest and attentive audiences in the open-air. I have seen the tears of repentance, and the smiles of hope. Truly, this is an essential and a useful means of evangelization. God bless it evermore.

XII. The Water Cure amongst the Poor.

It is a great help to one to know that God is ever ready to bless even what is not pleasant, such as the opposition just referred to—whether it comes from ignorance or wickedness, or from behind the priest's altar, as it often does; but it is well to try to improve the opportunity which providence may thus cast in one's way. This I have ever studied to do. For instance, our Evangelistic Association does not profess to give money, and so forth, to the people, *especially to bribe them to come to our meetings*, yet, as has been indicated, I try to get for the helpless the help to which they are entitled. Again, I endeavour to do for the people what they cannot do for themselves, such as by way of sanitary improvement. In some cases I have so pressed upon the authorities the necessity of putting the Act in force, to the great benefit to health, and that not the only result, respect and affection have been increased. But that which has helped me most in that way to the hearts and confidence of the people is, the use I sometimes make of my past experience in relation to the laws of health.

I have already referred to an instance in which some slight knowledge in the blessed art of healing was of some benefit. Never have I forgotten the sentence uttered by the person therein referred to. "They's the best missionaries as can help body and soul, as can employ hands and head." I had been very early impressed with this idea. For long these two ideas had run side by side in my mind—the desire to become a preacher of the gospel, and the wish to be acquainted with the human frame—to be enabled to be the means of giving light to the darken soul, and to relieve the sufferer from bodily pain. It was

with this view that, when a boy, I endeavoured to improve the
valuable opportunity kindly given to me by the late Dr Wood
of the village of Lochee, near Dundee; and it was with the same
purpose, some years after, even after I had become a popular
teacher, that I apprenticed myself to the chemist and druggist
in Kirriemuir. "We arranged that I should open the shop in
the morning and remain there, doing a boy's drudgery, selling
powders and so forth, till nine; to re-enter at five, and remain
till ten in the evening, compounding and dispensing medicines,
thus giving me between nine and ten to take breakfast and walk
to my school, a distance of about two and a-half miles, and from
four till five to retrace my steps and take tea; the only time I
had for reading and reflection being before seven in the morning
and after ten in the evening. I continued to labour this way
for about a-year and a-half, at the end of which time I resigned
the office of teacher, and devoted my whole time to the study
and practice of medicine." *

This was trying to the mind and frame, but I was anxious to
learn, and from the motive named. I am truly glad I did undertake these increased responsibilities. The result has been blessed
to not a few, even before I came to London; though I have not since
then had so much faith in drugs as before, yet the information I
had thereby, and by other means, attained, touching the laws of
health and the cure of disease, has been useful amongst the poor
and the sick with whom I am brought daily in contact. Of
course, I do not "practise," nor do I stand in the way of the
"practitioner," but only suggest some simple remedy when he
cannot come, or after his skill has failed. I say *simple remedy*,
and I mean it—seldom anything stronger than water, *sometimes
a little soap to let the water reach the skin.*

I soon found that in nearly every house in the localities into
which the poor are crammed, is some complaint—the "rheumatiz," severe and stitching pains, slow and fluctuating fevers, sick

* "Life Story," p. 60.

headaches, and every kind of sores. All this arises from the condition of the home, and from the want of proper food. This sad state of matters—even in relation to physical suffering—is sure to awaken pity, and so arouse practical sympathy as to cause one to say, What can I do even to lessen the pain? At least, so I felt, and so I feel, and hence I venture to do my best. All suffer greatly from this fearful state of things, but the aged and the children suffer most. What pictures of physical distress might be given as seen in the abodes of the poor! But I try to do good, especially when I first enter the locality or the house, by healing some sore. This takes to itself the shape of a visible proof of the power of my general remedy—*water*, carefully applied. For instance, an Irishwoman—a poor and wretched widow —with her four children, presented themselves to me one day· The mother had been a strong woman once, but was now much weakened. Her children were sad to look upon, especially the baby. "Poor child, it can never get better, but I must nurse it as long as it lives, and that prevents me from getting out to do a bit of work. There, that girl has not been able to keep baby for so many weeks, and she is so ill too; look at that finger, and that hand, and that arm," so said the mother, now pointing to her eldest girl, who had been, and was, suffering greatly. Having asked if she had sought advice, and been assured she had, but in vain, I offered some suggestions which were attended to, and, by God's blessing, the girl was soon able again to help her widowed mother to get out "to do a bit of work" as before.

I had no difficulty afterwards in urging this mother, and others in the place, to adopt a few simple directions which I then, and after, gave in other cases.

I remember one instance of the proof of the power of water when properly applied. It was past midnight when I heard of a particular sadness in a poor home. The baby was expected every moment to die. The doctor had said it could not live more than two hours. I went, and stated what they might try as a last remedy. They acted upon my advice, and baby recovered. It was simply the application of water.

This happy result spread in the neighbourhood, and many sought advice, which was also followed by results more or less successful.

In this place, one of the minor results was to change the name I had before received—the " little preacher," to the " preaching doctor." But this was nothing to the happy influence. That in which I rejoiced most, was the fact of the influence being coupled with the thought and the pleasure of seeing the suffering relieved, and of so gaining the confidence and affection of those concerned, that I had a better chance of directing them to Him who can save soul and body.

I mention this for two reasons—to show that by study and care, one may increase his usefulness by manifesting a practical regard for the comfort of the body as well as for the safety of the soul ;—and to mention this way of help as worthy of the consideration of those who meet with the people, especially the poorer portion of them. Without dogmatising, I would venture the opinion that one of the greatest blessings to the poor would be the introduction of the water cure in all its simplicity and power.

XIII. Use of Letters in the Good Work.

Few could believe the benefit of letters in efforts to be useful to one another. In my experience they served two purposes— they have informed me of those in need of help and encouragement, and enabled me to send both when I could not call. Out of many instances I may give these :—

I had been ill and not able to be about for days, and during that time a poor woman became so low in heart and strength, from poverty and sickness, that she thought she was about to leave what to her had been a vale of tears. She got a person to write to me; and I wrote to a kind and prudent lady, who not only called, but soon interested others in the poor woman's favour.

A dear lady having heard of me, and being unable to call, wrote to me asking my efforts in behalf of a family known to her. The demon strong drink was at the root of this family's trouble, but other consequent and sad evils were in attendance, as is always the case. I visited. The aspect was fearful, and at first seemed hopeless; but the effort was so blessed that in a few weeks there was such an improvement that one could scarcely believe he was in the company of the same family.

One who had suffered much pain of body, but who had given her heart to the Lord, met with a fellow-sufferer from like causes. There was this difference between the two—and a great difference it was—the husband of the former was sober and kind, but the husband of the latter was a drunkard, and had so far forgotten his marriage vows as to neglect her whom he had promised to cherish and protect. The more favoured woman wrote to me in behalf of the more afflicted one. By means of a letter—for he was so far distant that I could not call—I reasoned with the erring husband, and pleaded for a change of life, for his own as well as for her sake. He bethought himself; and such was the change soon after that his happy wife was able to record the fact, that by him home was preferred to the publican's parlour, and the Bible had become his study.

Sometimes I have occasion to write to the distressed in body and mind. On one occasion I visited a young person who thought her days were few. After reading a psalm to her, and calling her attention to some of its beauties, she said, " How sweet; I wish I could remember it." On learning that she was anxious to see me respecting it, and finding I could not visit her so soon as she wished, I penned for her the Scottish version of that psalm in metre. As it may be new to some of my English readers, and since it has been so favourably accepted wherever I have repeated it, a copy may not be unacceptable here :—

"The Lord's my shepherd, I 'll not want.
  He makes me down to lie
In pastures green : he leadeth me
  The quiet waters by.

" My soul he doth restore again ;
  And me to walk doth make
Within the paths of righteousness,
  Ev'n for his own name's sake.

" Yea, though I walk in death's dark vale,
  Yet will I fear none ill :
For thou art with me ; and thy rod
  And staff me comfort still.

" My table thou hast furnished
  In presence of my foes ;
My head thou dost with oil anoint,
  And my cup overflows.

" Goodness and mercy all my life
  Shall surely follow me :
And in God's house for evermore
  My dwelling-place shall be."

The comfort she derived from these lines cannot be named. "Often did she kiss your kind letter, and that sweet psalm you sent. It is all tears, but tears of joy," said her mother, referring to the last days and deeds of the girl.

And sometimes it is my lot to sympathise with the bereaved at their homes, and by letter. If a suitable hymn is not at hand, or if one is not at my memory's command, and I think it better to send a few verses, I give them new, from my pen. Here are a few such lines, which I have reason to believe were useful :—

" Little Louie !—dear wee child !—
  Play'd and laugh'd so sweet, so mild ;
And, by telling look or sign,
  Would her little wants define.

" Little Louie's gone to heaven ;
 There, to her, a crown is given ;
There, in robes of spotless white,
 Louie sings with pure delight.

" Little Louie, we shall meet,
 At the Saviour's glorious seat ;
There with all the bless'd to reign,
 Ever free from death and pain.

" That shall be a happy day,
 Then we shall love's law obey ;
Then with Louie, and the rest,
 We shall dwell for ever blest."

XIV. FINAL TRIUMPHS.

It is said that one of Wesley's mottoes was, " Never to strike Satan unless he thought it possible to knock him down," and there is much philosophy in this, not a little of which may be applied to the rescuing of those under his power ; hence it is well not only to *endeavour to rescue as many as possible*, but to see that the devourer does *not recapture them*. It is a grand thing to be enabled to leave the wrong path, grander still to walk in the right path ; but it is the consummation of all to endure to the end, to overcome all things, and, in holy triumph, die in the peace of believing. If such is the case with those whose lines have fallen in pleasant places,—and none will gainsay it,—how much more is it so when this joyous triumph is shared in by those who may well be called " brands plucked from the burning."

I have not been left without witnessing such, without such desired testimony in favour of efforts happily directed and graciously blessed, without positive proofs of sinners becoming saints, of the once fearless rebel against God becoming His truly loyal subject.

" Blessed be God, I see Jesus my Saviour again," said one

such during my last interview with him.   But just before that
he had been so sadly cast down that he called out, " Again the
mist is gathering round the cross ; I cannot see Jesus as before."
After a short conversation, and an earnest prayer, the " mist "
cleared away ; and just before I left his bedside, he added,
" Bless the Lord, as you say, He is the God of salvation."
Next morning he went home to realise that glorious and cheering fact.

" Though I may be asleep when you call, do not leave without speaking to me, I am so anxious how I may be saved;"
so said a woman whom I had frequently visited, and, up till
that time, without any apparent result.   Glad to hear these
words, I continued as if she were the only one for whom I was
labouring.   Day after day gave brighter hopes, till at last, and
just the day before she parted this life, she, in answer to a
question, said, " I *know* my name is *now* written in the book of
life by the blood of Jesus."

How cheering to believe in the " eleventh hour," for many to
whom the " good news " have been but lately brought, or at
least, *lately brought home*, only find life and peace at this
hour.   " Oh, to have only a few weeks in which to serve God,
to tell what He had done for my soul," exclaimed a dying
believer to me only the day before he died.   Doubtless, his
dear wife and sweet child would have been glad had this
earnest prayer been granted ; but they have this confidence that
he has gone to be " for ever with the Lord."   There are many
such ; yes, many who at the eleventh hour give evidence that
they are saved through Christ.

" My Jesus, my Jesus, I am safe in my Jesus," said another
man who had sent for me to bid me farewell, and express his
thanks for attentions paid to him and his family during sad
suffering and long sickness.   " God bless you and those who
have been the means of bringing you into this needful district."
He paused, and wept, and then added, " I go to my Jesus,

farewell." This was on a Sunday afternoon, and he went to rest that night about ten o'clock.

But such happy results have not been confined to the grown-up amongst those who have been brought under the influence of our united efforts. As has been seen, I have a " Bud of Promise," a society of children from five to fourteen years of age, which has the same relation to our Christian Instruction Society as the Band of Hope has to the Temperance movement. This, together with our Band of Hope, brings me more directly in contact with children. They not only wish and expect to be visited,—and the pleasure I have derived in doing so has been sweet and profitable,—but they also tell me of those who may be ill, and ask me to call upon them. Two instances of this kind will close these results.

A girl had been taken seriously ill, and removed to the workhouse infirmary. I went there to see her; and though about fourteen, I found her totally ignorant of the plan of salvation. She had heard of Jesus and of sin, but her only hope, if it may be called hope, was that she had " been baptized." Poor creature, how blind in the midst of so much light. Day after day I called, for she was some considerable time " on the slate "—that is, considered by the doctors to be so near her end that her parents and others might call any day and at any hour.

" I see *now* that Jesus is my Saviour," was about the last sentence she uttered. How glad I was to hear it, for it was with difficulty—and after sitting with her at her bedside—that I could get her intelligently to understand God's way of being the God of salvation.

Again, a girl who came to my out-door services, and who afterwards attended those held in a schoolroom, became very ill, and was taken to Middlesex Hospital. She was not long there when she expressed a wish that I should visit her. I did so.

"I have asked you to call that I may thank you for leading me to Jesus," were amongst her first words after I entered. "What a blessing your coming to our place of meeting has been to me," she continued, and the tears rolling down Annie's sweet face, for already it bespoke that calm repose and soft joy which tell of a changed heart, a saved soul. Her last words were these: by way of advice she said, "Seek God without delay;" and by way of consolation, she added, "I know *my* Saviour, and He says, 'Fear not, for I am nigh,' 'for I am with you alway, even unto the end.'"

XV. YET ANOTHER TWO INCIDENTS.

Before I close this chapter of incidents I shall briefly mention another two.

My literary efforts—if what I have done in that way since I came to London may have that name—except in one case, have not been alluded to. Save the *Weekly Record*, the *Ragged School Union Magazine* was the first periodical to which I contributed, but I have also written for the *Christian Cabinet, Christian World,* the *Revival,* and so forth. I have also added to my list of small books. As is stated in the preface of my "Sabbath School from a Practical Point of View," immediately after the publication of my "Prize Autobiography," I received many letters regarding the various themes therein incidentally referred to, such as the best means of gaining the ear and confidence of those most in want of sympathy and advice; the best way to gain the affection and obedience of children in week-day schools; and how to manage a Sabbath-school.

In relation to the latter question, the letters were so numerous that I found it almost impossible to answer them; and this also proved to me the necessity of a book touching the subjects or queries contained in these letters. Besides, as I have elsewhere said, I owe a debt of deep gratitude to the Sabbath-school. In it, "as a scholar and as a teacher, some of the sweetest and most pleasant associations arise in my mind, giving birth to gratitude and joy to my soul. The family altar is pleasant and profitable; may it soon be erected in every home. To see a whole family evincing an interest in their spiritual welfare, each one intent on eternal salvation, is a refreshing, an ennobling sight; yet the Sabbath-school is needed, especially for those who have not the good fortune to see the family altar. Such, whether of the outcast or the careless, may not hear the voice of Jesus saying, 'Suffer little children to come unto me;' but they may hear it in the Sabbath-school. I thank God I heard it."*

But apart from this obligation and these solicitations, I felt anxious to do all the good in my power for children, whom I have ever loved, and hence in that little work I have endeavoured to reach and benefit the scholar through the teacher.

Feeling grateful not only to God, but also to my Sabbath-school teachers, I dedicated the book to Mr Robertson, Dundee. He it was who first received me into that blessed institution, and gave me encouragement when most in need of it. The kindness and attention of this dear friend have been blessed not only to my own soul, but, I trust, to others upon whom I have been privileged to exert an influence in the Sabbath-school and elsewhere.

But this little book did not only afford me the occasion of indicating my gratitude towards my Sabbath-school teachers, and the interest I have ever felt in the welfare of children, it also gave an opportunity of writing to one who had specially manifested a deep interest in me—I mean Her Majesty the Queen. Because of what she had done I felt anxious to let her know that I had become more useful than ever; hence on the 17th of March 1863, I penned the following letter :—

* "Life Story," p. 20.

"To the Queen's most Excellent Majesty.

"Madam,—May it please your Majesty, it is with the combination of a fear of being considered presuming and a feeling of gratitude, I forward with this, by post, a copy of my 'Sunday-School from a Practical Point of View,' just published. The preface contains the reason why I have written the book, and I forward it to your Majesty, trusting it will be accepted as an humble effort from the pen that wrote 'Life Story,' the autobiography which your Majesty was graciously pleased to acknowledge, and which acknowledgment, in the providence of God, has helped to widen my sphere of usefulness. As was lately stated in the *British Workman*, I am 'now engaged in a useful mission amongst the industrious classes of London;' and this is the very work for which God was mysteriously and, as is now evident, kindly preparing me in Scotland, amidst the struggles I had and the hardships I underwent there.

"May He continue to guide, as well as preserve, your gracious Majesty and devoted subjects, is the prayer of

"James I. Hillocks."

Two days later I received the following reply:—

"Sir Charles Phipps has received the commands of Her Majesty the Queen, to acknowledge the receipt of the book which Mr Hillocks forwarded on the 17th inst., and to thank him for it.

"Windsor Castle, 19*th March* 1863."

My visit to Scotland is the other incident to which I refer. Who does not love a holiday? The great necessity of a little breathing time is only known to those who have to perform continuous and arduous duties. I remember on one occasion meeting with a city missionary who had come home earlier than usual. "I do not feel very well," he said, "and am now on my way to Hampstead Heath."

"To Hampstead Heath to get the air, whilst the masses are in such a condition," said I to myself, and felt inclined to scold my friend. But I was only newly begun to traverse the narrow lanes, the dirty courts, the crowded and sickly homes. Since then, many is the time I have been glad of a mouthful of fresh air, of an hour's relief.

Yet the past is the only year, as an evangelist, I have taken my holidays, and for various reasons. In North London I had not gotten my mission in that working order which would warrant my leaving it for a few weeks. In the north-west,—and though there co-operating with congenial workers—I felt the same difficulty during the first year.

"Better rest without the doctor than with him," said one of my friends, referring to my late illness caused by overwork. He was right, and I resolved to take such friendly hints into consideration; but then came a difficulty, which, doubtless, is often felt by many poor hard-worker—the means of getting off, of living away from home, and of returning. My difficulty, in the first instance, arose from being without a regular income previous to my engagement, so that we had to help the past out of our small income. And then, in the second instance, the difficulty became greater, inasmuch as we had, previous to my engagement at the north-west, been about six months without salary, and that in London! But being assured by my kind fellow-workers in connexion with our Evangelistic Association that every effort would be made to keep the machinery in motion during my absence, I thought of trying to raise the means by lecturing, where my services might be accepted, for the mere trifle which would clear my expenses. With this view I issued a circular, but found two obstacles in my way—the lecturing season had not begun, and some of the more fortunate of Londoners, or rather London speakers, had been in the country "starring." Yet, though one field was closing at the date I offered my humble services, and the other had not opened, I had as many invitations as enabled me to see my holidays would not take a penny from my other pressing claims. This being the case, I set out for Scotland, breaking my journey at Northampton and Carlisle, Dumfries being the spot whereon I again set my feet on Scotch soil. And round I went till I came to Edinburgh; but my time, because of my anxiety touching my London labours, being limited, I returned southward, broke my journey at Kendal, and arrived once more in London amongst my people, all of whom manifested a delight in seeing me the better for the journey.

So nicely did my income and expenditure tally, that, after all was paid, I had a balance in my favour of threepence. But that was not all; I was useful whilst I was being invigorated; and that which perhaps did me the most good was the cheerful fact that wherever I went the reception was warm, and my labours on Sunday were as successful as those of the week-day; whether in hall or chapel the audiences were large and attentive. And then I had the pleasure of meeting some of my old friends, as warm and hearty as ever.

Besides receiving a hearty welcome from the Rev. Dr Guthrie, Professor Blackie, the Rev. Wm. Reid, Dr Menzies, and others, this journey made for me new friends, whose friendship I value. In Dumfries I met Thomas Aird, the poet, for the first time. It was true, I know I had a place in his noble heart long before that, but to shake hands with, to speak to, to see the old dear man, was to me no small delight. And then there is Colonel M. Shaw, Fort Castle, Ayr, amongst the many new and genial friends whose friendship has been brought about by that journey. One of the newspapers referring to my visit to Scotland, said, " His touching and life-like ' Life Story ' has made him many other friends of whom he knows not, and secures him at once a warm welcome wherever he goes."

But not the least advantage of these holidays was the leisure it afforded me to review these chapters for the press.

CHAPTER VIII.

"GOOD WORD AND WORK," AND A FEW THOUGHTS THEREBY SUGGESTED.

I. EARNEST WORKERS.

THOSE I met with. This is a theme of itself sufficiently large for a work of no small dimensions. Were I to give a sketch of them, however briefly, the book would be as large, if not as interesting, as the fashionable three-volume novels. But this is not in my present plan. What I mean to do here, is merely to name a few of the workers, referring at the same time to the work they represent.

The few I may mention are not selected as superior to the many who here are nameless, but simply because I have been brought more directly in contact with them, or because there was something in their efforts akin to mine. "Like draws to like."

When I came to London I was favoured, by some of my friends in Scotland, with notes of introduction to the Rev. Thomas Binny, the Rev. Jabez Burns, D.D., the Rev. John Young, LL.D., (author of "The Christ of History,") and others, with whose warm friendship and kindly appreciation I have been honoured; but it was after I had promised to write some short papers on London agencies for Christian objects, and on making inquiry into this topic, that I formed a knowledge of more of the many good workers of London. These investigations revealed

M

to me, in a remarkable and cheering manner, that there were—what is generally admitted—many, many warm hearts and munificent hands in London; that, as far as charity was concerned, the goodness of the metropolis was equal to its greatness. Its warm generosity, natural gentleness, simple tenderness, and practical sympathy, are truly astonishing.

Whatever may be the result of this grand rising to the work of necessity and mercy—of this development of the high and holy characteristics of Christian love, God only knows; but this is certain, that efforts are being made to meet almost every case of suffering and sorrow, touching body and mind. We have above 700 charities in London, all of which are meant to contribute to the moral or physical melioration of the helpless, and even the hopeless; each society endeavouring, in its own way, to mitigate, if not to cure, the manifold forms of evil by which the erring and the perishing suffer. The generous kindliness of Christian benevolence has become so diffused throughout the metropolis, that her noble humanity, and warm generosity, have not only reached the sick and insane, the maimed and the thousands that are suffering from any of our many physical diseases; she has not only taxed her ingenuity to devise a cure, she has also, in many cases, taken a step in advance, in order, if possible, to arrive at prevention; and one of the proofs of her discriminating judgment is found in the cheering fact, that many of her devoted and self-sacrificing subjects have given their skilful attention to the spiritual destitution of the people, *as connected with their physical degradation.* The words, a man has a soul as well as a body, a body as well as a soul, convey no new idea; yet it is one that those who aspire to help to promote the glory of God and the happiness of man, would do well to keep in view in all their plans.

II. Two of many such Helpers.

It is admitted, on all hands, that the press is a powerful means either for good or bad purposes, and all agree that to social and religious reformers it is indispensable. Many have thought so and acted accordingly, and with good results; but it must also be admitted that the conducting of such is a difficult task. This arises from various causes, and one is, the difficulty of making a selection,—a difficulty which rises, not from the uniform superiority of the matter sent, but from so much of that prevalent desire to see one's name in print. How seldom the proprietor is independent! How seldom the editor can do what he thinks best! Often, if he did, he would burn more than half of what appears. I do not say so from any harsh feeling, I merely record the fact. Many write from a higher motive—to do good; but how many of such, even where talent is evident, find frequently to their astonishment, and sometimes to their annoyance, that their conceptions, however ably portrayed, are not appreciated by those for whom they had laboured. Whatever may be the leading causes of this, one is, many of those who thus write do not understand those to whom they address themselves. If not dependent on the pen, such writers offer their labours as a free gift; and if they are wealthy, they can, and often do, offer to purchase so many copies of the number in which the articles appear. From this arise the temptations to which editors and publishers of such publications are subjected. Wealth and talent, a noble purpose, and a useful effort, may go hand in hand—they sometimes do; but the talent may not tell under such circumstances, especially if put into the wrong channel, and the purpose, however noble, may be thereby frustrated. Alas! this is often the case, and hence the numerous failures in regard to the good object the well-disposed have in view. Good hearts are needed, and wise heads are indispensable, in all efforts on behalf of the people; and the goodness and wisdom must be manifest in doing that which is right, at the right time, and at the right place. If any class of leaders of the public mind ought to keep to this rule, surely they are the editors and proprietors of publications, the grand object of which is to advise and to encourage the sons and daughters of toil in that which pertains to their comfort, and peace. There are not a few such in our day,—God give their proprietors encouragement and their editors wisdom! I refer not only to those recorded as more directly religious, but to those also that aim at social improvement as well. Of those useful to me, I may here name two of the monthlies—the *British Workman* and the *British Workwoman ;* and I mention them because of their connexion with my work, and because of my meeting with those who are associated with them.

At the commencement of 1861 might have been seen, in the streets and in the booksellers' shops, placards upon which was the question, "What would the poor do, were it not for the poor?" and to this query was appended the words—"See the *British Workman* for January." On turning to that number, it will be seen that the paper under the title given, was a long extract from my "Life Story," just then published. This led to my first interview with the friend with whom that excellent publication is associated. And again, but some time after, my efforts at North London attracted his attention, and glad was I to see him amongst those there who regularly attended the monthly meetings gathered to hear me read extracts from my journal, touching the nature and results of my labours. On these occasions, he evinced a large share of common sense, and a considerable knowledge of humanity, together with an evident desire to do the most good.

My acquaintanceship with the friend whose name is identified with the *British Workwoman,* has not been so long in duration, but to me it has been interesting and pleasant. It was just after he had thought of starting that publication—which has been issued with the view of aiding in the improvement and ele-

vation of woman as the centre of all social influence. This he
proposed to do " by the exposition of Bible truths, by sketch
and essay, anecdote and biography, fact and fiction, prose and
poetry, to arouse and sustain, in the minds and hearts of British
workwomen, a sense of the responsibility which rests upon them
to make plain how honourable is virtuous industry, and how
much of true happiness may be secured in a very humble condition of life." When we couple this noble aim with the great
truth contained in the noted sentence uttered by Earl Shaftesbury—" I believe that any improvement which could be brought
to bear on the mothers, would effect a greater amount of good
than anything that has yet been done"—it must be evident that
the conception is a good one. And—as is the case with the *British
Workman*—I can add, I know it to be a useful one. From the
manner in which I know it to be received by daughters, wives,
and mothers, I feel assured they had felt the necessity of a
medium through which their feelings and duties, wants and trials,
might be known. The truth is, interesting and useful as the
*British Work*MAN has been, and still is, to the husband and son—
especially in relation to the pictures—it was not meet that
he should be alone, it was necessary he should have a helpmate,
and he has found her in the *British Work*WOMAN. As has been
well said, " Let them go on, side by side, as man and wife." As
such they are helping me in my work, and I find the one intro-
duces the other. " I like the *Workwoman* for myself, please get
for me the *Workman* for my husband," is a declaration and a
request I often listen to with pleasure. God bless this " man
and wife," and the conductors of both, and that because both
publications are amongst those which aid in the social and religious improvement of those who need such help.

III. Another Couple of Workers.

Woman ! there is poetry in the word which finds its way to

our bosoms in youth, and retains its influence upon our hearts in old age. Her empire is the heart, in which she reigns, conquering and to conquer. When in her proper sphere, she adorns the creation, advances society, and glorifies God. The real nobility of her mind enables her to rise above interest and ambition, and the tender sympathy of her heart strengthens the hand of man for the struggle and bustle in the battle of life. Whether wife, mother, or sister, her actions, sentiments, and feelings are ready to sustain those who are destitute of home, friends, and kindred; and thus in every position in life her activity is experienced in every place, and her sympathy is felt wherever she is found. Holy, beneficent mission! to make man happy and useful by her watchful care, worldly prudence, tender affection, and wise counsel. Her position is generally considered one of humility; but her vocation is truly one of love; and how willingly does she lend her aid to rend the clouds of passion, and chase away the advances of sorrow. True, there are those of the fair sex who foolishly give the most of their time and attention to those fashionable shows which constitute the amusement of the world, who are ignorant of domestic duties, who, from false notions of gentility, are ashamed to take part in the household affairs, who imagine that their affected learning and pedantic accomplishments will atone for their want of a practical knowledge of domestic economy, who love the drawing-room or the parlour more than the nursery or the kitchen, who would handle the cryon or graver with more pleasure than they would attend to the instruction and comfort of their household. And there are too many mothers who are daily adding to the moral and physical weakness of their offspring. This is the effect of blinding ignorance and the corrupting habits of society. It is said, and I am sorry to add, with truth, that there are indifferent, fickle, inconsistent, and false women to be met with; but these women, by the artificial existence to which they are bred, have lost the most of the finer sentiments which endear woman to man.

Such are ignorant fools, who deserve not the name of woman—they are a disgrace to the sex and a stumblingblock to society. It is the good and useful woman—she who knows her duty and does it—that is worthy of praise and confidence. Whatever be her position in life or rank in society—her natural endowments or acquired accomplishments, if she moves in her own legitimate sphere, and proves herself worthy of her holy vocation, she is entitled to the endearing appellation, *woman*, and, next to God, she becomes the centre of all delights of sense and soul. Do we enter the palace of nature? then the soft glories of her tender soul shades an unfading lustre over the beauty and grandeur of all around us. Is a flood of cares like to overwhelm us? then does she not—frail bark though she be—help to bear us over the billowy sea of fortune to the hoped-for haven of joy? Do we give over our "labour of love" because blighting calumny has wounded our hearts, and foiled our best intentions? then she, by her healing virtue and tender sympathy, re-enlists us in the patience of hope. Who can know the full value of a truly good woman? None but He who giveth every good and perfect gift. "Her price is far above rubies;" and the poet, addressing her, exclaims,—

> " There is in you all that we believe of heaven—
> Amazing brightness, purity, and truth,
> Eternal joy and everlasting love."

When this powerful influence is exercised for good, what a blessing to mankind! And this is done in our day with grand results. Thanks to God, there are women in these isles of ours who are working for God. In the course of my labours I have met with many such, but I shall only name two here.

Amongst the first invitations which I received, after my arrival in London, was that from Captain and Mrs Bayly. I had heard of this good lady, and her noble efforts amongst her neighbours; and glad was I to have this opportunity of seeing her, and hearing from her lips the nature of the efforts which had been so greatly blessed to those in need of the blessing. She had been suffering from over-work, and was yet ailing; but she did me the favour—yes, and the honour too—of making a good cup of tea, all the sweeter by her presence and conversation. Nor was this all. At the festival-meetings, then being held, I had the pleasure of addressing the "rescued,"—mothers, fathers, and children,—every meeting being more interesting than another. These were pleasant scenes. What a glorious sight to see those who, in all probability, would still have been in the ways of wickedness and misery, now on the road to comfort and happiness! The sights I saw there, night after night, did my heart good.

And the results of these labours of love were as cheering as they were pleasant; they proved that none are so deeply fallen that they may not be lifted up. Not a few in that interesting group were *seeking* the means of improvement. One instance may be given.

The most aged of them had lived seven years alone in an old van, and at that time still continued to creep over Nottinghill, calling, "Chairs to mend! chairs to mend!" He had become a firm, an earnest total abstainer, declaring to all to whom he spoke on that subject that strong drink made him "wicked and miserable." When reflecting on his past life, he would say, "Oh dear! oh dear! oh dear!" He loves to have the Scriptures read to him, and hopes to obtain forgiveness.

What a change! thought I, as I loomed on the past and beheld the present. What may not yet be accomplished by these working and united social and religious reformers; and that amongst many of those who, to all human appearance, were utterly helpless! Out of all this earnest work, great blessings have since sprung,—one of which is a "Working Man's Hall," in which are centred noble and prudent efforts for the elevation of the people; and not far from that building is another,—a handsome "New Tabernacle,"—built by a tradesman of the neighbourhood, Mr Varley, and dedicated to the Lord and evangelisation.

It was not long after I went to North London that I had the pleasure of meeting Mrs Ranyard, the Honorary Secretary to "The Bible and Domestic Female Missions." She had just read my "Life Story." Little did I think, when in tears I was revising that autobiography for Charles Dickens's inspection, that it would be said, as I lately read, it has made many friends whom I knew not, and secured for me at once a hearty welcome wherever I go.

"It is truly remarkable," said this lady, "how in Scotland you should be so trained in the providence of God for such useful work in London," and then went on to tell how she felt when reading the "Story." Never shall I forget the impressions fixed on my mind during my first conversation with this gifted and high-principled lady. The common sense, the happy thought, the ready utterance, with which she is endowed, and which is manifest in all her generous efforts in behalf of women, were evident and impressive. There was a pleasing frankness, nicely blended with a becoming dignity; and our after-meetings only served the more to convince me that these rare and useful qualities were wedded to Christian charity, fearless honesty, and earnest benevolence.

And how happily all this is associated with the great work with which her name is inseparably connected! Before that time, I had known something of the Bible-woman's work; but since that lady laid before me her plans, and revealed the motives which led her to action, I have had a better opportunity of considering the necessity and of observing the usefulness of such efforts. *Suitable* Bible-women can do for their sex what no other agency can; and they *have* done what, to a great extent, without their help, must have been left undone. The object of this useful mission is to talk with the outcast poor, to help them to improve their homes and habits, to make kind wives and good husbands, careful parents and tidy children, useful and happy families. And its bases may be recorded in these words—

"Nothing is of decisive use to them (the people) that does not help them to help themselves."

God bless all such work as these couple of workers—with many others—so ably represent!

IV. Another Couple of Efforts.

A card of invitation to a *conversazione* in connexion with the Working Man's Club and Institute Union was the means of introducing me to some of those interested in such like efforts. Upon that card, along with others, was the honoured name of Lord Brougham ; and that of itself was to me a proof of the sincerity of these workers in behalf of the working man.

As is now well known, that association "is formed for the purpose of *helping working men to establish clubs and institutes*, where they can meet for conversation, business, and mental improvement, with the means of recreation and refreshment, without being dependent for these purposes upon the public-house ; the clubs at the same time constituting societies for mutual helpfulness in various ways."

That this is needed, all must admit; and that it has been useful wherever attained, is a fact which is telling favourably on society. The council state that the aim of the Union " in all cases is to *help working men to help themselves*, rather than to establish or manage institutions for them—this being as essential for the moral usefulness as for the permanent success of our endeavours. But it is not one of the least recommendations of this movement that it is pre-eminently calculated, in every stage of it, to promote that *mutual sympathy and friendly intercourse*, as well as that interchange of benefits between the different classes and sections of society, which is not more stringently required by Christianity than needed for the preservation of social order and national progress."

And these friends of the people admit a fact worthy of consideration when they say, "The working men of this country, greatly as they both deserve and need our sympathy and help, are by no means so easily helped as some persons imagine. *Innumerable failures in all parts of the country* prove this only too painfully. The very anxiety to help them, combined, as it too often is, with ignorance how to do it, frequently forms a formidable hindrance to most praiseworthy efforts. In addition to pecuniary help, which is needed as capital for the first outfit of the clubs, there is yet greater necessity for gathering in a common centre experience, information, and personal influence, to be employed throughout the country in that *impartial, unsectarian spirit* which has hitherto characterised the Union. Unless this continues to be done, there is manifest danger of the movement becoming stunted or misdirected, sectional in its spirit, spasmodic or feeble in its action, and most discouraging in its results."

Still, with this difficulty staring them in the face, they are persevering, and succeeding remarkably. In Mr Solly they have an active secretary. His intense earnestness, his anxiety to learn more than he knows, and his readiness to impart to others what he does know, became evident to me at once.

Willingly would I offer some remarks here touching the nature and management of such clubs; but limited space compels me to deny myself what might otherwise be a favourable opportunity of giving my reasons for and against some points involved in their management.

Of the necessity there is for such clubs, or whatever name such gatherings may have, for promoting the social, mental, and moral welfare of the people, and for the *healthful* recreation of the working classes, there can be no doubt; but the *mode* is a debatable theme. Yet this I can say,—workmen particularly, and society in general, are much indebted to the efforts of the "Working Men's Club and Institute Union" on behalf of a large mass of the people; and sincerely do I hope that the Spirit and will of God may be evinced in all its undertakings.

The other effort I refer to here is in the same direction as that I have indicated. This may be disputed by some, especially those who may have a word to say in favour of the pipe; but of this I am certain, that the aim of the one is as noble and as disinterested as the other, indeed the aim is the same—the welfare, the moral and social well-being, of the people. Both institutions may occasionally manifest errors in judgment as to the mode of gaining their respective objects; but that object is a good one. I refer now to the British Anti-Tobacco Society, of which Mr Reynolds is the earnest secretary. He, as well as those able and good men who support this society, has heartily espoused this, because, as is well known, "in no instance is the sin of the father more strikingly visited upon his children than in the sin of tobacco-smoking;" and "that smoking is a main cause of ruining our young men, pauperising the working men, and rendering comparatively useless the best efforts of ministers of religion." In this opinion I most heartily concur. I believe, with the late Professor Miller and other eminent medical authorities, "that every man, woman, and child who uses tobacco unnecessarily, to any appreciable extent, is thereby injuring himself or herself morally, mentally, and physically, more or less." One of the objects of this society is stated to be "incidentally to promote the object of the great temperance reformation," and this word "incidentally" is a very modest way of putting the statement. I have no hesitation in saying that this society, through Mr Reynolds, and its other promoters, and means of diffusing knowledge on the point at issue, *directly* helps the cause of total abstinence from strong drink. "I gave up the pot, and then I soon broke the pipe," is a statement I often hear from working men when giving their experience touching the fearful bane of our nation, *drunkenness*, and the pleasing antidote, abstinence; and so is it with regard to the pipe. Let the intoxicant tobacco be given up, and the chances are many that the other intoxicant, alcohol, will soon be forsaken. And let it never be forgotten, that the common and general use of tobacco is one of the many, if not the largest, sources of that dashing and deadly stream,—intemperance,—which is rushing and rolling through our land.   There is death in the pipe as well as in the pot, and there is death in the pot as well as in the pipe.

With this, as with the other effort, I wish it all the success possible, knowing that both are worthy of consideration.

V. RAGGED SCHOOLS.

There are now many good efforts. Not a few are being useful, and none more so than our Ragged Schools. In their own way, they not only " pluck brands from the burning," but also become a means of preventing many from going into the " burning." If ever a movement obeyed the Divine injunction—" Lift up your voice for the young children that fainteth for hunger at the corner of every street "—it is this effort, to " rid them out of the hand of the wicked," to

> " Gather them in from the lanes and streets,
> Gather them in from the dark retreats ;
> From the haunts of folly, the dens of crime,
> Gather them in their early prime."

Long before I came to London, I felt interested in such efforts. It had been my fortune to know something of the nature and working, the object and usefulness, of the Ragged Schools in Aberdeen, with which the Rev. J. H. Wilson was happily associated, and of those with which Dr Guthrie's worthy name is connected ; but it was in London where I began more thoroughly to examine the movement and watch its results, and that with the view of helping as I had opportunity. Through the kindness of Lord Kinnaird, I was introduced to the Rev. John Garwood, of the London City Mission, who kindly introduced me to Mr Gent, secretary of the Ragged School Union—" established for the support of free schools for the destitute poor of

London and its suburbs." The result has been favourable, I hope, not only to myself. Though I have only met with Mr Gent in his official capacity, and I merely mention his name in connexion with the office, yet I have been with him often enough to convince me that it is with him a special object to try what can be done for the children of the destitute poor. On one occasion, I referred to the idea expressed by Henry Mayhew, that " ragged schools are of more injury than good to the community;" and though more than ten years had passed since that statement had been made and refuted by Lord Shaftesbury and Mr Anderson, he had ready at hand the multiplicity of facts, the ever-increasing facts, which prove the reverse of Mr Mayhew's proposition. And these facts he handled so as to indicate that he had made them his own, and that for the purpose of defending the institution in connexion with which he was labouring, and is labouring, so earnestly. This gave me the necessary confidence; and whatever instruction or help I needed in relation to ragged schools, I went for it to No. 1 Exeter Hall, and found in Mr Gent a readiness to render all the assistance in his power, which to me was a benefit; for I have found not only that the movement is one of the many parts of a practical system of benevolence, but that the ragged school and all its surroundings also forms a useful theme for the social anatomist.

And besides meeting with Mr Gent, and others more or less directly connected with the Union, I have met with other friends having the same noble aim in view, who support and manage ragged schools chiefly by private or individual kindness and exertion. By the efforts of such, the aid of a few more anxious to do good in that way, and an occasional help or countenance from the central body, much good is being done. Amongst the many instances of such, I may name the Hindes' Mews Ragged School, Marylebone Lane. I mention this field of earnest and successful labour in behalf of the young, because I have long had the pleasure of the personal friendship of the generous super-

intendent, moved as he ever is to deeds of kindness by the best of Christian motives—a man who by many will be long remembered after he is gone, and especially by the young of that neighbourhood—a man who has not only laboured with all his might in whatever he has conceived to be for good, and who has not only gone forth with willing and open hand to the rescue of the outcast and neglected generally, but who has also had influence sufficient to gather round him other earnest and active workers having the same generous aim. But I also name this seat of thoughtful effort because its condition and position are remarkable, and because they are a fair representation of many such institutions. In its report for 1860, I find these words :—
" Could we take our position at a sufficient height, immediately over the school-rooms, a tolerable idea of the neighbourhood by which it is surrounded would be obtained. Fashionable squares surrounded by the mansions of the wealthy, flanked by the stables for their horses ; and then almost immediately adjoining the courts and lanes, in which are found the abodes of another, and a no less numerous class of the community, from which the ' raw material' for our ragged schools is supplied. Interwoven are the dwellings of the rich and the poor ; but not so with the inhabitants, they live and move as two different tribes, except where the influence of self-interest on the one hand, or philanthropy and Christianity on the other, brings them into occasional communication with each other. This is the situation of this field of labour." Here, then, is week-day and Sunday-schools, a Band of Hope, and a mutual improvement class, a penny bank, and other means of attraction and improvement ; and this is the kind of useful machinery, more or less diversified and extended, in connexion with this system of practical and valuable benevolence. In addition to the value of the ragged school, as doing that which no other school can do, there is generally connected with it a variety of other labours that are being blessed to the neighbourhood. Indeed, I find that the

ragged school is frequently the centre of our various evange-listic efforts. But apart from this in itself, its claims on the public are numerous and strong.

The child is sweet, winning, and beautiful; and if a spark of love is within, the child will draw it out, not bit by bit, that is impossible; for if the heart is in the right place, and the mind in the right state, unbounded love gushes forth towards him. See these sparkling young eyes! do they not rivet your attention and cause an inexpressible emotion to come quickly from the innermost soul? Look again at that gem of a rounded dimple in the rosy cheek! and then—what a glorious thought!—think of what makes that eye so bright, that cheek so fair; what reveals that beauty, which words can never describe; what makes that form not only a lovely, but a loving child. He is a subject of intense pleasure and happiness, receiving and impart-ing both. His wonderful frame bears the impress of divinity, bespeaking the wisdom and kindness of the Creator. He is not only a living, but a never-dying soul; a sinner, without doubt, yet he may become one of the successful candidates for eternal bliss; since for him the gospel provides and offers a Saviour, in every way suited to the exigencies of his case. Often have I gazed with intense pleasure on the beauties of the rose and the lily in balmy nature's calm repose, and I have felt as if I could wish that they might retain their beauty. Their sudden or gra-dual change, however, reminded me of the sad fate of many boys and girls. How many, in early childhood, who were interesting because of "their amazing brightness, purity, and truth," have found that " life is as tedious as a twice-told tale, yielding nought but shame and bitterness!" I have thought of the dear, sweet pet in its mother's lap, receiving daily its " thousand and one" kisses, safely and trustingly hanging "on love's delicious breath;" then came rushing in the thought that others, who had been once as that babe, had progressed in sin and misery as they had grown in years. I have thought, too, of the child at play, where it would seem that "all its life's enjoyments rest." There it is, in raptures of glee. A moment more, and the temper is ruffled, the passions are fired, the brows are knit, bad words are exchanged, and, mayhap, hard blows are given. Is there not something mysterious and seemingly contradictory here? for if there be any one creature on earth innocent, is it not the child? And yet there it is, now all love, and then all hatred; now excessive in acts of kindness, and then fearful in deeds of violence—the child is said to be father to the man, and *man is a sinner.* This solves the mystery. He belongs to the universal brotherhood, and is properly called the "crown of creation;" and he will be better and brighter in heaven, where simplicity and love will be pure and lasting; yet, in this probationary state, he soon proves what some one has said what that glorious old book, the Bible, long since declared, that "human nature is broken down and degenerated;" that sin has cast a dark shade upon that beauty and glory, which innocence and excellence imparted before the fall.

And in addition to this there is another consideration. There is not only a family likeness in all that pertains to fallen humanity, the child is remarkable for his susceptibility. He, like soft wax, receives, and often retains, the impression from that which surrounds him. He is not only moved by inward impulse, he is affected by outward circumstances; and what are the circumstances which often surround the ragged-school boy? I have seen such enter the school. All that covers his dirty figure is not worth twopence at the rag-store. At first, he feels as strange and as timid as a mouse in a trap, and as anxious to get out. He has scarcely heard a kind word in his life. The name of Jesus he knows not. He never heard of it, except in cursing and blasphemy, and his parents are nearly as ignorant as himself. Here, in a Christian land, he is as unenlightened as a pagan. Such a sight is enough not only to picture to the mind scenes of the most thrilling interest, but also to fill the soul

N

with ideas intensely suggestive and momentous. Yet ignorant as he may be, or wicked as he may be, he is one of those for whom Jesus pleads, such as He asked to be brought unto Him, such as He may, by the means of grace, place His hand upon and bless, and of whom He may yet say, " Of such is the kingdom of heaven." " It is not the will of our heavenly Father that any of these little ones should perish." And how gladsome it must be to the friends of children, how pleased must be the children's Friend to think that so many are not willing that any such should perish, and that, like the Sabbath-school, the ragged-school has been established and is maintained to rescue the children—to feed His lambs!

V. "Go and Do what you Can."

But notwithstanding Sunday-schools and ragged-schools, and other efforts to rescue our young, many grow up wandering far from God and peace. To recall the wanderer and to bring back to the fold, we have home-mission efforts, and they are useful, but I think not so much so as they might be. It is long since good and brave men entered that field and valiantly penetrated the abodes of poverty and suffering, of vice and crime, and yet these are strewn thickly, the gaunt places are as dismal as ever. If one fever garden becomes less conspicuous in the bills of mortality, another black alley stands in its stead. If one family is led to feel the dignity of independence, another whines because, as is too often the case, the hypocrite secures the dole. If one is lifted out of the "slough of despond," another sinks deeper into the filthy mire of social and moral degradation. To say how this comes about would require more space than I have at my command; but this I can say, before there can be the desired, the effective improvement, those engaged for the avowed purpose of religious consolation must widen their field of usefulness; they must help more than ever to remove the stumbling-blocks.

Nay, more, they must, more than ever, be less encumbered with undue restrictions. "Go and do what you can," ought to be the injunction as they start upon their difficult and dangerous journey.

For one occupying the place I do, that of an evangelist,—one whose duty it is to visit as well as preach,—this is a delicate point upon which to speak; but if this renders it difficult, it also gives me an opportunity of knowing what really is; and this urges me to speak for the sake of the glorious cause which we all seek to promote. And happily for me and my increasing usefulness, the edge is taken off the delicacy. Thanks to God, and those dear friends with whom I am congenially yoked, I am so far free to speak that what I say cannot be regarded as special pleading. With the utmost confidence those with whom I am associated say to me, as was said to Mr M'Cree, "Go and do what you can;" and, like him, I am at perfect liberty—indeed I am encouraged—to take the life and words of Jesus as the basis of my mode of evangelisation.

I have here associated Mr M'Cree with this idea, and I have reason to do so. In London, as elsewhere, I have met with many an earnest brother in the Mission work,—with those, too, whose labours have been blessed in no ordinary degree; but I confess it has not as yet been my lot to meet with a worker with whom my sympathies ran more in unison, nor with a work the mode of accomplishing which is more in accordance with my ideas as to how we may best *reach* and *improve* the people. Shortly after my arrival in London I heard of him, but did not have the pleasure of meeting with him till 1862; and that warm attachment which I feel and cherish towards him was not brought about till 1863. Since then, we have had an opportunity of meeting more frequently; and I have thereby become better acquainted with him and his work in St Giles's—a locality which, like Bethnal Green, is associated with fetid air and fusty smells, old clothes and old bones, lazy women and dirty children, shabby

loiterers and lounging drunkards, dark alleys and brilliant gin-
shops, ignorance and degradation, moral and spiritual destitution.
Such are a few of the rougher outlines of the Seven Dials—Mr
M'Cree's "diocese." There he labours and superintends labour;
and all the more effectively that he has the liberty to go and do
what he can to the bringing-in of many outcasts, to the joy of
souls made happy in the peace of believing. He visits sometimes
day and night; he preaches Sunday and week-day; he sees to
the bodies as well as the souls of his charge; he is grave and
gay; and I am glad to add, he, as is evident, is "merry and
wise." I have been with him on Sunday and week-day, on an
ordinary and festive occasion, and such is the impression he has
left on my mind. Doubtless he has had the great advantage of
a long stay and of hearty encouragement; but he has proved
himself to be worthy of both, worthy of the liberty to do what
he can. *Might not hundreds more be the same, and do the same,
if they had the same opportunity?*

At the commencement of a lecture delivered by Mr M' Cree,
June 21, 1862,—touching this important point and his coming
to London,—he said, "Fourteen years ago, it pleased God to
send me up to London to work among the poor. I was invited
by the Rev. W. Brook of Bloomsbury Chapel, who wished me to
try what I could do to benefit the lower classes of the great
metropolis; and after considering the offer for about four weeks
I resolved to accept it, and set out to see what I could do for
man and for God. When I arrived, I inquired what I was to
do; and the answer was, '*Go and do what you can.*'"

With this call from God, and liberty from man, he went forth
to visit the poor from day to day, endeavouring by all possible
means to teach them the way to peace and love—Jesus Christ.
He is successful; and doubtless this arises as much from the
" liberty" to go and do *what* he can, *when* he can, and in the
best way he can, as from his ability and sincerity. His friends
and associates in the good work, like mine, have done as others

should do. I have no hesitation in saying, for those who engage the services of one who wishes in this way to work "for man and for God," the first question is, or ought to be, Is he "born again?" then, Has he the secondary but essential qualifications, ability and prudence, energy and activity, earnestness and aptitude? Having satisfied themselves on these points, let them *trust* the one sent forth; as with one, so with the thousands. I am aware that it is said there may be, as there have been, dishonest and disqualified evangelists and missionaries. This I admit, just as there have been and may be dishonest and disqualified clergymen and ministers; but will undue restraint or unreasonable demands take off the prefix "*dis?*" By no means. It is the opinion of many well-disposed persons that injudicious and unnecessary restraints tell against the progress of real and effective mission work.

To those who really know the difficulties connected with the efforts of our home missionaries, it is evident that the "making-up" of the "journal" is one of no ordinary nature, especially when the worker is expected minutely to tabulate results as well as efforts. What must be the state of that man's mind when he has been from house to house striving with all his heart, with all his mind, and with all his strength to do good, to serve the heavenly Master,—to whom he can in all conscience say, "Lord, Thou knowest I have done my best;" and yet when he reaches home he finds it difficult to present such an account as may satisfy his earthly masters! What more pitiable sight can there be than the anxious and exhausted, the plodding, often-saddened, and sometimes suspected, worker in the vineyard sitting over his "journal" at home, and being harassed by the thought that *on paper* his day's work will have but a shabby appearance; and that though in the sight of God, and in reality, it may have been glorious as to starting-points, tending to happy results, that which saddens his heart and surrounds him with temptation, is the thought that his fitness for the work may be calculated by what he can put on paper; that it is very probable his situation and his character depend upon the number of visits paid, of times the Scriptures have been read, of children sent to school, of people sent to church or chapel, of the number of "conversations," and such like "special cases"! If he does not make the best of it that night, if he is enabled so to resist temptation as to keep imagination from the point of his pen, he may by a process of reasoning, from facts known to him touching the case of others in the same work, be induced, almost compelled, next day or days to *drive on* at his labour as if he was operating on inanimate matter instead of mind, surrounded by elements almost all of which are opposed to those results looked for, and by none more anxiously than the visitor.

I am aware that it has been said, and is still said, that subscribers wish to see that work is done for the money given; and there is something in this, if they regard this work in the same light as the builder does the erection of a house, if it were possible and in the power of the visitor and preacher to render his efforts as visible as the bricklayer and mason. This is not the case, as must be evident on the least reflection; and hence we are driven back to the application of the same rule in relation to the conductors of mission effort, as has been named in connexion with those who go out and in amongst the people. The generous wealthy ought to have faith in the intelligence and honesty of those whom they directly or indirectly appoint to the management of the *business* department. This I believe is the case, with but very few exceptions, and this sends us back to those at the head of the work. And what is the effect of the effort to show results? It is a well-known fact that many subscribers are in the habit of deducting from twenty-five to fifty per cent. off the figures in the reports. And this is not only calculated to injure the societies whose directors may wish to MAKE THE VERY BEST APPEARANCE in order to augment their funds, but it is damaging to other societies, however conducted; it is creating an increasing want of faith in what really is a work of faith, and to some degree a labour of love.

I say *labour of love*, and that too on the part of those workers who are paid—that is, receive a salary for their work. I have no hesitation in saying that a very large majority of such have entered the field, feeling convinced that God sent them; and that many of the really qualified of them—of the able and earnest, the honest and devoted, the soul-loving and God-glorifying—could, with less labour, less danger, and in some cases more independence, increase their income by applying their talents in another direction.

But this pressure—to record minute, and certainly for the purpose named unnecessary, details—does not only harass the pious and faithful worker, ultimately weaken the faith of the generous subscriber; it hinders the progress of mission work by destroying the confidence of the poor in the worker. Find out the leading reasons why the poor object to calls, why they are distant, why they are reserved, why some of them act the hypocrite when they think pious pretensions will bring some pecuniary reward. It will be found for one reason that what may pass betwixt the visitor and the visited may be recorded,— that even the innermost secrets of the heart may be read first by one, and then another, and yet another. This is one reason—and a leading reason—why so many of the poor and the ignorant suppose they see in this worker all that understood by the word "jesuitic"—one possessed of great cunning, craft, and deceit, so as to be able to insinuate into favour, with the view of imposing upon those whose attention or affection may be gained.

"Now, sir, before you sit down, tell me if you are like those who put everything they hear in a book. If you are, you'll get nothing here!" Such was the salutation with which a newly-appointed visitor was lately met. And though others may not be so plain spoken, it is the feeling of many. Nor is this all. I know it has entered the minds of many of the people that one

of the reasons of the minute recording of visits, and all other
things therewith connected, is to prove that the visitor has done
his duty; hence they infer that the employers have not confidence in him. This, being coupled with other notions, goes
direct against his success; for one of the first essentials to usefulness is to gain and retain the people's confidence. Of course,
the worker with wisdom and tact may do much to counteract
the injurious pressure of such hindrances to usefulness, but
those at the head of all mission effort can do much more, and
the first step in that direction is to " *trust*" the worker.

But, in addition to all this, there is something more connected
with the injunction, " Go and do what you can." This does
not only imply confidence in the person appointed that he will
do his duty, it also means that he knows best (being on the spot,
and having experience) not only *how*, but *when*, to work. This
liberty can only be given where there is confidence, but the first
is as essential as the last. For instance, suppose the blacksmith at the fire to be considered a journeyman, and regarded
by the employer as able for his work and likely to be faithful in
the performance of his duties. He has a piece of iron of which
he is to make an article named to him. He puts that iron into
the fire, heaps on coals and makes the bellows roar. Near to
him it may be, but in an enclosed box or office, is his master.
He hears the roaring of the fire, but he does not see the effect
upon the iron. He may know that it must not only be red-hot,
but white hot; he may know that at the proper stage of heat the
iron should be struck, but he sees it not, and yet he calls out,
" Strike, *now* is the time." Give it so many strokes in so many
seconds, that is his rule. The man obeys; the shape wished
may be obtained, but it is just as likely—nay, more than ten
chances to one—that the form is not that which is wished.

Such is a fair specimen of what too often is the case when the
worker in the mission-field is restrained and constrained by
rules made by those who have not seen, and heard, and known

for themselves; those who doubtless are well-intended theorists, but who, if put into the field, would find it very difficult, if not impossible, to carry out what they lay down as a guide to others. If the journeyman blacksmith and his master would so bungle the conformation desired, certainly the moulders of minds would, under similar restraints, commit errors much more serious. In all kindness and humility would I ask that these matters be considered by the proper parties. Most readily do I admit that those who are hired are responsible to those who pay the money; that the employed ought to seek to know the mind and wishes of the employer, and that with the view of carrying these wishes out: nay, I go farther, and say that instead of objecting to laws, I can believe there is, in some cases, with man as it is always with God, love in law; but the laws of man, though often well intended, are not always wise and suitable. They may be made for a good purpose, but—as has often been the case—framed by those who had only examined one side of the question, and that imperfectly. Where such is the case, the result cannot be what the best intended expected. Where rules are needed, let them be few, and short, and wise. And if ever this ought to be true in any instance, surely it is in the case of mission work; but once more I say, where the right man for the right place is found, the best rule for him is,—Do what you can, but take the words and life of Christ as the basis of the work of evangelisation.

What I have just said refers chiefly to the management of mission work; and I do not mean to qualify more than I have done, even one sentence. I have said only what I felt bound to say, and that for the sake of the grand and common object every Christian has in view; but I have reason to add that the errors, however brought about, do not all lie on one side. The difficulties to which I have referred create others, and all unite in surrounding the worker, circumscribing and disheartening him; but he is the servant of God, and as such is accountable to *Him*, as well as to those by whom he is employed.   This is an important consideration for all, but especially for the worker in the mission field, whether he is designated a missionary or an evangelist, a minister or a clergyman.   With him the question ought to be, " What can promote the greatest amount of good of the greatest number in need of it?"   As those by whom he may be appointed cannot lay down rules for him at all approaching to infallibility, so neither can he frame for himself rules after the Medes and Persians' fashion.   In all matters pertaining to the vicissitudes of life, its various and ever-changing surroundings, immutability in relation to modes of action must be fatal to the best intentions.   In all such cases there is no rule without exceptions; and where this fact is ignored, injustice to some one, or some thing, is done.   In all plans—especially for mission work—there must be room left for exceptional cases, and these cases frequently outnumber all others; hence the difficulty of providing *beforehand*; and yet this in some measure must be done.   There must be an understanding of some kind, and this must be made on the broadest ground possible—the enlargement and prosperity of the Church of Christ must be the leading principle of action.   In the evangelist, anything short of this is sure to cramp his soul, and lead to results not to be desired; but starting from this unsectarian point, and ever keeping it in view, he helps towards the greatest good in being able to unite heartily with others already at work.   He can more easily give to them the same latitude of opinion which he desires for himself; but, alas! how frequently it is otherwise! how unwilling many are to concede to others the least particle of liberty of conscience, if by doing so *their* views—often very narrow—are called in question!

And besides this narrowness of view, and attempting to dictate to others in the absence of this grand principle, there is too often a petty jealousy which is sure to wither the souls of those in whose bosoms it dwells.   This leads to the forming of opinions everything but favourable in regard to other workers; and being formed and fostered, they are soon uttered and spread to the injury of the victims, and the lessening of their usefulness. And this scandal soon reaches the ears of those for whose benefit the workers work. If the person of whom the evil is spoken thinks it proper to vindicate himself, then the battle rages more furiously, and whoever fights most valiantly, whoever is in the right, it matters not, alas! for the results. With the pauperised class, those who have been taught to whine out *religion*, he is the best man who for them can go the deepest into the pockets of the wealthy. This gives a personal triumph, and causes a soft smile to play upon the bland face of the victor, but the results are disastrous. What a pity there are any who so far forget their duty as to act so far contrary to the spirit and letter of the law of God! What a position this is for those who profess to be intrusted with the " word of reconciliation!" Again, the absence of the noble wish—to promote the greatest amount of good—makes room for another great error, the desire to decide for others as to church fellowship; instead of leading to Jesus, always insisting on the claims of some church. The man who said there were a "hundred Christianities at King's Cross," only conveyed the idea which thousands have—an idea implanted by those who cater for a system. What a difference there is where the worker labours to bring the sinner to a Saviour, to be instrumental in God's hand in rescuing the slaves of sin, and leading them into the kingdom of God! What a difference there is between the system defender and provider, and the lover of souls, who with life and love goes to work for man and for God! God help all of us that we may be filled with a loving and catholic spirit; without this there can neither be singleness of purpose nor devotedness of heart, usefulness nor happiness.

I might here give instances known to me of the absence of the Christ-like spirit, and of the sad effects which are ever sure to follow, but I merely wish to mention the matter and pass on, trusting that the day is not distant when the workers shall work for the Master on the broad ground which He has graciously mapped out; when the glory of God in the salvation of souls shall be the universal object; when light and zeal, faith and energy, shall go hand in hand; when to that liberty of conscience and latitude of opinion, which ought to be interchanged by all, there may be given by the employers to the employed that freedom of action which amounts to the liberty embodied in the words—"Go and do what you can."

VI. Preaching in the Open Air.

I have been criticising instead of recording, and I must continue this ungracious work yet a little longer. But I am referring to what I know, and what is immediately connected with my labours. I have been speaking of the errors of those who may be said to be more or less under control, and doubtless the same class are mixed up with open-air preachers, and therefore, in some measure, share the blame and praise connected with open-air preaching; but the open-air mission may be regarded as made up of those who are under no control but their own wisdom and desires—the latter doubtless are good, but the former seems not to be always of the most approved stamp. Of course I refer to London, which is certainly the greatest field for this useful and essential mode of evangelisation. Open-air preaching is not new, but it never was so prevalent, so generally recognised, as now. I am told that no farther back than twenty years, if a man was heard talking loudly in the streets, he was at once set down as a fanatic or a demagogue. Though many sneers, and not a little opposition frequently meet the person who steps forth to arrest the attention of the "loungers" or passers by, yet it is now fashionable to preach "out of doors." It is now believed to be "orthodox" thus to preach; but who will undertake to define the "orthodoxy" given forth from time to time by all classes and degrees of preachers—from the Bishop of London to that earnest person who calls himself a " young convert ? "

Listen to that " preacher." He is speaking energetically. He is truly earnest, but who can make out what he means? " Words, words, words!" The people stop. They hear the words, " Jesus," " sinner," " hell," "damnation," over and over again, but in what relation? None can say. One declaration he is sure to make again and again, and yet again—that he has " come out depending on the strength of the Lord "—which, by too many such speakers, simply means going forth to speak on what they know not, and, therefore, without reflecting even for a moment. How absurd! how damaging to the cause they stand forth to represent!

Pass on to that other group. A preacher is in its midst who has gone into the Bible. Night and day he has made it his study, but, as is soon evident, he has not done so with the view of learning from God how matters really stand in relation to the Creator and the creature, but rather to see how well he can maintain his favourite point—often of small importance to those addressed. He dogmatises and abuses; the simple truths of the gospel are seldom heard from his lips. What good can he do?

" Move on." Still another group and another preacher, but *he* is labouring hard, not to give a reason for the hope that is in him, but to prove that reason is opposed to religion; he is under-valuing *all* human efforts in matters pertaining to our eternal interests. What good can he do amongst the people?

Once more, pass on to that open space where another preacher is shouting loudly. He is quite opposed to that class of speakers who condescendingly " come *down* to the understanding of the people " (?) He is born, he thinks, to bring up the people to his elevated standard (of the English language.) He has studied, but evidently his theme has been how best to employ his stock of big words so that he might make a display of *his learning*. He has not only balloon-shaped nouns, but crinoline adjectives. His immensely-blown expressions he scatters broadcast, and generally in a most ludicrous manner; and hence he is regarded, and not improperly regarded, by the more sensible of his listeners, as a piece of affectation, empty as a tenantless shell, and as useless.

And, as might be expected, there is open-air speaking which does not claim to be called preaching. The truth is, it is often the opposite, for atheists, deists, secularists, and so forth, claim the attention of the public in the streets and open places of London. There are conscientious sceptics, who honestly wish that their doubts may be removed; and it becomes the enlightened Christian to reason with such at the proper time and in an intelligent manner; but there are others who wish to shine and gloat over personal victory. Such go to the street to oppose, and if possible browbeat the preacher, especially when the latter says something very foolish or out of place, as is too frequently the case. They are as subtle as they are numerous. I have watched their movements, and followed them up, and I mourn to say the ridicule they raise against the gracious truths of the simple gospel is calculated to make one tremble for the result.

See that strongly-built man, muffled up, as if afraid lest he should catch cold. His hair is gray and somewhat long; but his face and words do not permit of the qualifying term " reverend," which his age and aspect might otherwise suggest. I saw him first at King's Cross, but he goes all over London, at every preaching station—now at the " Brill," then at Paddington Green, then back on Towerhill. He moves about from group to group, watching his opportunity and biding his time. Being an old stager, his experience gives him every advantage not only to know on whom, but when to pounce. Where the preacher evinces a weakness or a want of guardedness, there this cunning prowler is sure to place himself. When his opportunity arrives, he draws himself up with apparent kindness and an expressed anxiety to "*learn* something." It is soon evident that he has turned his question to a point of infidelity to which he has devoted his attention and to which he has frequently given utterance. When it so happens that the preacher has not reflected upon that theme, or is unequal to the occasion, this enemy to gospel truth and real happiness triumphs at the expense of all that is sacred. Having succeeded, he tries to clench the nail he has driven, and doubtless, in his frightful career, he has done much in the way of forming and confirming infidels.

But much harm as he and others of the same stamp have done, dangerous as they are to virtue and to happiness, I feel convinced that though the *avowed*, they are not the *worst* enemies to the promotion of the gospel by open-air speaking. From what I know,—having heard for myself and heard from the lips of many of the people,—I hesitate not to say that such preachers and preaching as that of which I have given four specimens, do more damage to the spread of the gospel in the open air than the most cunning of its wicked enemies. Yet, let me add, I should not be doing justice to open-air preaching, nor to my convictions touching its manner and influence, did I not readily and gladly admit that within the past two years I have observed a decided change for the better. Though such errors as I have named are too numerous, yet, side by side with them, are efforts made which God is blessing, *because they are done in the name and in the spirit of the Saviour.* These latter efforts are daily increasing, and much of this improvement is due to the earnest and prudent efforts of the "Open-Air Mission," the office of which is at No. 1 Robert Street, Adelphi. Whatever faults there may be connected with the preachers who consider this society as a centre of operations, it cannot be denied that many of them, "kind hearted and sensible," are, by God's help, doing much "quiet and useful work" in lanes and alleys and far-off back streets.

But there is yet room left for improvement; and how to bring this about, is an important question upon which I cannot enter, although I cannot break short here—I must at least say, that one prevailing error in relation to open-air preaching is the false idea that the office is not so sacred as that of the pulpit. What is preaching? Is it not proclaiming God's will in relation to man's salvation and happiness? and what can detract from its sacredness? None can value more highly, none can feel more solemnly impressed, than I do, in the sublime homage at the stated assembly of the people before the Almighty, known as the ordinary means of grace; but worship is worship wherever the heart's adoration ascends to God; and, to tell the truth as it is in Jesus is to perform a duty, which is as sacred on the dirty curbstone as it is in the most gorgeous pulpit; and yet how many take upon themselves the responsibilities of the open-air preacher, evidently without thought and certainly without preparation! I ask not that the open-air sermon be a brilliant production evincing literary labour. Profound compositions would be as useless in the street as they often are in church or chapel; but surely this cannot justify the absence of brain work; certain am I that in all preaching there should be mind as well as heart; if not, it cannot be effective. It is readily admitted that superior talent and cultivated eloquence are of small avail, if the speaker feels not what he says; but he must not only evince a real sympathy, he must also be able to express his emotions and sentiments intelligently before he can urge effectively. The preacher, wherever he preaches, must first know the truth as it is in Christ and feel its influence on his own heart; but his next duty is to seek, by prayer and preparation, to be able to present that truth in the most interesting manner. The out-door preacher, as well as in-door preacher, has to bring the soul face to face with its Maker; and if he does his duty, he will seek to know the wants and temptations of those whom he addresses, and so treat the facts and acts of life as they might personally affect the hearers. Without this, no preaching can lead to profitable results, and hence the necessity of the preacher being not only earnest but able. Let our friends who go out to the highways and byways to preach only think of this, and remember that their duties, *as preachers*, are as sacred and solemn as if they spoke in the house of God to a stated assembly.

In asking this, I only plead for what I have myself endeavoured to do. As is known to my first pastor and to others, the duties and responsibilities of the preacher gained from me no small consideration from the first time I felt the desire to fill this sacred office. I am reminded of this by glancing at some of my letters to these friends. In one of them I find these words:—
"So intense has grown my love and devotion towards my God —Creator, Preserver, and Redeemer—that again, and perhaps more than ever, I feel almost impelled to burst the fetters of custom so as to come out to tell the ' Sacred Story;' but the consideration of the solemnity of the preacher's duties, and the hope of yet obtaining a collegiate education, have as yet counterbalanced my enthusiasm. Though I am convinced that one may be called to preach, and, with the help of his Master, do much good without the commonly prescribed education in all its branches, yet I feel convinced that the more real learning and proper knowledge a man has, the better able will he be to perform his duty. I love education as I love truth, for its own sake; and I believe that when it is of the right stamp and properly applied, it leads to a desire for the refined in taste, the delicate in feeling, and the fair in nature. All this I long for; but chiefly that I may be able, when the time comes, to speak with persuasiveness."

And allied to this error is another of the same kind, but connected with those religious services conducted in schools and other small places of meeting where those who attend are poor. How often it is that speakers at such gatherings, especially where

O

they are thin, speak as if they had not even known the passage of Scripture upon which their remarks were to be based! how often such an audience is addressed as if anything was good enough for them! Is not each individual soul as precious in the sight of God as if its frame was encased in the best of rich silk or black cloth? Is it not in need of the Bread of Life? Why then be careless, or, at least, thoughtless? A story is told of a minister who had prepared a sermon with much care, but the Sunday following happened to be rainy, and the hearers few in number, so he would reserve it for " a *better* occasion." At the close of his made-up medley of a sermon, he noticed a celebrated doctor of divinity who had slipped in unobserved, and how sorry he was because he had given such a " shabby sermon" before such a learned man! Alas! too many act after the same manner in relation to such gatherings—giving the " shabby sermon" to the poor and often thin audience, reserving the " well prepared" for " a more *suitable* occasion!" Where such is the case, the sacred nature of the preacher's duty is forgotten, and the consequences are sad. Let all preachers think.

But having referred to the Open Air Mission, perhaps I ought further to add, that whatever success has attended my humble efforts as an open air preacher, much of it is due to the fortunate incident which providentially brought about my first meeting with Mr Kirkham, the secretary for that society. A sorely tried, but I believe a true Christian, lady was the means of introducing me to this mild and happy friend and fellow-labourer; and that introduction has resulted in a friendship which is as true as it has been useful. From the first, he produced a favourable impression upon my mind, and his practical prudence, coupled, as it ever is, with a cheerful piety, has fixed and deepened that impression.

As some of my readers know, this useful society was established in June 1853, for the purpose of encouraging, regulating, and improving open air preaching, and that with the view of more effectively taking the gospel to the masses assembled in the streets, at races, fairs, and public places, in or round London— wherever people can be met with out of doors. And besides the ordinary efforts during the year ending June 1864, the preachers visited twenty-six races, forty-six fairs, seven executions, (at which fourteen criminals were hung,) and six special gatherings, such as the Shakespearian Tercentenary, and so forth.

But this society owes much of its success also to the liberal spirit of the honorary secretary and the managing committee; and one of the many proofs of this combined wisdom and catho- licity is evident in the manner in which the monthly conferences of members and friends are conducted. From the number that attend these meetings, the position of many of those who take an active part in them, from what is there said,—from all these and other indications, it is evident that open air preaching has become an institution, and that this portion of effort in this direction is recognised by the wise and good of Christ's Church. I go to these meetings to learn, and many a useful hint I have picked up and applied to good purpose.

CHAPTER IX.

WITH THE FALLING—THE CAUSES OF THE DOWNWARD COURSE.

I. THE FALLING.

NOTWITHSTANDING what I have said, especially in the fourth and fifth portions of the previous chapter, I readily and heartily admit that much is being done in London, as elsewhere, in behalf of suffering humanity. What I have therein pointed out are but blemishes—visible and telling, and therefore important blemishes—in the grand picture of Christian benevolence. Beside the quiet, private efforts made in behalf of suffering and sorrow by thousands of warm hearts and munificent hands, there is in London above seven hundred charities. Only think of the anxious care, the unwearied perseverance, and the amount of money involved in the management of these institutions! and to this add the cheering fact, that whatever faults there may be connected with some who belong to these societies, there are profound thought and powerful light ever emanating from the mental resources of master minds, imbued, as many of them are, by enlightened and elevated piety. Men of common sense as well as mental power have come to the rescue. They (of course I mean women as well) have brought sound philosophy as well as earnest feeling to bear upon their work; and many of these efforts are not only benevolent, they are also intelligent, and hence the results are frequently telling and useful.

Let us rejoice in all this with thanksgiving; but let us not forget that, even yet, we have with us the *falling*. I refer not to that frightful aspect which stands up in ghastly ugliness before one after the harrowing and sickening study of the lives and habits of those who have made up their minds to live upon that for which others have laboured—to the professional thief, the vulgar garotter, nor to any of that class which carry out their sagacious devices in their war against society, that they may become "lucky," and their victims unhappy. Nor do I allude to those fearful pages upon which are the names of those whose success speak of knavery triumphant, which tell of fortunes made without honest industry, of widows and orphans reduced to beggars by large-minded schemes. No; at present I neither refer to the hoards of theftdom nor the swindling fraternity—much as the latter have polluted the stream of commerce, and brought to poverty and misery many who have been warmly cradled—I allude to the great mass of the falling, yet struggling people.

Falling! See that poor fellow. A number of his enemies are determined to hunt him to death, and farther if they can. Weakened as he is, he would beat any single one off the field, but they have united, and hence their cruel power. He is driven from his position and is pressed backward. He tries to stop, but his enemies find that their power increases as he becomes weaker. At last they drive him to a precipice close to which is a sloping bank. On this bank he is determined to fight, as it were, for life. There he struggles, but his enemies are the stronger, and he falls. The sloping bank is slippery, and this is against him, but he clings to it with hands and feet. The agony of despair covers his face, but his enemies know nothing of pity. Victory is that for which they are pressing, and they snap off one hand. He still clings with the other, and they snap it off too. One chance more he has, and only one. Though lying on the bank, his face to the ground, his hands chopped off, yet, in desperation, he fixes his toes in the earth, but another crushing blow, and the toes and earth yield to the pressure, and down he falls to the bottom of the precipice crushed and bleeding, and anxious to die.

This is not an imaginary picture. I know all about it. I have been pressed and crushed after the same manner, and scarcely had my own wounds ceased bleeding, when I was binding up others.

II. WHERE I FOUND THE FALLING.

In the cottage by the way. Yes, in the cottage.

"It is a struggle, sir, with us. There is nine here, and we have not had much more than my husband's wages, and that is only ten shillings when he has work and able to work. He has been more than three months of the year out of work, and ailing. I goes, when he's at home, to gather stones, but there has not been much of that. I gets a sixpence a day, and that is something; often all we have to keep us. Then we fall back with our rent, and has to make it up when he gets work. Our place is all of a muddle, for I have been away in search of work. There is some people as be kind, but we have a great struggle, sir."

So said a woman to me in one of our country towns. As might be expected, I listened attentively. Observing that I sympathised most heartily with her, she related her history and that of her parents. The story was such a detail of life in the country of one continued conflict with a hard, hard fate—the sufferers being almost always down—that I could scarcely keep back the tear.

"How can you make out?" was a question which came from my lips before I was aware of it. Here is one of her replies. "In our ordinary way, I makes out to get a good dinner at supper-time. Sometimes I gets three-pennyworth of bone and outside bits of meat, and sometimes only two-pennyworth—as I can. I gets a turnip for a ha'penny, and sometimes a little rice, if I can. I put all this in a saucepan with plenty of water, and lets it boil for hours, and then I buys two-pennyworth of stale bread and cuts it very small. It boils till it becomes thickish. The children, poor duckies, cannot wait till father comes home in the evening, so they gets their share about four o'clock, and we gets ours when he comes."

This was "a hero in the strife," one not easily put aside, but who can say how long she can stand out? "I am not so strong as I was; and sometimes I feel as if I must yield," is the melancholy admission with which she closed her story. She is begun to fall, is every day less able to resist the downward pressure.

In the "yards" behind the streets of our clean-like country towns, we find the falling in large numbers. Some are yet struggling, and others are feeling as if they had no heart to meet the pressing events. I have entered these back yards, and found there erections called houses, and which are inhabited by the poor of the place. It matters not which one of these hovels we enter—they are nearly all alike; but we may look into that one in the corner. Of course it is a clay or mud floor, in which are not a few holes. None of the four walls are entire, but the most of the holes are covered with pieces of coarse cloth or matting. As for plaster, there is very little of that, and the bricks are black— a dirty black, as if just taken from a semi-fluid dung-pit. The windows—or what are called windows—have very little glass in them, but its absence is supplied by bundles of filthy rags. It is not easy to pace the floor without stumbling, but when it is done it is found to be about ten feet by ten, perhaps a little more or less.

In this hut *dwell* a family of seven—I dare not say *live;* for surely existence in such a place and under their sad circumstances is but a living death. The furniture—if we can give the few things that name—is in conformity with the hovel. There is but one resting-place, which gets the name of a bed, and such a *bed* for this large family! By the side of the fireplace the mother is seated upon a stone brought in from the field, for there is neither stool nor chair in the place. She is lean and pale, and seems to have no heart, no courage—to have forgotten the use of her hands. She stares so vacantly and pitifully that one cannot help feeling for her—impressed as when one looks upon a helpless idiot. She is so ignorant that she knows not the letters of the alphabet; but she is a British mother—a mother of seven children, five of whom are with her, all of whom are as ignorant as she is herself. Her husband is a farm labourer, and is not much better than any of them. His wages are so small, and the family wants are so many, that they are always on the point of starvation.

This is by no means an exceptional case, nor is it connected with an exceptional part of the country. That very town has the advantage of having within itself the means of improvement, and never did I see benevolence more abundant, earnest, and active.

I would not here speak positively, but I fear that the second example represents a large, if not the largest portion of our industrial country poor,—yielding and sinking beneath the weight of adverse circumstances. After they thus yield they feel no heart—the hands often fall when the heart sinks. Many a town looks fair and flourishing outwardly, but behind the streets, in the " back yards," are scenes truly heart-rending. This might be expected, considering the nature of the wretched hovels into which the poor are crammed, and that the more so, since it is too evident in all parts of England which I have visited. Spiritual destitution goes hand in hand with social degradation.

In our courts, alleys, and so forth—in the metropolis as well as in the provinces—yes; where the poor are crammed—there we find the falling in large proportions. One day, shortly after I came to London, whilst standing at the foot of Ludgate Hill, and beholding with amazement the rushing stream of life, I asked myself the question, "What is the condition of these sweeping masses? Are not many of them dwellers in shambles?" In a short time I was in search of answers; that is, I was soon traversing the back streets, passages, and courts where the masses dwell; and what I then beheld—even without entering one of the places called *homes*—was truly harrowing. Though not a stranger to such sights, yet they presented themselves to me in a somewhat different, and (may I not add?) in a more ghastly aspect than I had previously seen elsewhere. I had long and carefully paid attention to the important subject—the dwellings of the poor—and had read somewhat of such in London, but I was not prepared for what I then and there beheld. I did not ask the question whether or not the Canongate or Cowgate would be a match for St Giles's or Bethnal Green, in regard to the manner in which the poor are crowded in narrow and filthy places. Two blacks do not make a white; but long before I had discontinued my inspection of the gloomy rookeries in the grim backways and squalid alleys, I was compelled to feel, that however much we may boast of our palaces and mansions, never, while the masses are crammed into wretched hovels, in fever-breeding localities, can it be said that either Edinburgh or London has done its duty to those who are thereby the more immediate sufferers. Most readily do I admit that I felt the more keenly on this point, because during my first rounds of observation my own wounds were not quite healed up; but certainly the sights and sounds were such, (and, alas! to this day, *are* such,) as to wring sympathy from a very hard heart, and to make sorrowful the gayest of the gay, *if seen by them.* The yellow and sunken eyes, the pale and leaden complexions, the meagre and miserable forms, the tattered and filthy garbage which the visible dwellers presented—and that without even entering a dwelling—were heart-rending.

Since then I have not only traversed such byways from time to time, but entered the most miserable and horrible of the hiding-places of poverty and crime; and there I have found the falling struggling and dying in the fight—sometimes the good fight of faith, but many more in sad darkness. I have met with people as truly religious in a back and black hovel as ever I met with in the most spacious and splendid drawing-room; but I must say that I found here, as elsewhere, that the condition of the body has something to do with the state of the mind; that strong minds and good resolutions have yielded under demoralising influences, and that the cramming of the people into places unfit for homes, is to encircle them with what frequently tells for harm to body and soul. Some there are who resist with a grand heroism the force of such unfavourable circumstances; but, alas! how many more, even after long and painful struggles to rise, give way, and sink till the last particle of anything approaching to decision of character is lost.

I can believe that some of the mortality which is attributed to overcrowding in dense localities is due to other causes than the absence of *fresh* and the presence of *foul* air. I am aware that drunkenness and its many attendant evils—want and misery, cruel usage, and broken hearts—help greatly to enlarge the dreadful mortality in those districts into which the poor are crowded; yet those who really know life amongst the lowly, know that such terrible cramming is injurious to the morals as well as to the health of the sufferers. It cannot be otherwise than detrimental to both. The dark, damp, and filthy hovels—with their poisonous effluvia, within and without—gulp down thousands at a meal, by tainting the blood, weakening the body, and producing virulent diseases. This manslaying effluvia not only corrupts the fountains of life, but it sticks to the victim while life lasts, and will not die with death. To the victim it practically and emphatically says, "Where thou liest I shall lie, but when thou diest I shall not die. In thy ignorance or from thy necessities, wrap me up in what thou callest thy bedding, and I shall wait thy return to restlessness. And where thou goest I shall go, even to the street and the workshop. Rise in the morning, pale, sickly, and cold, and bottle me up in thy garments, to which I have affectionately clung, and I shall go with thee in search of my kindred."

We are ready to give vent to our indignation at such a state of things, but how often are we content with big-word denunciation without entering into details. We properly call overcrowding a "national curse," and as properly speak of its effects as "wholesale murder," but how seldom do we go into the operation of one cause of this social murder. My conviction is, that wholesale speaking only gives general or surface ideas, which cannot be the most practical for useful purposes. For instance, how long and how often have we had the horrors of war described in a general way, and yet to little purpose? We speak of hacked and mangled bodies, of the agonies and groans of the dying, of the hatred and revenge amongst the living, and all this is very strong, but it only becomes forcible in proportion as we follow it up; we will become the more anxious for peace, when we behold first one and then another writhing in awful torture, slain, dying!—when we turn from the murdered son to the mourning mother, the murdered husband to the distracted widow, the murdered father to the helpless children! And it is the same in relation to this overcrowding and all other evils; to tell the more effectually against them by being the abler to meet them, we must become less general and more particular. Listen for one moment to one of a thousand of many thousands of Nature's knocks of warning. A poor fellow-creature is struck, but he does not see the enemy, nor does he at this moment anticipate the effect of the blow. He staggers a little, grows sallow, feels sickly, cannot see as he did, makes his way home, goes to bed, expecting to be better next day. Not so. He receives another blow, and again he reels. His dear children are astonished, and weep. The wife of his bosom tries to revive him by bathing his temples and laying wet cloths upon his aching brow. All in vain; he is down to rise no more! Now insensible to all around; no repose for him, though at times he is held in a stupor; so vacant is that hazy eye that was once so bright and intelligent. And those parched lips and clammy hands, how distressing for his bosom friend to look upon! But she is there, with beating heart, glowing with affection and swollen with sympathy and grief. God help her and her little ones; for soon she is to be the poor widow, and they fatherless as well as helpless. The purple spots appear, the lips are inky, the tongue will not rest, for it seems the nearer he is to the gates of death he is more intent on the things of life. He has not a moment to spare. Now furious and incoherent, now calm and profound, as if listening intently to some soft whisper. He is dead, and his widow soon goes to meet him, some of the children accompany her, and the rest are sent to the union.

Multiply this by thousands, and, if you can, look at the heap, and cast down beside it the previous sufferings and miseries known only to God and the victims. What a mass to look upon in a Christian country and in the great metropolis!

But what is that, even that, when compared to the effects of overcrowding on the morals of those whose bodily powers are thus not only enfeebled and deformed, but whose mental faculties are depressed and weakened? Thereby the mainsprings of human life, of thought, and of action are affected, and in some cases fractured; but there is such a close connexion between the lungs, the stomach, and the mind, that physical impurities and moral impurities frequently go hand in hand. Those who have not seen the wretched dwellings of the poor, who do not retrace effects to their causes, are astonished when they hear of the vast amount of vice and misery, of moral as well as physical diseases, (both of which are contagious,) of theft, burglary, garotting, and murder; but let them go out and in amongst the victims as evangelists and missionaries do, and the astonishment will be the other way. From what I know, I am surprised that crime and misery are not even much more prevalent, more horrid and appalling than they are. We begin to look aghast at the dimensions and features of prostitution, and while there are various other causes, primary and secondary, I hesitate not to say that here, in these dens of the poor, its seeds are daily scattered on fertile soil. It is no colouring of the sad picture to say that, in many cases, sons and daughters and lodgers daily and nightly herd together like swine. And as to the extent of drunkenness—notwithstanding the efforts made to diminish and demolish it—is it not even yet rioting and devouring its victims? It is; and one reason why it is so, is the overcrowding of the people. I am a total abstainer, and I go for prohibition of the liquor traffic; I have done my best, and I shall ever do all I can, while it is needed, to destroy drunkenness, because it is the parent of so much that is evil; because it dams up the present, and lessens the chances of future happiness; but I know this, that in these hotbeds may be found not a few of the seeds of intemperance. Apart from the drinking customs, apart from the temptations of the drink traffic, there is here an inducement to drink—to drink frequently and largely. Here the weak naturally wish for strength, the feeble need energy, and many, from no bad motive to begin with, seek them in what they, and too many more, call the " use "(?) of alcoholic drinks. Because of the short but false excitement, they suppose they find relief from the swallowing of this liquid fire. And, without the least reflection as to the nature and tendency of strong drink, they run to it as often as their means permit, and oftener, until they bring down upon themselves the disgusting epithet " drunkards," and until they, in addition to the evils of overcrowding, suffer those of drunkenness also. I offer no apology, I ask no quarter for drunkenness, but I plead for the drunkard, especially when he has been led to the drink from the false idea of finding that relief which good house accommodation and proper ventilation would have given.

In the mud we meet with the youthful falling. It is said,

and it may stand good as a rule, that as the homes so are the habits. Though, as has been readily admitted, it does not follow that because a man is found in a bad house he is a bad man, nor does it follow that though a man occupies a respectable house he is therefore a respectable man—that he is a more virtuous man than the other who, by various causes, has been driven into the shabby abode in a sloppy alley, yet, as has also been indicated, and as is too well known, the home has something to do with the inmate, just as the condition of the body has to do with the state of the mind; and yet some there are who withstand the unfavourable influence in a manner truly remarkable.

Some of these grow up and become useful, but others only triumph for a little, and then begin to fall. This commencement manifests itself at various ages, and in both the sexes. In the class of abodes just referred to are to be found a large number who leave their homes in the daytime. Parents leave for various reasons. The father for his work, or the less honourable, to skulk about the public-house doors to watch for prey—for there are a large number of men who live by chance jobs, others by what they can make by any means which may not be called robbery, though, if found out would be so, by sly thievery. Many mothers leave home as early as possible, also from various motives. Some to work, some to gossip, some for the low beer shop or glaring gin palace. They do so from custom—others, like them, have done so for long; from habit, the exodus is as regular as sunrise, from the instinctive desire to get out of the fetid air. For a stranger to enter such homes in the morning, as I have often done, he feels a sensation more nauseous and prostrating than sea sickness. And there need not be any surprise here. It is said that every time an adult breathes he requires about a pint of pure air; this is needed to vivify the blood in its passage through the lungs. And these crammed up creatures, like other creatures, exhale as well as inhale, and every breath sent forth being poisonous, vitiates, or makes bad, about eighteen pints of the surrounding air. Hence our wise and kind Creator has ordered this gaseous poison to ascend and seek an outlet, which it does, if it can get off. So that there must be sufficient space and proper means of ventilation. Therefore those who are acquainted with these matters say that an adult requires at least five hundred feet of breathing space; that is, two persons living or sleeping together would require an apartment ten feet by ten, and ten feet high. Now think of five or six, seven or eight, nay, sometimes more, in one small apartment for a whole night, surrounded by this exhaled and other poisonous gases, and ask yourself if you would not instinctively seek for breathing room at least. This, I believe, is one reason, perhaps the chief reason, why the hovel is forsaken as early in the morning as possible.

But if the parents are off, where are the children? Getting their education. Where? Some in the ragged school, thanks to God, and good friends; but many more are having their lesson in the street. And what a swarm of children gather in and romp about these seathing and festering dens! This may arise from various causes. One, and perhaps the chief one, is the fact, that those who are reduced, or begun to fall, *and have children*, find it difficult to secure apartments even in those houses just a degree superior to those to which they are driven. " I never thought we would have to come to such a place, but we could not get a room anywhere else because of our children, and they must be where we are," is a true tale to which I have often listened. But whatever the cause, there the children are, already begun to fall, learning the downward way. What a sight! masses of children hastening to ruin and destruction! At first, I was astonished as well as saddened. Never can I forget my first visit to a London back court.

" Who's it you wants, sir?" asked a boy as I entered. He was, indeed, a sharp little fellow. He had no cap, but his head was well covered with plenty of hair; which would have hung

in beautiful ringlets had it been clean and combed. Greasy
dirt covered a naturally well-formed face, which otherwise would
have been pleasant to look upon. The tattered jacket being
fastened below the waist, and only by a pin, left exposed the
upper part of his shirtless form, as dirty as his face. His
trousers were as tattered as the jacket, and his feet in keeping
with his head, and this in winter! Being taken by surprise,
and not having my answer ready, he added, "I knows all here,
sir. What's the number, sir?"

After a few words by way of answer to his inquiries, he put
his hand to his brow in a manner which showed it was not the
first time he had done so. I understood the meaning, but did
not give him anything till he assured me he had had "*nothink*
to eat since yesterday morning."

As soon as he got the copper, off he went, and before I had
time to leave the court, more than twenty of his kind were
surrounding me, telling their sad tales. Of course, I was not
able to supply the wants of this group of pauperised wretchedness; but I asked myself, "What must be the condition of this
kind of London society when the giving of *one penny* to one of
its wretched members would bring out so many about this same
age, equally ill, and some of them even worse, prepared for the
keen winter? Where lies the root of all this? What will be
its ultimate result?"

Not long after this, but in another locality, I had an occasion
to distribute some small bills telling of a special lecture to be
delivered on the following evening. I make it a rule to do anything to forward a good cause, and I have found it a source of
usefulness in giving out such notices where bill-posters would not
care to enter. As usual, the children were numerous, and I had
little difficulty in bringing them round about me. The bills were
small, and in the shape of " a ticket-for soup." This at once led
those who received them to think they had had a gift, and in an
instant of time I had hundreds of children round me calling out,

"Please, sir, a ticket-for-soup!" "Please, sir, my father has no work to do!" "Please, sir, mother is ill!" "Please, sir, we have not had anything to eat all day!" and many more such appeals were made as fast as they could be uttered. But I would not give a bill during the clamour. Though jostled here and there, I waited till I could be heard, when I told them the contents of the paper. Then it was that I witnessed the climax. From the midst of this gathering of human squalor rose up additional proofs of the pauperised and wicked spirit that often grows with the growth of those who are huddled behind the main streets of this wealthy metropolis. Not a few tore up the papers before me, and fearful were the oaths that were uttered by the girls as well as the boys. But the event did not pass without good coming out of it. At last I was enabled to obtain a hearing and to exercise that influence, even with such children, which God has given to me. The result was, some took the papers home, some of the parents attended the meeting to which the bills referred, and ultimately a happy change began to manifest itself in some of the homes.

But this is only one feature of this downward course, for a pauperised person is a falling, an ever falling, person, be he or she old or young. Were I to follow these boys and girls throughout the various phases of their strange lives from five to fifteen years of age, what scenes might be depicted? but I shall only give two or three sketches as specimens of thousands of others—not, indeed, of the lowest stamp, not of those who are said "to subsist on nothing and who reside nowhere," but of those who have had something to eat and somewhere to go—specimens of the many, many thousands whose parents live in the hovels previously described.

"What is this that has so upset all of you?" I asked, on entering the house of one who had been rescued some time before. Everything was out of order, hearts were like to break. "Father has broken his pledge;" and that which caused it was

P

a source of great grief to "mother," as well as to "father." He had for long lived the life of a drunkard; the mother, too, had been in the habit of being much from home. The home had had no attractions, the children, as well as the parents, being seldom there, save for a few hours at night.

"Do not press that question, sir!" said the mother, wringing her hands in agony. I did not press for an answer; but the father before I left told me all about it, and it is such that I dare not narrate here. It related to the conduct of one of their daughters (in the company of others of the same age, not long entered in their teens) in front of one of the lowest of our low beer and gin brothels. Speaking to his wife, he said, "This is the result of leaving the children in the streets, and of leading them to such places. Like the rest, she was taken there by you, and now she goes in spite of us; and hence the awful scene I had the mortification to see, and which so upset me, that I rushed in out of sight, broke my pledge, and tried to drown my grief and shame in strong drink; and here I am again on the road to ruin;" and the poor fellow wept bitterly.

"You see, sir, when one is in the way, these places and these things do not appear so bad," said the mother, by way of apology.

"It is true, too true," added the sorrowing father; "but we know now to our sad experience that though we ourselves may repent of our ways, and even forsake them, we cannot get the children to unlearn with us what we have taught them in our thoughtless wickedness."

Lately a woman called at one of our meetings, and said she wished to take the pledge again. I asked her what led her to break it, and she said,—

"Vexation. My boy was in trouble, and I had to go to the magistrate about him. My neighbour advised me to take a drop of gin to give me courage, and I did so. She went with me;

and when coming home we had some more, and I stopped not till all I had saved was spent, and here I am as wretched as ever."

In reply to other inquiries, she added, " Well, I am to blame. When they were all young I left them at home, but they went out amongst the rest, and learned the fearful lessons they are now practising. We wish them to do better, but now we cannot control them. I says to my master, (her husband,) we are to blame. When children get so far when young, we cannot get them back, though *we* may do better."

Again, when I entered one of those large houses in which from twelve to sixteen families dwell, a poor woman pressed my hand and said, " I am glad you are come; I know not what I am to do with that boy, he has kicked me so."

The boy was not more than fourteen years of age, but he could fight and curse " like a man." In answer to the question how he had become so determinedly wicked, she added, " When father spent the most of his wages in drink, I had to go out, and the children were left in the streets. He had these lessons there; and now he will not be advised to go to work, nor to school, nor any good. His father is now doing well, but *he* will not be advised. I fear his end, wicked boy that he is."

We may be horrified even with these faint appearances of results, the effect of causes already indicated; but we need not be astonished. If any are, let them go with me three steps further on, *not to what is considered the paths of crime,* but having reference to what is daily manifesting itself and yet often unnoticed.

There is a crowd, and it may be thus divided—1. Into fools with some cash, and who are always looking out for bargains; 2. Those who relish rude wit, especially at the expense of all that is good; 3. Many of those children who are left alone by their parents to pass the day as they best can. In the centre of this crowd is an itinerant auctioneer, who is busy disposing of his wares and showing his *cleverness*. He is treating his gaping audience after the genuine Cheap John fashion. Almost every other sentence he utters is such as to make any one tremble who has the least respect for modesty, virtue, and religion. One or two illustrations will suffice to indicate my meaning:—"Here's somethink—the very think you need," he says, pulling a yard measure from its case. "Here, take that back till you are out of sight;" and a man takes one end of the measure, and goes back to the full length of it. "Come back," was the next salutation; "that fellow has gone to hell with it. I told you it was the very think he needed. Come, now, buy, buy—cheap, good, and useful; it will go to the bottomless pit, and if you put a hook at the end of it, we can pull you up from the flames."

The laugh was elicited, and the measure was sold. Two pictures are next offered. "Here is a picture of Jesus' mother. Well, *that* is strange; he was better off than I am, for I never had a mother," and great roars of laughter follows. Taking up the other picture, he continued, "Here is the match. It is the 'Breaking of bread.' Well, here again he is better off than I am, for I have not broken bread to-day;" and again the loud laugh follows, but the pictures find no "bidders."

Still on he goes, using language so obscene and blasphemous that I dare not mention it here; and that, too, in Christian London. Truly this is a school for children.

Think of the likely result of this kind of teaching, and you will not be astonished at this:—About ten o'clock one evening I was making my way home, when I observed a group of children, boys and girls—the eldest not more than fourteen and the youngest eleven. Even before I came close, I could, from what I heard, know that their conversation was so very rough and even rude that it would be unpleasant to pen. They seemed happy, for they sang as well as cursed, but the most of their songs savoured of the music hall. They sung others, but that which attracted my attention most was the one in which this verse occurred—

> " Old mother —— lived up stairs;
> She sold apples and I sold pears;
> What she got I cannot tell;
> I went to ——, she went to hell."

These blanks are put where I missed the word by not hearing it. For about half an hour I waited at hearing distance from this group, and what came from their lips made me ask what kind of men and women these children would make? Soon after I approached them and began to speak to them, they dispersed, but nearly all went one way—to a locality such as I have described at the commencement of this chapter. The homes to which these children belonged I visited afterwards, and found in one of them a drunken father, in another a drunken mother, in a third both parents drunken, and in the fourth a struggling widow, who had to leave her children in the morning and did not get home till nearly ten at night—all were of the uninviting species of homes.

But these fearful sights and sounds, even amongst the young, are not confined to week-days. Juvenile depravity, all the varied symptoms of the fearful falling, appear in all the seven days of the week. For instance, one Sunday, in a large crowd, chiefly of boys and such lads as love to encourage fights, I stopped and witnessed a Sayers and Heenan scene in miniature. The united ages of the boys pitted against each other would not have been more than twenty-six years. Caps, jackets, vests, and shirts, such as they possessed, were thrown aside coolly and carefully. The shoes and stockings were also taken off, and the trousers tucked up. It had not been their first encounter. They went through the civilities of the ring in a perfect manner. Each had his second, according to the most approved fashion; and after the stretching out of the arms, drawing the elbows back so as to get them into an elastic temperament, the signal was given, each gave his bare bosom a significant slap with his palm, and then they went at it. "Cut away!" "'it 'im!" "Pitch into 'im!" "Walk into 'im!" and many other similar exclamations went the round in rapid succession, while the juvenile combatants were prancing about as systematically as if they had been dancing a new reel. At last they really did "go it" after such a savage fashion—tearing, beating, and kicking, until they fell. They were soon up and prancing as before, but I now saw the blood, and could stand it no longer. To interfere is to run the risk of personal injury when men are engaged, and no little danger even when boys are fighting. I did interfere, and succeeded in stopping the battle, but the duty was not an easy performance. Of course, I was threatened and challenged, but neither ruffled my temper. I could not accept the one, so I had to risk the other. Two or three pokes in the ribs by fellows behind me was my payment; but I am glad to add that one of those who were very rough towards me ultimately became a member of one of the societies connected with my labours.

Such is a passing glance. What may be expected from such children? Do we get as much as we can well look for, all things considered? Looking at what I have seen, I say we get more than what we are warranted to expect. Whatever may be said by way of blaming the poor—and doubtless there is room for blame in some cases—whatever of their failings may be visible, (the most and worst are often visible,) there is no denying the cheering fact that many rise above crushing influences with a determination truly heroic, and with wonderful elasticity. It is worthy of remark that though—as amongst all classes—there are some who are lazy, and who would do anything rather than work for the bread they eat, yet, as a rule, the offspring, even of those who live in the localities referred to, are worthy of the honourable title—"industrious classes;" though some never master the bad habits acquired under such unfavourable circumstances, yet the great majority try as soon as possible to get some work to do. And this applies to the female as well as to the male portion, extending to those who are considered higher in the social scale. But how fares it with those who go to work? Are the temptations less? the helps to improvement more?

What becomes of the boys? I do not mean the "Wild Arabs," as they are called, but the boys who go to work. Many rise to usefulness, some to a position, others to a fortune; but the sad experience of real life tells that there are more who fall, or feel their existence to be a drudge and a drag, than all the more fortunate put together. Why? Truly, this is a big question, but it may find its answer in these simple and awful facts. Frequently, alas, they are beyond paternal control previous to their leaving home. Almost all have acquired habits difficult to conquer. Nearly all have been trained to the ruinous drinking customs of our day. The workshops, or other places of the kind, generally act according to these customs. Many employers remember number one, and forget their responsibilities. Some of those in charge catch the same spirit; and if vice is not encouraged, it is not checked. The boy apes the man, and often the man is beerised. He, too, must go to the public-house like the rest, and drink like the rest. He marries when yet a boy, and his *mis'es* is more youthful. He may be a good workman in his way, or be in favour with the foreman—a favour some think worth purchasing, even with beer. If this young husband has met with a worthy wife, he may survive and revive, especially if he has had any good impressions when a boy. If not, he soon comes down, and down, and down, to degradation and ruin.

So much for the artizan; but there are the shopkeepers, a very large class in London. They, too, rise and fall. Some rise rather rapidly, and some fall unexpectedly. "We are trained to this kind of thing," said one to me who had fallen fast and far. He referred to the way of doing business. "The truth is, sir, a big shop, some credit, and plenty of bounce—selling one or two things, as leading articles, below cost price, and charging forty or fifty per cent. of profit on all other things—that is the art of making business pay." So said one who had been long in business, and who knew what he said. Of course, as a truthful and sensible man, he admitted, what is only just to admit, that there are business men who have honest intentions and who still stand out for integrity amidst much temptation to follow in the wake of those competitors who believe in "commercial puffing." It is true that honesty is the best policy, but it is difficult to put the theory in practice when those who love it and who wish to practise it are side by side with members of the "puffing exchange." On first thoughts, the *economical stranger*, and sometimes the *sharp cockney*, think they are greatly indebted to the latter fraternity, they "do the thing" so cleverly; and, were it not for the injury *done to all concerned*, one would almost admire the sharp practice. Talent is often called in and paid for in the carrying out of this polite robbery, and hence the representation is often such that black is almost made white, that shillings are all but sovereigns. I would not say that all take to this for the purpose of enticing and entangling the unwary. Perhaps if we knew all, there might be some exceptions; some who only act upon the principle that when we are in Rome we must do as Rome does,—some who may have been forced into this mode of dealing by competition and other circumstances; but this does not alter the nature and tendency of the advertising system now so extensively practised—a system which may, in the main, be characterised as "lying." It may be true that Messrs Cheap John & Company endeavour, *to all appearance*, to wish to bestow upon John Bull favours not only too numerous to mention, but too generous to conceive, even to convert "commercial distress" into "glorious news." Indeed, so anxious is this large and long-established firm to be careful lest the eye of the ticket reader be not offended by a presentation of the whole truth *at once*, that the article *shown* is not only "cut to the lowest farthing," but the lesser portions of the price are, as much as possible, put in the shade. For instance, here is an article of dress; it is "worth £4, 4s.," but this firm, "for the public good," cannot, *in conscience*, take for it £2; they therefore ticket it thus: "**£1,** 19s. 11¾d., formerly sold at FOUR GUINEAS!"—the 19s. 11¾d. being in the lightest possible pencil marking, whilst the £1 is black and bold—the odds being of no moment to the purchaser *till* it has to be paid! Frequently have I listened to groups gathered round the flaming bill and flashing ticket, and what they said gave me to understand that it was very possible they might soon be victimised.

I have given an instance referring to an article of dress, but I do not mean that those who deal in such are the only, nor the worst amongst this noted class of dealers. Who that has looked about him has not seen that such efforts to induce a sale, *and thereby confer a great boon upon the purchaser*, range far and wide—from shrimps to salmon, from "cats' meat" to roast beef, from the "gold" watch to the old nail, from the "finest" coat to the roughest slop, from the richest silk to the coarsest calico, from Harrow Road to Bow Common, from Brixton to Highgate?

Now and then our newspapers lecture us concerning "mock auctions," and tell us to beware of those "ladies and gentlemen" who make up this firm which is always selling off and is seldom sold out; and this class frequently do much harm, feeling, it may be, that they have as good a right thus to be "selling off" as their "commercial brethren." Now, without entering upon the comparative demerits of either, I must say—what I know—that such dealing, such a mode of transaction, connected, as it generally is, with petty dishonesties, becomes the root of much that is vicious and criminal, the first step to fraud, to ruin in morality and business.

The master cannot cheat without the servant knowing of it; indeed, some of the latter help the former in such works. "I had part of the sin, and I had a right to part of the profit," said a boy who had been put away for pilfering. As sure as a mother corrupts her child by doing and saying that which is wrong, so is the master "making haste to grow rich" sure to corrupt his servant; and once break the ice, there is no saying how deep he may fall. Many date their ruin from their being thus connected with dishonesty.

And if they make out to resist the force of such examples and power of such temptations, they meet others of another species at their lodgings. How many fall there! In London we have two classes of lodging-house keepers—those who take in a young man to help to take off part of the heavy burden of rent and taxes, and those who live by being lodging-house keepers. Into the hands of such, and sometimes into the hands of worse, the young man falls when he comes to London. Such young men are of two classes; those who can pay a good rent, and those who are compelled to be as economical as possible; but, in the case of either, the lodgings are seldom homes. In too many instances it is the money, not the person, that is wanted; and this is much more frequently the case in places where the lodger is not able to pay for "rooms." And even then, how many fall because of those they meet at the lodgings, and the loose manner of living there? In too many such houses Sunday presents scenes horrifying to any who know anything of the claims of that holy day. And as Sunday is spent, so the week is often ended. "I do not believe I can live long in London. What between my workshop and my lodging-house, I am nearly driven mad," said a young man who had lately come from the country. He then went on to say how that in the workshop religion was mocked at, and how he was treated at his lodgings—not even having his food made, but having to go to the coffee-house for it. It was fortunate he met with a friend to whom he could tell his story; and yet it was with difficulty he was rescued, for he was then in the act of listening to infidel sophistry and of yielding to sore temptations. Though from that time he entered a

Christian and comfortable home, yet, having to labour in the same shop, full of theoretical and practical infidelity, he became a doubter, and, to use his own words, " was on the way to hell." But God blessed the means which have led him back to the Shepherd's fold and made him happy in the Lord.

I have often said I wish I had a fortune, and that for the purpose of doing good; and one of the many ways by which I would attempt this would be to have safe and comfortable homes for such young men as come to London. I do not mean that I would need to spend a fortune on them, for such homes would be self-supporting if wisely conducted. Some employers have done much to remove such hindrances to real success and domestic comfort; but I meet with many who know many others who would be glad of a home to which the term Christian could be applied. Not a home with prison rules, but a place filled with winning kindness and healthy liberty. How many fall from want of such a place—a retreat from temptation, a Bethel wherein to meet with God and the godly?

The falling amongst our young men *from the country* may be seen in the streets, round and within those dens of iniquity where the land sharks put up. Here many of our youth are nipped in the bud,—they fall at once,—and in their turn become members of the same rascal class, of those who took from them the feet of manliness and honesty. To the observer, this forms one of the many horrid characteristic features of the streets of London.

From inquiry, as well as from observation, from the lips of the victims, I soon learned that not a few of those who make up the bulk of this hideous formation are those who had come to London from these three, amongst other motives: Those who had come on a visit, with the view of returning in a day or two; those who had left home to go abroad, but who must first see " London sights;" and those who had come to push their fortune. Whilst I write, what a horrid mass of awful pictures touching this ruinous feature of London life re-pass before my mind, each one of which says, "Stranger, beware!" Seldom a day passes without the record of ample proofs of knavery triumphant. With the exception of the loss of a few handkerchiefs, and having my watch-guard cut three times, I have escaped scot-free, but not without running risks; for the traps to catch the stranger are so various, and so cunningly devised, that even a *canny* Scotchman may be caught, especially if napping, or ready to accept an invitation to "have a drop." Here is one attempt to draw me:—

"How long is it since this church was built?" asked one of the gentlemen of winning frankness, drawing closer and closer by my side, and appearing as countryfied as possible—quite an innocent rustic in *his* way.

Having answered him, he began to comment on the wonderful changes in London since the last fifteen years, he being (as he said) all that time closely engaged as a "Dorset farmer." By way of continuation, he added that he had "been compelled to leave Dorset on a very unpleasant affair;" that his "man-servant" had prevented him from getting a splendid bargain of a nice brougham, which a friend—the steward of the Right Honourable Lord ——— (I shall here call him Lord Blank)—had for sale.

His story was so well told, that it had all the appearance of being a truthful one; but scarcely had he detailed his case when the "steward" suddenly appeared, as if he had fallen from the clouds. The latter commenced the same story just where the former left off; and how nicely the two ends met!

Of course, I must be politely introduced "to his lordship's steward," who, addressing me, continued,—"The fact is, sir, I am expecting to come off well at his lordship's death. Between you and I, I am his lordship's nephew, though this is not known; I would not offend him for the world. But may we not have a friendly glass, anyhow, and a talk?"

"Certainly, certainly! but our *friend* may not wish anything save wine. But we will get the private parlour. Come along; do us the favour to be a midsman," chimed in the farmer, at the same time pointing out how I might be useful to both parties by purchasing the brougham from the "steward" and giving it over to the "farmer," the latter giving me the £20 with which to pay the former!

Had I gone to do this *favour* and been inclined to *wine*, doubtless I would have found that there were some "flash cash" in the way. What would I have thought if I had yielded, and an inspector of police had been under the necessity of stating what one lately said at Worship Street Station,—only putting in the designations, the farmer for the one named, and the steward for the other,—certainly it would not be an extravagant supposition to suppose that the report would have read thus:— Inspector: "I was at the station when the prisoners were brought in and searched. On the 'farmer' were found a packet of sixty-eight Bank of England £5 notes, a £10 note, three flash notes, a bag containing 114 medals *to imitate sovereigns*, a metal watch in imitation of gold, an eye-glass, key, knife, 4s. 11½d. in money, a duplicate, and some papers. On the 'steward' were a purse containing two sovereigns, some silver and copper, nine imitation sovereigns, six imitation cheques, fourteen cards, twelve playing cards and two business cards, a duplicate, pocket-book, chain, seal, three receipt stamps, and other articles."

But I did not think it proper to assist this "farmer," ready as I am to render help; nor did I think it proper to accept the offers of the magnanimous "steward." Doubtless the publican, into whose back private parlour I was invited, would have been very serviceable, the wine plentiful, and of the *proper* sort! yet I would not be tempted.

I thought of this attempt to entangle me when I read the description of another such dodge, wherein a Scotchman became the victim. "It appears," says one of our dailies, "that D—— (I omit the name here) was addressed by a respectable-looking person at Charing Cross, and an acquaintanceship commenced which ended as might be expected. The two friends adjourned to a public-house in the locality of Artillery Row, where they were soon joined by a third actor in the domestic drama. The new comer, with a winning frankness, expatiated on his good fortune in being left £1500 by a relative, out of which he was to give £100 to the poor of any four parishes. D—— was no doubt anxious that the poor of his own parish should benefit by the generosity of the munificent Saxon, and it was arranged that he and his friend should show some money to the stranger as a proof of their respectability, before receiving the £25. They went home for the purpose of procuring the amount, and D—— on his return proved his title to be trusted by exhibiting £60, and his friend presented a purse full of gold. But, besides getting the £25, the Scotchman was to be engaged by the stranger as a farm-bailiff, and he and his friend were asked to obtain a receipt stamp for the £25, and one for £10, which was to be paid in earnest of service. It was only proper, however, that the £60 should be left as a pledge that D—— meant what he said, and would return to his new master. This was done; but when D—— came back, sooth to say, he found neither money nor master; both were gone, and he was left alone to reflect on the proverb that a fool and his money are soon parted."

But this, like the other case, is only one of the many ways, one of the various traps, set everywhere in London to catch the stranger. Another class who live on their wits, to the injury of society generally, and young men in particular, is that which more directly seeks the co-operation of the traffic in strong drink,—a large class, which seldom appears at a police court, at least for the base and ruinous offence to which I allude. To indicate one of many instances, see that young man—a stranger —bewildered as well as amazed. He is in search of a street, but has lost his way. Seeing one of those whom he thinks is a public servant, but who sometimes turns out to be the publican's servant, he asks his way, and the policeman sends him, not to the place inquired after, but to a neighbouring public-house. Alas! even this class of such social plagues are ever near at hand. With all confidence in clear buttons and helmet caps, the poor fellow obeys the injunction. To the place named he goes, and is there surrounded by a host of *kind friends*, ready to tell him anything or go anywhere, to drink anything or even "stand treat," so that they prove themselves to be to strangers courteous. His gratitude is roused; and being brought up to the drinking customs,—"the *fine* home-brewed country ale,"—he shows his appreciation of such manifestations of kindness by treating all round. "He is wrong, sir; I knows best," says one of the by-standers. To this the other replies somewhat angrily, and is prepared to stand by and fight for "the stranger—a good *fellar*." Sparring preparations are made, but of course the matter is suddenly made up; another public-house is entered, and the stranger is more than ever generously inclined. The *friends* in turn treat him; he drinks and feels queer,—is taken to *fresh* air down an adjoining court; he awakes next morning *minus* his purse and the best of his clothes,—is almost delirious,—has fallen, never to rise again.

Where are these *friends*—the sharks? Again at their post, waiting for another victim at the dens where victims are caught.

How many are sent to such public-houses to be entrapped! How many of those thus ruined in their turn sink to the lowest scale, and at last help to swell the number of those who look out for the stranger and simple, to rob and ruin them!

But there appears to me to be something strange in all this. Knowing the nature and tendency of the strong-drink traffic, I am not astonished that there are amongst those engaged in it some who would thus help to entrap and ruin the unwary, and, it may be, share the spoil; but how it comes about that the police lend such publicans and such scouts assistance in sending strangers to such places to make inquiries, is to me a puzzler.

It may be said that the potboys and barmaids may know the neighbourhood; but can the policeman not know—ought he not to know it as well? Does he not know of such work—partly the result of his sending strangers to such places? Surely he ought to know of it, and use his influence to crush it, instead of thus fostering it, intentionally or otherwise. I can believe that there are amongst our London police men of honesty, of feeling, of intelligence, men who act from a sense of duty; but from what I know, there are sad exceptions; and this would suggest the question,—Is it the case that some are base enough to connive with such publicans, and the gang which prowl about their dens, to catch and crush the stranger and the thoughtless?

Nor is this the only chance these heartless publican and ruffian scouts take of the falling young men. I might, as the result of observation, give many more such cases. See that young man up from the country for a few days to see London, but, like many more, goes to see it at the public-house. His friends go with him, and he is flush and boastful. To pay for what he has ordered, he pulls out all the cash he has. An "accidental" commotion is made, just in time to knock his money out of his hand. A scramble, in all anxiety to *serve* the stranger, is the result. The money is gathered, and some of it is given to the owner, and he must "stand treat." Those who have *helped* him (themselves) wish him to leave with them—would have him off, either to be treated or "stand treat." This his companions—who had come merely to have a friendly glass with him—will not permit. *They* knew the sharks who are around him, and what will be the result. Having hinted at this, the fellows pretend to feel insulted, and a fight is proposed, to *prove* their honourable intentions. The young man interferes, and assures his companions that he was not robbed; but the re-assurance, that "that sponge had just given a *yellow-boy* to a woman," was resented by a flourish of arms.

These are scenes I have myself witnessed. For the purpose

of rescuing such thoughtless young men, I have entered the beer-shop and gin-palace. I have frequently found that it is not easy to meet the tiger in his den, surrounded, as he generally is, with such vile leeches; but then the thought of the possibility of rescuing a fellow-creature gives courage and strength.

But, powerful as these efforts to ruin the young men of London are, there are other traps even more dangerous: I mean those set by the proprietors of what are called our "Licensed Places of Amusement"—the tea-gardens, music-halls, and public dancings.

> "Who steals my purse, steals trash; 'tis something, nothing,—
> 'Twas mine, 'tis his, and has been slave to thousands.
> But he that filches from me my good name,
> Robs me of that which not enriches him,
> And makes me poor indeed."

So said the poet; he is right. His remark applies to all classes of seducers, whether of boys or girls, men or women, but especially to the large and increasing class just named. I have already referred to this class; and would again ask my reader to turn once more to Chapter IV., and, suppose the stranger young man in the midst of the scenes therein slightly indicated, ask if he is not in danger of falling. If any yet doubt, let them be reminded of these two facts:—

1. Strong drink, with all its insinuating power, is there.

2. That fallen women, with all their aided influence, are there.

In short, they are the hotbeds of drunkenness and prostitution. A "licensed place of amusement" is just another name for a "brothel." If there are instances in which the former and the latter are not one, there is even in such cases—*if such there be*—an inseparable connexion. And young men—of course all kinds who will come into the net, but especially young men—are the chief object of attention with the waiter and the strumpet; and is it to be wondered at if he is caught and lost to society, to all that is honourable, dutiful, and hopeful?

Q

And scarcely has he left the train or the boat when he meets with invitations, in the shape of flaming announcements, referring to these places, and at all the arriving and landing places, upon blank walls, under arches, in windows, yea, and frequently in the "*coffee*-houses." Those who rent and own such places of "amusement" are not insensible to the amazing credulity of many who can be misled by sensational lying, and hence they, too, adopt that means of attraction; but how many, to their sad experience, find that instead of pleasure, amusement, and entertainment, the ultimate results are ruin and misery, death, and the unforgiven sinner's doom! How many young men, once promising but now miserable, have found that this class of vile seducers, of all others, do not only *draw* from the thoughtless good money, but also steal that good name which is the immediate jewel of the soul. When too late, they find it matters not how many lies are told in flaming characters, nor how large the space they occupy, almost everywhere. "Tea-gardens," "pleasure-grounds," "music halls," and other such names, simply mean vile drunkaries and dens for assignations—traps to catch and fleece the unwary.

What the young men have to withstand by way of temptation in London—as indeed almost everywhere—who can tell? But, being aware of what I do know, I must say that I am not surprised when I find the falling in almost every workshop, office, and street, and that in all the shades of degradation and destitution. Poor fellows! God help them; and help us to do our best to help them to help themselves!

But what becomes of the girls? This is another question at which I can only glance briefly. Some of them rise to usefulness—becoming honourable women, loving wives, and careful mothers; but how many fall! how many are falling at this hour! What an idea is that conveyed by the words, falling women! One, *even one*, of the most wonderful and beautiful structures known to have come from God's hand—one of the most precious and useful creatures on earth—falling; going down to ruin, to be miserable—perhaps, eternally miserable—what a thought, and yet how many such fair blossoms are being plucked, cast out, and thrust into early and loathsome graves! how many are being lost to peace and happiness, to usefulness, and to heaven. When I think of this and remember what I have heard from the lips of *the fallen* in their hopeless anguish, I feel as if I could curse and extinguish those who live by engendering and fostering the causes which bring about such an awful destruction. But how comes this about? is the important question. Doubtless partly from errors connected with training in childhood. There is much practical wisdom in the divine injunction, " Train up a child in the way it should go, that when he is old he may not depart from it ;" but there are many inducements to go out of the way, even after he or she has been well trained. In London, this applies more to the daughter even than to the son. See that infant girl, pure, gladsome, and confident. Life and hope beam in her fair young face. A year or two elapse, and intelligence gives dignity to her infantine beauty. A few years more, and the sweet girl merges into the bloom of womanhood. Then she enters life, but soon she finds, to her sad experience, " there is nothing true but heaven." Still nature is favourable. Beauty and grace combine to adorn her handsome form; and there is something about her face and manner that is truly womanly. Every way is she worthy of a lover capable of forming a just estimate of her moral excellence, able to give value for value received, able to prove himself worthy of her heart and hand. But, alas! alas! hers is not " love that meets return" —she is betrayed. By the vicious of society she is led into temptation. That young man has some time since presented himself as one who loves her " most sincerely," and promises " most truly" to be to her " most honourable." Representing himself as of high station, he, with all the polished grossness of the fashionable rake, has availed himself of the opportunities which his base assistants have afforded him. First he gained her ear, then her attention, and then her confidence.

The scene has changed. She has gone. Where? Ask her parents. At the private ball? No. At the tea-gardens? No. At the Haymarket? No. At Ratcliff Highway? No. In succession she has passed from each of these scenes. Look on that loathsome bed that frequently terminates the career of the vicious. She has just left this also. "Where, where is she gone?" sobs her father. "Where, where, where may I find my daughter?" cries the mother.

The Thames is blackened by the midnight cloud, and this once virtuous girl is on "The Bridge of Sighs," where so many of England's fair daughters have stood, and from which they have taken the fearful leap in the awful dark. It is her time. She is there, her hopes blasted, standing aghast at the future of sin and shame stretched out before her, and goaded on to utter despair, fearless of the " terrible shape" of the " phantom of grisly bone," she looks below, and suiting the action to the word, she cries—

> "Anywhere, anywhere,
> Out of the world."

Alas! this picture owes nothing to the fancies of imagination. As many parents are sadly aware, it is an awful reality,—a small extract from the fearful pages of every-day life amongst our sisterhood. Well may parents tremble!

But we must again come to the question, What are the remote causes of this going out of the way, this falling on the part of daughters? If we say idleness, then figures refute us. In the short summary of work dated 1864, and published by the friends of the London Female Preventive and Reformatory Institution, we find that of 1478 cases only 53 were of no occupation. If we, as is generally done, put it at the door of gaiety, love of dress, and liberty, we are again here reminded that of 226, only 24 are against this cause. And of the same number

226, only 39 stand against destitution. What, then,—inebriety and bad company? Only 53, of the 226, stand against this cause; and opposite to the words, " breach of promise of marriage," we see 62, of this same 226. Here, of the causes of fall assigned, we have four which may be set aside in pairs: destitution and breach of promise of marriage, 101; intemperance and gaiety, 77—showing that a considerably larger number fall by causes over which they have little or no control, than by causes which they might, or at least ought to, have extinguished. And this fact is all the more worthy of notice, inasmuch that the customs and habits of society sow the seeds of this twofold cause. Daily, both by precept and example, the love of gaudy dress and of strong drink is encouraged and strengthened, so that at least fifty per cent. of the blame—or rather of those who have fallen—may be charged against others; that is, of the 178, arising from the four causes, not more than 38 can be said to have yielded to causes which might be called preventable.

Having seen that neither idleness, a love of dress, nor a desire for drink, is a leading cause of this falling, we are driven back to the same question, and this same paper helps us to the answer. Out of 1478, no less than 1020 had been *domestic servants!* Think of that. Surely it is startling to those who knew it not, and certainly it is worthy of the consideration of all concerned. Why is this? ask parents. Why is this? ask moral reformers; but only God and the victims of this social wrong know why, that is, to the full extent. I cannot here enter minutely into this very important investigation; yet I cannot but admit the existence, in some cases, of what is designated "the depravity of employers." I am sure that many of the honourable and virtuous—and surely they form the large majority—would be glad if it became a custom amongst those who bring the employers and those they employ together, to ask as to the character of the former as well as that of the latter.

The worthy would have nothing to lose by such inquiries, only the worthless need fear it. But though it were admitted,—what all of us would rejoice in the possibility of believing—that this "depravity" was but a false rumour, there are other causes which also help to account for such a striking statement as the fact, that out of 1478 females promiscuously gathered into the institution mentioned, 1020 had been domestic servants.

Here is one of the keys which open the mystery. I had observed a large number of servants had to go for "the supper beer," and it occurred to me that I should watch the result, first at the thronged places and then in the new and quiet streets. In the latter locality the results become more apparent. In one such, I took my stand for seven successive nights from nine to eleven o'clock. It was a short but a fashionable street, and from the house near to the centre came forth a good looking, clean, and tidy servant about twenty years of age. As regular as the clock she appeared, jug in hand, and walked slowly along to the public-house, which, of course, was at the best corner of the street. One of the nights I observed that she kept behind one who perhaps had once won her bread by honest labour. She seemed pleased with the shape and sweep of the dress of the one before her. Another night a fop is also on the way. He makes up to her, and words are exchanged, but she passed on. Next night he is waiting, but this time he takes the cigar from his mouth and tries to kiss her. The next night, as she entered the "jug department," he saluted, she smiled. Soon he had his hand upon her shoulder, and in such a manner as would have made some females break the jug upon his head, and served him right; but a roar of laughter is all that is heard, and soon he "stands treat," and then accompanies her to the gate of the house. A few words are exchanged and she hurries in with the beer. But before weeks pass, she has left. Before months pass, she is like that one whose silk dress she seemed to admire, whose apparent liberty she seemed to envy. Those whom she served drank the beer, doubtless seeing no harm in it, thinking it had been paid for, and that was enough. True, they gave the money to purchase it; but the cost of it lay not only in the cash,—the loss of character and virtue must be added, and to these it is possible that ere this, and thereby, a lost soul may be thrown into the bargain. Let those who must, after this manner, have their beer, but let them count the cost, and ask, What saith the Lord?

Sometime after I made this observation, I had occasion to read it and others to a number of gentlemen interested in my labours. It took some of these friends by surprise; but one of them, who knew society well, said it was "nothing new, it need not surprise, such *fearful work and awful results* are manifest every night." Of course, he referred to the 40,000 prostitutes that nightly walk our London streets.

And, perhaps, that which led him to put so much stress on the words, "Fearful work and awful results," was the impression that our streets make on the mind of the observer. I make this supposition, because the two series of thoughts run side by side in my own mind. In the open streets, at noonday, we meet with the falling,—those who have been so prepared as to become the prey of those whose chief business or study is the art of seduction. This is a terrible fact, and an acquaintance with some of its incidents induces me to refer to it here.

I was not long in London before I observed the ways of our *gentlemen* prowlers—gentleman coarse and brutal, as well as rich and refined—refined as he is refined, who can "smile, and smile and be a villain." After careful inquiry, I found these *gentlemen* to be thus divided—the rich rakes, and those who strive to ape them. The latter spring from various sources. Far away in the country a family are living on frugal fare. Mother not only works hard, but tries to save as much as possible. Father toils almost night and day, and his object is, that his son may occupy higher social status than has been his lot. The boy advances in years only to increase the family hopes. Already some of the hard earnings are spent upon him for his special education. He is equipped for London, for he has views of a situation. Mark the difference between this lad and that of the father when he was the same age. "Truly," says some by-stander, "this is an age of progression; if the next generation improve as much as this rising one, what must be that young man's children?" Good wishes go with him, and he arrives in the great metropolis. He is amazed, bewildered, and alone,—but not long alone; he gets a companion a year or two older, who knows a "thing or two" about town. They meet others who know a little more, and he soon becomes the "gentleman;" but the parents severely have paid for his training. Their last penny is spent, their last ray of hope is dimmed. The parents sink in sadness. The hair is gray with grief more than with age. Only a few years more and the son is gone to an early, dishonoured, loathsome grave; but how many has he ruined before this? He aped the gentleman prowler after fresh prey, and run his short and filthy career to the corruption of society, as well as to the sadness of many a heart and the loss of many a soul.

But he is only one of the many, and after all not the worst of those whose example and footsteps he followed, as far as his parents' means, and others derived from dishonesty, permitted him. I say this class,—though large and ruinous in their way, to the extent of their power,—are not the worst. The rich rakes, besides having the same base desires, have the means at command. They have not only the will, but the power to put that will in force. Though I use the words, "rich rakes," yet I would be harsh and unjust did I convey the idea that in all instances, or even in the majority of such, these two words must accompany each other. This would be as far wrong as if I were to assert that all the young men in London were such as the one I have, from life, described. He represents many; but there are many more who live and act far otherwise; many more who are useful and happy, and an honour to their parents;

yet we cannot, we ought not, to forget the fact that the *gentle-men starers* are numerous, and that from amongst the rich may be found the most powerful, if not the most wicked, of this species of corrupters. I do not pretend to know all the outs and ins of the wealthy and titled—my walk is amongst the poor and the helpless—but I know enough of those who are highly favoured as regards this life, to be aware that amongst them may be found the gallant and noble, the gentle and pure; yet it would be cowardly—since the matter is broached—here to omit the appalling fact, that from amongst those that have the means, the riches, are not a few whose chief purpose seems to be to apply their vast resources—of which they are so shamefully unworthy—to aid them in obtaining the base desires of their jaded luxury. It is too well known that these vile vagabonds are more dangerous to society than all classes and degrees of theftdom put together. To steal a poor man's purse is the lowest kind of theft, but to rob him of his daughter—next to her mother the apple of his eye, the pride of his heart, the joy of his soul—oh, how base! and yet society bears with it, and mothers there are who countenance those vile wretches who do so day after day.

I refer not now to the midnight pavements, to the ordinary, nor even to the extraordinary courses of devised debauchery which ever runs riot after the sun has left the sky. I allude to the shameful doings of a large number of those whose entire occupation is seduction—not only at night in the haunts of vice, but in the open day, and even in the busy streets, before the eyes of the people.

The women thus *stared at* may be divided into two classes—those who court such *gallant* attention—and those who feel hurt because of it. It is the latter class—our industrial daughters—the innocent—that obtain the most attention from the " staring gentlemen." These licentious miscreants (that is their title) prefer to hound down fresh prey. They follow those who, when

in their element, when at home, " fill the air around with beauty."
So brazen is the stare, that it brings to the cheek of the pure a
blush of shame; it gives to the virtuous woman unspeakable
pain.

Many more of those thus stared at and followed hard up might
escape from the poisonous fangs of these base and rotten vermin,
were it not that they have help at hand. Having fancied, they
seek and find assistance in their carefully-organised system, and
thereby too often secure and entangle, ruin and make miserable,
their prey. Thus many of God's best blossoms are plucked, thus
many of our social gems are lost, thus beauty becomes deformity,
and happiness is exchanged for misery. And yet society winks
at it, many of our guardians share the profits derived from
sources which aid these seducers, brothers and fathers are silent
while their sisters and daughters are in danger, and even
mothers make welcome to their houses such a vile and terrible
scourge as the starer!

Thus it is that it has become positively dangerous for a woman
possessed of those exterior graces, which generally encircle the
virtuous and the active, to walk the streets without a protector.
What between the " stare " of the rich libertine, and the " snare "
of his base procuress, it is really unsafe for the sisterhood to walk
in the streets of London. Thus it is that these vile villains
and their slavish accomplices sap the foundations of purity and
chastity—ruining the character and prospects of as many as they
possibly can of our industrial and virtuous daughters, who have
been enabled to conquer the numerous, formidable, and sickening
obstacles to bodily strength, mental vigour, and moral purpose.

The same remarks apply to railway carriages, as is well known
to those who read our police reports. Lately I was travelling
third class. The low roof of the carriage, and the manner in which
we were cramped up, led to a conversation as to the comparative
comforts in first, second, and third-class carriages. One of our
fellow-passengers who spoke was an interesting young woman.

In reply to one who remarked that the difference between the third and second-class fares was not much, she said, "*I would not think twice about the matter of fares for the sake of the comfort, but there is* NO SAFETY IN A FIRST OR SECOND-CLASS CARRIAGE. *These monied rakes follow* UNPROTECTED *women, as a hawk follows the bird.*" What a meaning there is in these words! What a disgraceful state of things. And the disgrace on our national character, on our common manhood, but especially on the part of the base villains, is increased, when we reflect on the fact that those selected for seduction, as a rule, are the helpless—the poor, the fatherless, the motherless, the orphans, and deserted girls. From the figures already referred to, we find that of the 1478 females who had shared the benefits of that "home," 263 were fatherless, 231 motherless, 470 entire orphans, 89 uncertain if parents alive,—showing that only 405 of the whole had living parents from whom to receive the least protection. So that, independent of the sin, the vile wickedness, of entrapping and betraying, and ruining these helpless, and others perhaps as helpless, there is a dirty cowardice, and that on the part of many who are regarded as "gallant gentlemen." And, again, to this add the well-known fact that it would seem as if our social arrangements were invented so as to accommodate these rakes and other of the same class. Females, as well as males, are not only being prepared when young, from infancy, by training and example, social errors and social wrongs, by bad habits and ruinous customs, but they are almost—in many cases, altogether—*driven* to give attention, if not to court, such *staring* from such *gentlemen*, whether at service in the "*desirable* residence," or in the street passing to or from her work, or in search of it.

This might be made even more manifest by an examination of various unfavourable circumstances which surround those who earnestly strive to live by honest labour, however hard to get and ill remunerated when received. The tales I have listened to—which, on inquiry, I found to be too true—touching this point, are very harrowing. Next to domestic servants stand those called needlewomen. Out of the 1478 already mentioned, 399 are placed against this class. This opens what is now regarded as a theme worthy of consideration. However inconsistent it may appear, and really is, to practical people, as we call ourselves, the steed must first take to his heels before we begin to discuss how best to shut the stable door. This is applied to the most of our social matters. There must not only be a special sacrifice, but it must also be of such a nature as to *force* itself on public attention. We have hearts amongst us—many who can feel for others' woes; but we have others who purposely shut their eyes and ears; and hence, always for the latter, and sometimes for the former, it is necessary that the half-hidden evil burst in upon society so as to confound it,—that the evil be brought from the quiet and dangerous darkness to the light of day. A proof of this, touching the condition of needlewomen, was evinced in the case of the late Mary Anne Walker, one of the many victims of the combination of the imperial behest of fashion and the grinding rapacity of commerce. Had any person, even in the name of humanity, been induced to step forth, only a few days before that murder, and speak of the awful power which lurks in the fearful combination of fashion and selfishness, he would, by not a few, have been branded as a very discontented person, unable to see the beauty and worth and grand results of our " rational liberty," and " humanising civilisation," as one unwilling to appreciate the education and enlightenment of an age which has made the human race what it never was before. But as soon as one of the victims of social wrongs was set free

> "From slavery's sad abode,
> No more to hear the oppressor's voice,
> Or dread the tyrant's rod,"

that the glaring evil of horrid cruelty towards thousands of thousands of our sisters *forced* itself upon the public gaze, it became fashionable to speak and to write strongly on the overworked and underpaid dressmaker. Nor has the sensational eloquence been lost. It has not only forced some employers of dressmakers and milliners to follow the example of others who, without that pressure, had done something to make their workwomen comfortable, it has also ended in the formation of a society whose object is to diminish, as far as possible, the dreary burden of excessive toil, and lessen the horrors yet connected with the system. These ladies, to their honour, have at last found that Hood was not a dreamer, and they are determined, in their way, to help those needlewomen employed at the most prominent and fashionable millinery and dressmaking establishments of the metropolis, especially those at the West-End. But what of the other needlewomen, those who don't get to the west, who are also overworked and underpaid—the shirt-makers, and so forth? Are they to be forgotten, that they may become the easier prey for the " staring gentleman?" God forbid!

A clergyman and his *lady*, like many more, hear of the strength and activity, the virtue and endurance of " Scotch lasses." They make application through one who believed in their honesty and piety. The girl arrives in London, goes to her place, gets her orders, and things go on smoothly for a time, but at last the children manifest their usual bad habits. She is expected not only to bear with them, but to control them; a task, indeed! for they, as it suited their taste, would kick and curse their parents, calling them all kinds of bad names. The girl, too, is kicked and abused; and at last the mistress does not think that she is a " perfect nurse," a qualification which the girl never assumed at the engagement. The term is broken, the girl is set adrift in London! For aught this *lady* and *gentleman* cared—I speak on the strength of their deeds—this girl might have gone to seek her bread and bed anywhere. But she was virtuous, and was not friendless.

For a time she was taken in, and, efforts being made in her behalf, she got another place, and there remained for some time; but Sunday cooking and Sunday work being too much for her, and giving her no time to attend divine service, not even to read, she had to leave.

At last, she became a needlewoman, one of the shirt-makers, or rather, those who did what the machine could not do. Without going into details, I might simply state that she found it impossible to earn as much as would pay for thread, candle, and lodgings, not to mention fire and food. But she was virtuous and had friends.

Again she applies for service, and, being strong and active, she obtains a situation. Not to speak of hard work during the week-days, Sunday, as before, is the killing day for cooking and working and running for beer and gin and cabs—a hell on earth! But besides all this, the son visited the kitchen and had to be ordered off by her, and the father meets her "*by chance*" when cleaning out the rooms, so that she has to be firm and threaten to call out before she gets free from his rude grasp and vile glances. But she is virtuous, appeals to her friends, and again leaves, thankful she has escaped.

Had she not been virtuous, what then? Had she been friendless, what then? How many are sent for and treated as she has been? How many such have striven and at last yielded? And this, together with other baneful influences, gives the key to the secret why that, of 1478 females gathered in, 1123 were domestic servants and needlewomen.

And what is the use of telling these fearful facts? I do so because the more I know of them I become the more active in behalf of all concerned; and I can believe that my readers are likely to be so directed. Whilst it is well and proper—a duty— to care for the *fallen* in every possible way, surely it is better, a more imperative duty, to see to the *falling*. *Prevention* is better than *cure*.

CHAPTER X.

OUGHT WE TO THRASH THE ROTTEN STRAW? YES. AND WHY.

I. Some of the Tender " Straws."

HAT were they? Children. The mother, the real mother, knows what is meant by that—beauty and simplicity—sweet innocence and rich instinct—a happy energy and a telling reality—the graceful as well as the lively—the divine as well as the human—the teacher as well as the pupil. Children! the special object of Christ's attention. " Suffer the children to come unto me and forbid them not, for of such is the kingdom of heaven," said the " holy *child*" Jesus. Never did one, born of a woman, retain the sweet simplicity, the graceful innocence, the angelic nobility of childhood, so long as He who is emphatically called " *the* Son of God"—from His birth, throughout His life, and at death. Still young, still beautiful, still grand, still divine, He gave up His life; and with childlike earnestness, and in childlike faith, said, " Father, forgive them; for they know not what they do." Children! precious plants, just sprung from the maternal bosom; ready, *if they had the opportunity*—if not *forbidden* to go to Christ, their Saviour and example,—to unfold their rich and valuable blossoms.

What have they undergone? A change. With thousands, and tens of thousands, social wrongs, human folly, or affected art, soon begins to *trim* and to shape, and the tender plant yields. They are too often influenced and bent by those who are foolish enough and vain enough to try to check and mend the God-given instincts. The minds of such being filled with absurdities, they commence their operation with something approaching to silly cruelty, and ere long the last traces of the divine beauty of the child begins to disappear. The young plant is trained, " educated,"—that is, remodelled,—but how ? The tender and sweet have become coarse and rude ; the simple and grand have become complex and hideous, vicious and violent, unholy and horrible—to become the members of the " dangerous class ;" to be abused or punished by those who have no feeling, or who contemplate severity rather than reformation ; in some cases, thanks to God and humanity, to awaken tender pity from kindly hearts.

Can such be rescued ? Are they worth thought and efforts ? I have thought so, and acted accordingly. The sights I have seen, touching what is called juvenile depravity, in such localities as have already been described, and on the part of many who have had more favourable training, have pressed heavily on my mind, and led me to ask, Ought we to thrash the fragile straw, " rotten" though it may be ? Oppressed with concern, I brought into being the " Christian Instruction Bud of Promise," which is already developing its rich blossoms.

In a back place, with parents far from intelligence and piety, and in a poor bed, lay a sick child,—a member of this Bud of Promise,—not long picked up from the mud in the street. She thought she was dying, but felt safe in Jesus ; yet she was unhappy respecting her parents. " I never knew so much of Christ before. My dear —— told me all about Him ; and I have come to your meeting to learn more," said her mother to me one night after my address.

" Grandmother is very ill, sir. I know she would be glad to see you. You'll call soon, sir ; won't you ?" said one of this youthful band, the tears of affectionate entreaty and hopeful anticipation gathering in her eyes.

I was only too glad to comply with the request; and I found that the additional manifestation for grandmother's spiritual interest and temporal comfort at home was remarkable. I could have wept with joy, but I suppressed the tears.

"You hear, Mr Hillocks? You like to hear about Jesus and heaven? That you do, grandmother," said this child; and the dear girl kissed the furrowed cheek of the aged woman in such a manner as to tell that she was able and willing, *in the name and spirit of Jesus*, to

"Wash the feet of poor old age."

And the same, in its way, may be said of my Band of Hope. The good done thereby is cheering; not only to the children themselves, but through them to the parents.

"Will you come to see father?" asked a young member; "he drinks so, and beats mother so." I went and found that this child had been paving the way for me; that she had there carried God's warning in relation to strong drink, and God's pleadings with the sinner to return. By her help, with God's blessing, the desired object was gained. The drunkard became a man, a husband, a father; and comfort and peace came back to that home once more.

Again, I have to rejoice in the remarkable evidences of the fact, that the fine traits of humanity and the holy elements of divinity re-appear under good influences. With these children—gathered in from the streets, the courts, and alleys—I have felt as at the very gates of heaven. How delightful, after calling their attention to the words and life of Christ, to hear the request—"Please, sir, do let us sing the hymn, 'I want to be like Jesus.'" Yes, like Jesus; and as one of the many instances of their Christ-like sympathy for others' woes, these children have united and formed "The Children's Friend-in-Need Society." It would do one's heart good to see them drop their pennies, half-pennies, and farthings into the box, to help those of their own age, who may be more friendless or sick or otherwise help-less.

Nor are such results confined to the Tolmer's Square district. A dear brother and hard worker hearing of our success called on me, and, after a conversation on my plans, formed in his own district a "Bud of Promise;" and the intelligence which he gives me from time to time is very pleasing and encouraging.

Hence, were it asked of me, " Ought we to thrash the rotten straw?" I would answer, Yes, and give these and other facts relating to the tender "straws" as a reason why.

II. The Difficulties in the Way.

Touching the difficulties in the way of "thrashing this rotten straw," I have been met by words something like these—" All very well, so far as children are concerned, especially when they are thus brought in contact with other children who may not as yet be classed amongst the youthful portion of the 'rotten straw.'"

The difficulty I can, and do, readily admit. I meet it every day. Those who know human nature, and the effects of unfa-vourable influences upon it, are aware that it is more difficult for age than youth to bend in the right direction, more difficult to get into the right way, to keep into the straight path. The longer one is in the ways of wickedness, in the slough of corrup-tion, it is the more difficult to shake off the corrosive filth which makes the so-called "hopeless" hideous. And may the admitted advantages of the more favoured mingling with the less favoured children, not stand out as a hint which the moral or religious reformer may well consider in relation to adults? I think it might.

One of the leading difficulties in the way is the absence of a manly independence on the part of many, of anything like a desire to be honest to themselves and honourable to others, of that which inspires the moral hero. This, together with the pauperising tendency of many of the efforts in behalf of the poor, leads to the cultivation on their part of the art of deception—an art in which many of the young are adepts, in some cases equal to the adult.

"I have no parents. My mother was a *Scotch* woman, and was killed in Scotland. She worked at a thrashing-mill there, and the machinery tore her body to pieces. My father is English, and he was sent home to London. We came with him. He got work, but became so ill. Our things were taken for the rent, and he died broken-hearted. I do not know where my brother is; but my sister, four years older than I am, is on the streets. I have not slept in a house for two months, and I know not where to go. I am hungry and cold."

So said a lad to me one rainy, cold day. He was about thirteen years of age, and of a rather strong make. He had scarcely as much upon him as cover his body, and what he had was dripping wet—a wretched aspect, indeed. Believing his tale, I took him to my home, where he was fed, warmed, and in some measure clothed. I also gave him a letter to one of the managers of a ragged and industrial school, telling him that I would call there next day. I called, but he had not been there. For some time his case concerned my mind much; till one day, on entering a noted back street, I found the same lad amongst others of the same stamp.

"Why did you not deliver my letter?" I asked him.

"I knew a trick worth two of that," was the reply.

"Is your mother alive?" was my next question.

"As much alive as you are, sir," was the prompt reply volunteered by another boy.

"Is your father dead?" I asked, keeping hold of him.

"He is dead drunk, sir; that is what I meant," he said, giving a knowing wink to the rest of the boys, and offering to prove the truth of his statement by taking me into his house.

"When may I see mother?" I continued somewhat firmly; but he was able for me. His reply was—"Mother goes out to work every day save Sunday; and then she is so drunk she does not see nor knows nobody."

Subsequent inquiry taught me that almost every word of his first story was false, and without foundation; the only truthful particles being that the sister was on the street,—that the brother, like himself, was often from home, living the same kind of life and telling the same kind of lies,—the parents were still in the land of the living, but "dead in trespasses and sin."

This is what may be expected as a result of what is being done every day by parents; it is merely the natural, though awful, consequence of precept and example, as is sadly proved in every-day life. What can we look for when mothers forget themselves, and depart so far from honesty and womanhood?

"Please, sir, you have passed by one of the rooms in this house; do come to see a poor starving creature in it," said a woman, as she followed hard after me.

True, I had passed that room because the door was shut, and, as I afterwards learned, purposely shut, to give time for the arrangement of the "shifting scene." Thinking that I was to blame, and believing in the truthfulness of the sad tale of "utter starvation" related to me, I went back and beheld a harrowing sight. In the back corner of the room was something in the shape of a bedstead. On it was a mixture of shavings and straw, thinly spread, and over which was an old and ragged covering. Upon it sat a mother, hair all dishevelled, the most of it thrown back, but as much left—and *placed*—in front as to give the desired effect. The face *rather* pale. A tattered piece of a shawl is thrown over her shoulders, but in such a manner as to expose her breast, at which a baby, without even a shift, is sucking, or trying to do so. No fire. All sad, and the aspect dreadful. But one of those who make up the ghastly group by the side of this bed was reading from the New Testament; and so *earnest* was she, that I had to ask her to stop till I made some inquiry.

"She is dying, sir, and is in need of consolation, and I am doing my best in my humble way, for I am no scholar," said the reader.

"The Lord is good to bring you here, sir; may He bless you!" said another woman.

"What can be done, sir, for this dying woman?" added another, the tears running down; and in this weeping the rest heartily joined.

I felt my pockets, but I knew my purse was very light (how can the pocket of a poor evangelist be heavy?) Yet it was not just empty. "Get some warm water," said I, and was making my way out. "But, sir, there is no fire; a few pence will get some coals," was the reply. I gave the cash, and left to procure some tea, sugar, bread, and so forth. When I came back the coals had not come; but I handed over what I had brought to the one who read to the "dying" woman. An effort was again made to get more money from me, "to get something of clothing for mother and child," but I had no more; and, believing that she would soon have a good cup of tea, I left to call again.

I did call again, in my simplicity, and was glad to find the woman *restored;* but three weeks after that I met the same *reader* in another house, and as *religious* as ever. After she left, the person in whose house we met asked if I remembered being in such-and-such a house, and met her there. Of course I answered in the affirmative, and then received from her a statement to the effect that the whole was a "make-up;" that during the very time I was procuring, with almost breathless haste, what I thought was necessary to prevent "starvation," these wretched women were drinking stout—having a pot below the bed referred to; that the money I left for coals went for beer;

nay, that even the sugar and tea were converted into gin. I made inquiry, and found that I had been taken in and done for; that I had not been sent "by the Lord of all the earth," but brought through the *land*-lord of the stout and gin—one of the lords who would, I fear, rather *curse* than *bless* me.

But women are not the only deceivers on this score. There are men, not a few, who not only wink at such, but who take part in the proceedings. It is Christmas Eve. A number of those who are *supposed* to spend profitably the coming day are assembled for prayer and praise. One there is whose voice rises above the rest, whilst they sing

> " Rock of ages, cleft for me,
>   Let me hide myself in thee."

"Bless the Lord for his goodness and preserving care," says this one as he parts with the rest; but what has he done? He has had throughout the year about £2 per week in the shape of wages, and might have had £2, 10s. if he had kept more from the public-house. Besides, he has had a share of all the charities going in the neighbourhood; and on this occasion he has had a triple " Christmas share "—one from three different sources. One parcel he sells for 3s. 6d., and with this he *retires* for the night into one of the lowest of the *low* public-houses, to join in other songs than " Rock of ages." Of course, next day he was whining religion at three different places, and the phrase " Bless the Lord" was frequently uttered by him after the most approved fashion.

And this wide-spread, and, I fear, spreading, pauperised, and ruinous spirit runs through almost every strata of society. " If I had a child dead, I knows who should bury it," said one of a group of men whom I had just been addressing, and urging to imbibe a manly spirit of self-support and independence.

" If I were ill, or off work a day, I should pretty soon see a certain gentleman at the Union," said another.

" The same here," added a third; " and here," chimed in a fourth; and so on, till I felt astonished and sorrowful.

"I don't say as you're not right, guv'nor; but these clergy and those men as goes about just speak to us working men to save the gentry, who should see to the poor," said another, addressing me; and the responses which followed indicated that he had given expression to a sentiment to which all the rest thought they could bear testimony, as most of them tried to do.

I mention these cases from life, and known to myself,—each one, alas! serving as a representative of thousands of its class; but I only give them here as a proof of what I have admitted,—namely, that there is a manifold difficulty in the way of improving and elevating those who are far down socially, and deeper down morally. But this is an obstacle in the way for which those who are so reduced are not alone to blame. We have this class in our midst much as thoughtless and selfish parents have naughty children—they have been trained to err. There is a noble independence in man; but it may be extinguished, and then what is he?—"like the chaff which the wind driveth away" —soon to be bundled up amongst the "rotten straw," and by some to be left in corruption; but this ought rather to lead us to ask the question, What has taken away the dignity of independence? "Sin," says one, and doubtless he is correct. "Poverty," says another, and he is not altogether mistaken. But there are sinners, as is generally understood, who are not so reduced; and there are those steeped in poverty who believe in self-support, who will not do as those whose words and deeds have been indicated. What then? "Bad house accommodation," says another. "The drinking customs and drunkenness," says a fourth, and they too have many sad arguments to prove their statements. But again; there are some noble souls in bad homes, though strong drink almost always devours all that is manly. Others could come up and state other causes, and with truth. Perhaps some would be astonished were one to assert, as has been asserted, that a leading cause of the existence of this difficulty lies in what are called the Charities of London, or at least that portion of them which are so managed as to become such crutches to the people as ultimately deprive them of the use of their limbs. In this opinion, as in the others named, I concur, and my every-day observations confirm it.

Wherever we go, in London, we do not only find the poor and needy, in every sense of these terms, but we also find a large proportion who make it their chief study how to shift about without providing for themselves otherwise than by appealing to every visitor and applying everywhere for relief. They are encouraged in this by two classes of givers—unintentionally, it may be, but most effectively—those whose kind hearts cannot withstand an appeal, and those who wish and study to add to the numbers of the particular sect or denomination to which they belong, by holding out gifts conditionally. "Unless you can bait well, you'll catch few fish here," said one of experience in *mission work* in the district to which I had just gone. Within these words lies an awful truth. Scarcely had I penetrated into the depths of poverty and misery there, as elsewhere, when the question, What and how much I could give? was, first indirectly and then directly, put to me by many. As has already been indicated, I set my face against all this, determined to stand or fall by this principle,—which I here repeat,—namely, "that, noble and needful though it often is to relieve the wants of the poor, it is still nobler and more needful to help them to do this by their own exertions; and to deepen in them the sentiment, that, both for time and eternity, God helps them who help themselves." A knowledge of human nature, of existing facts, and a love towards my fellow-creatures—together with a sincere desire "to discourage everything of a pauperising tendency and to encourage and develop self-respect and self-help"—made me form this resolution; and these, as well as other inducements, have urged me still to carry it out. Of course none of my readers for one moment can suppose that I speak against the development of prudent and timely help. God knows there are many honest poor who need and deserve more help than they get; oh that the kind-hearted of the wealthy could but know those who suffer most and deserve more! To give *because a person is in want*, is charity of the highest stamp; like unto seasoned mercy,

> "It droppeth, as the gentle rain from heaven,
>   Upon the place beneath; it is twice bless'd;
> It blesseth him that gives, and him that takes."

But *to give to serve a purpose*, is to make the gift a bribe, whatever that purpose may be, and bribery is ever associated with corruption. Need we be astonished then if the poor, pressed, as they often are, run after the loaves and the fishes, when they are held out as inducements, as bribes, to follow a party or a sect? It may be said, "It is for a good purpose." Well, suppose that is admitted, "are we to do evil that good may come?" "But is it evil to give to the poor?" is the next question; and to this I reply, that all depends upon the motive and the manner. I repeat, if it is help, *because* they need help, it is good, and may be useful; but if it is—as is too frequently the case—a gift, given on the condition that the receiver goes to some church or chapel, hall or school-room, "mothers' meeting" or "religious service," then it is evil,—a bribe,—and carries with it all the consequences of wrong-doing. I may be told of cases where people have gone for the loaf and felt the influence of the gospel, and there may be instances of results which for a time appear to be favourable; but balance these apparent changes with the positive injuries done to others, and we are driven back to the same conclusion. I have no hesitation in saying that there is not a greater source of hypocrisy than this bidding for the people, this holding out of bribes that they may go to a particular sect. If the devil is the father of lies, certainly this is the mother; and what a number of such liars we have between the two! Surely it is time that people naming the name of Christ should pause and think. Those who have seen and heard for themselves are aware that those who thus bribe are more to blame for the absence of self-respect and self-help, than those who are now so reduced as to depend upon bounty.   Such bribers, in their strong desire, by *any* means, to advance the claims of their church or system, do as much, if not more, to drive the once honest poor into the pauper class than all the mismanagement connected with our poor-law system.   The former, even more than the latter, destroy everything like stern principle, everything like manliness, in those who yield to inducements to go to any place of meeting on the promise of a loaf, of tea and sugar, of a coal or bread ticket, or a Christmas treat.   Hence this class of the wealthy, however unintentionally, give rise to one of our greatest difficulties of elevating those who are degraded, ignorant, and almost hopeless; but are we therefore to leave them to the sad results—present sorrow, and, it may be, future woe?   I know that many are now so far reduced that their recovery is all but hopeless; but are we to give up even the worst of such cases?   We know that Jesus did not cast away such as we may call the " rotten straw ;" that such had faith in Him, and that He forgave them.   When He did this, why not we?   Surely it becomes us to forgive and to help not only because we, who name His name, ought to follow His example, but also because we are co-offenders with them both in the sins of omission and commission, in doing that, *in relation to them*, which we ought not to have done, and in not doing that which we ought to have done.   Who of us are not in some measure responsible for our social wrongs, our spiritual destitution?   If we have not helped to bring some of them about, we may not have spoken out respecting error, selfishness, hypocrisy, and their results.   Who of us can wash our hands in innocence? A holy God can accuse us; yes, and these degraded ones too can bring home their charges against us, against many, but especially those who—from ignorance or selfishness, or a love of proselytism—destroy the dignity of independence, and place the victims of their attention in that position which learns them to look for gifts instead of help. Surely it becomes all of us, but especially the latter, to repent of our errors or sins and forsake them, to turn sail and run to the rescue even of "rotten straws."

III. It is Possible and Useful.

I have admitted the difficulty of thrashing the "rotten straw," but I must, in justice to my conviction, based on facts known to myself, refer to the other side of the truth—that a *difficulty* is not an *impossibility*. I have already spoken of the children of such, and what can be done in their behalf, and what they can do by way of return, and that in the midst of the obstacles indicated. I might go farther into the condition of those more advanced in years, from the merely giddy to the professionally "gay." Suppose we look again into the paper containing the figures already referred to, touching those brought into the institution then named, what do we find in favour of the word possible? Out of 1765, no less than 1244 became hopeful—863 had situations provided, 346 were restored to friends, 23 were married, and 12 emigrated. Nor were all the rest hopeless; indeed we find that 40 are all that stand against the sad word "dismissed."

This is not the place to enter into that portion of the rotten straw which belongs to what we call the social evil; but knowing all I do concerning some of its causes and consequences, I confess that, hopeful as I am of good results following proper work, these figures astonished me, and, to my mind, they go a great way in asserting the claims of those "homes for friendless and fallen."

But leaving this class, and again going out to the thousands and tens of thousands amongst whom our clergy and ministers, but especially the evangelist and missionary, and a host of others labour with zeal and energy. And here, too, results are surprising and cheering.

" Oh, sir, I cannot think of any one speaking to him, he is so strong, and becomes so angry. I 'll rather remain as I am than run the risk. You may be kicked down stairs. Oh, here he comes!" and the poor woman became pale as death, and trembled as an aspine leaf.

It was the man. I need not here enter into details any farther than say I succeeded, by the help of God, to get a hearing, to obtain a promise to come to one of my meetings. Then, of his own accord he came to other meetings. Drink was one of his many sins, indeed the besetting sin. In three weeks he signed the pledge, and instead of spending his Sundays and leisure hours in the public-house, he was seen at almost all our meetings, and in the house of God.

This was a work of time, but there was no bribery; nor was he and his wife and children the only sharers in the comfort and joy of this change. It was but the other day that I incidentally heard how he had been successful in his efforts to lead others in the right, in the rescue and comfort of another man whom he designated as " awful a blackguard" as he himself had been.

" After the reclaiming of that man, what may not be done? " said a friend to me, who knew well what he was and what had been previously done for him. Who that knows the joys which fill the heart when convinced of being the means of leading a soul to Jesus, would not climb any hill of difficulty in the hope of rescuing another at the top? It is not easy—it is sometimes dangerous—it requires strength and courage and perseverance of no mean order; but help is promised and given, and there is the reward.

One Sunday evening I had just passed through one of those severe conflicts which I have had to contend against when preaching in the open air, and I felt completely knocked up, but one of the friends reminded me of a promise I had made to open a new station that night, and that it was possible some might be expecting me. On we went, and I asked this friend to read a few verses to the people from the Bible, whilst I took breath. He did so, and began to say a few words by way of comment, when, lo, the audience became one scene of commotion, and the people came running from other parts, many of whom being of the larking cast joined in the fray. I lost sight of my friend the reader and my friend the singer, and was about thinking that I had no strength left for such an occasion, when I mounted a stair of three steps to look for my friends, and the idea of appealing to the people entered my mind. This idea was carried out; and, it being successful, I spoke on, taking Matt. xi. 28 as the basis of my discourse.

At the close, I asked if any who were there present felt the heavy burden, and if any of them wished the rest promised? For a time all were silent, and again I asked the same questions somewhat enlarged, that those present might be reminded of what I had previously said.

" Yes, here. I am a poor, awful sinner. I need Christ," called out an old woman in the crowd, making her way to me in a sad state of distraction. " What am I to do? what am I to do?" she again and again exclaimed. And after trying to calm her, I replied, by first repeating and then explaining to her and the crowd God's answer, " Believe in the Lord Jesus Christ, and thou shalt be saved." Afterwards I preached from these words for about another hour, and with happy results.

A friend accompanied me to this poor woman's *home.* " *Home !* "—well, that is the only word, and yet what a home ! She led us through a passage, and down a back stair, but not even to a back kitchen,—only to the back ground or garden. There, between the ash-bin and a bush, was a hollow in the earth, upon which was a piece of rug, all that kept her from the cold damp ground. " That," she said, " is my bed. There I have been for nights, and I shall continue to lie there rather than go back to him."

The " him " referred to the man with whom she had lived for

more than thirty years. They had quarrelled in drink, and were thus parted for the time.

At the proper quarter I interceded in her behalf, and glad was I to find that my wishes were acceded to, and that she was as ready to act upon my suggestions. Soon after this she came to our temperance meeting and took the pledge, and has kept it ever since. "I was a fearful drunkard, sir," she would say, "but with God's help it is all over now. I would not look into a public-house to see the time; if I did, I might see some of my old acquaintances and be drawn in. God is helping me."

Then she came to our mending-home society's meetings, where again she was encouraged, not only by me, but by the kind ladies who take a deep interest in it.

Then she came to our Thursday evening religious services "to be fed by the bread of life," as she phrased it, and she meant it.

But she has not only been rescued, she has been useful. She is not only connected with every one of our societies, but she has brought others to our meetings—even children, to our "Band of Hope" and to our "Bud of Promise." And one of those she brought was the man with whom she had lived in sin. He seeing her changed character thought of changing too, and the meetings were blessed to him.

"We have thought of getting married, sir, as the best way of forsaking our past sin—as you say, we must forsake it. I have forsaken drunkenness, and I know God has forgiven that sin—I am so happy that burden is away, sir. Do you think we may be married?" Such was the manner in which I was addressed one evening at the close of one of our meetings. Appointing a time to meet both to talk the matter over with them face to face, I went, and found that he too was also sincere. They were soon husband and wife, though their united ages made nearly 120 years.

"I bless the Lord for that Sunday, sir; I hope you will be

long spared to tell many like me that Jesus said, ' All ye that labour, and are heavy laden, come to me and I will give you rest.' He can take off the burden, sir." So she said, and wept as she spoke.

Need I again put the question, ought we to thrash the "rotten straw?" But though the results were not as I have exemplified, —though they only extend to the benefit of the individuals— straws here and there rescued from this hideous sheaf—there is another plea,—another reason why the effort ought to be made. These straws are not merely various parts of charcoal. However burnt up, however corrupt, if you will, there is something more than straw—there is a gem amongst the rubbish—a something which Christ came to seek and to save, and shall we slight this gem? God forbid!

CHAPTER XI.

SOME OF THE MANY THINGS THE WELL-DISPOSED MAY DO TO HELP THE GOOD WORK.

I. RETIRE AND LOOK BACK.

WHEN the voice was past, "Jesus was found *alone*." The poet has said—

> "Oh, solitude ! where are the charms
> Which sages have seen in thy face ?
> Better dwell in the midst of alarms
> Than reign in this horrible place."

There are some who dread to be alone, who are miserable in retirement—afraid to look into themselves, or to depend on their own resources. There are others who, for a time at least, long for retirement. Having held to all the voluptuousness of active life, and drained the cup of pleasure ; having thereby shattered the body and weakened the mind, they babble of green fields, pretty flowers, lovely streams, lofty mountains. But soon they find that, for them, these have no beauty, no grandeur ; that in them they neither awaken thoughts that are lofty nor aspirations that are holy. Finding no benefit, being unable to meditate, and fearful to pass an hour alone, they again long to mix up with varieties of life, to share in its noisy pleasures and tumultuous joys. But I ask not either of these classes to retire with the well-disposed,—those interested in the spread of the gospel, the recovery of man, and the glory of God ; and much as I think of the advantages (to those who can enjoy them without injuring other fellow-creatures) which may be gained by leaving for a time the extreme urgencies of business, the undue restraints of society, the more tumultuous scenes of life; much as I can sympathise with those who really enjoy, with fond and quiet satisfaction, the refreshing and invigorating delights of solitude— the outpouring heart, the reflecting mind, and the uplifted soul,—yet it is not this kind of retirement that I ask for here. I ask not a total and continued seclusion from the world—in a convent, a country village, a mountain top, nor in lonely vale; but I ask retirement and reflection, if it is no more than half an hour, but let the mind be entirely absorbed by the thoughts which present themselves for reflection. And oh, let us at the same time try to catch the divine spirit and the unity of purpose which characterised Christ's lonely moments—alone, and not alone, in communion with the Father, on the Father's business, to seek and to save that which is lost!

It is now my lot to have very little time for such retirement; but when I can snatch a few moments, when I find I have been "in the Spirit" on these occasions, I have gone forth strengthened for work, and found that many of my best wishes in relation to our Father's business have soon been amply gratified. And one of my helps has been looking back on past experience and observations. I am aware that it has been said, a brave soldier never looks behind, and this may stand as a rule in the art of that warfare—the science of slaying our fellow-creatures; but even in such case it would not be *always* safe, not even *prudent*, to carry it out to the letter. If the soldier of the cross was sure that all his enemies are before him, by all means let him have both eyes in front; but if they are behind and before—on every side—surely it is his duty to watch not only both ways, but in every direction. Let us feel convinced that it is our duty not only to wage war with whatever *stands out* in opposition to the comfort and happiness of the people, but also with that which may be yet *hiding itself* and secreting its subtle power, even more dangerous than the visible enemy. I know, because I have felt it, that such contemplations are almost overwhelming; but are we, as heroes in the glorious strife, to allow the word coward, even for once, to appear in connexion with our reflections on the best mode of reaching and improving the people? Surely no; then let us retire to our closets, and look back upon what we know of the virtues and failings, the wants and wishes, the trials and triumphs of those in need of help.

II. Think of the Homes of the Poor.

Having thrown aside everything like *self*-centred isolation, and being filled with the spirit which banishes pride and misanthropy, let us cast our thoughts into the homes of the people. "The people and their homes"—what a theme!

Some say they are fond of botany because of the beauty in which the herbs and plants are arrayed, and yet they may regard entomology as unworthy of their attention. Surely they forget that the science which treats of plants and that which speaks of insects are united; that, however beautiful and elegant the plant may be, there are round about it, and often upon it, insects large in number and infinite in variety, each one bespeaking the skill and kindness, wisdom and care, of the Maker of them all, the Preserver of them and us. Again, some there are who profess to study entomology, and who look at the insect without noticing its habitation; who contemplate the structure and habits of the bee without looking into its cell. Now both of these species, or rather portions, of our botanists and entomologists go to work in the wrong way, or rather, neither goes far enough. And I am afraid that some of our social and moral reformers err in the same way—in going so far, and not going far enough. As there are many who speak of the sweetness of the honey and conformation of the cell, and yet forget the bee which carried the one and formed the other, so there are many who speak of the wealth and grandeur of a county or a city, without noticing the people who made the one and enhanced the other; and how many, if they notice the people, forget to look into the people's homes!

In connexion with this theme, let us not only consider what *is*, but what is constantly, *transpiring*. At best, London houses are not of the most durable kind. In building, the art of so arranging putty, paint, and paper so as to look well, to begin with, is very successful; and hence time, tear and wear, soon tell against their appearance and convenience. Those who can better their condition leave the old or reduced houses for semi-detached villas in a more healthy locality; but these houses find other tenants, who do not occupy a floor, often only a room—nay, sometimes one apartment has to serve two families for scullery and cooking, living-room and bedroom. It is not rare to find nearly a hundred souls crammed in one house of about sixteen such apartments—the house being originally constructed for two families. This is bad enough; but for some time past the bad has become worse. This poor property, or the property in which the poor are crammed, is certainly easier purchased by those who wish the space for other purposes, and hence the more restless and *enterprising* of our railway directors, in their desire to pierce the suburbs and penetrate the city at every possible point, have broken up streets and pulled down whole neighbourhoods, driving away the small tradesman, the little manufacturer, the better-paid artisan, the poor labourer, and thousands of others still lower in the social scale. "No great hardship this; all the better for those who have lived in these localities, and for their neighbours," say some, but surely without reflection. Some there may be who escape to more breathing-room and fresher air, by migrating to the outskirts; but these are few. The masses, thus ejected, must squat down somewhere, as near to the "clearance" as possible, as these sad facts prove:—1. It is said that within the last ten years the number of persons per house, in the poor neighbourhoods which have as yet escaped the railway ravages, has been nearly doubled.   2. So powerfully has this told on the health—and of course, as has already been seen, on the morality—of the condensed and suffocating people, that the annual returns of fever cases show an increase of cent. per cent.   It is true, we hear not only of compulsory but of voluntary trains for "working people," and this may help to take a few from the lodgings in the slum to the cottage in the suburbs, from the alley mouth to the little garden.   But, looking at things as they are, even through the brightest of visible prospects, is it at all likely that these cheap trains, without other helps, will diminish the crowd crushed in our fever localities throughout London?—I ask is it probable that such inducements to ride will bring matters even to what they were before the daring and pitiless of our railway directors became the striking and irresistible destroyers of houses, squares, and even streets?   We know what is being done; what then can we look for ?   Surely it becomes us to think of the " *homes* of the people," if we expect to reach their hearts and improve their minds.

III. THINK OF THEIR DRINKING HABITS.

I say *their* drinking habits; but it would be wrong to infer thereby that those generally considered fit subjects of help are the greatest and the basest drunkards.   Comparisons are invidious ; but all who know the people are aware that if the working-classes follow the drinking customs, they are sure to suffer the more in pocket, person, and mind, because upon their time, strength, and means there is a demand often greater than the supply.   All, more or less, find that strong drink is bitter to those who take it; but this class or classes suffer the more severely because of the general character of their unfavourable position and sinking condition.

This is not the place to enter into an argument touching the great temperance question. The facts of science and the theories of politics, the influence of classes and the interest of individuals, upon which the *pros* and *cons* in such a controversy revolve, are too numerous and conflicting to be taken up in a record like this; but I may state in passing, that of this I feel convinced, that I have been more useful than I could have been had I not been an abstainer from all kinds of intoxicating drink.

"I am saved through the mercy of God, by the blood of Christ, but I would have been in hell had it not been for teetotalism," said a dear old saint to me. This I know to be the experience of many now in glory, of many yet making for the celestial city.

Not far from King's Cross is a gathering of dear friends. By invitation, I have met frequently with them, and the refreshment I have found at these meetings has been reviving and strengthening. What a blessing it is to meet with earnest, intelligent, and working Christians, such as gather here twice a week! Their only object is to lead souls to Christ, and to strengthen the weak. "Come, and welcome," is their motto. But our meetings have not been confined to these ordinary gatherings. After talking of drunkenness and its hindrances to every good cause, I met, by appointment, a few of the more active of them to talk about righteousness and temperance, and how best to promote them. At the close of this conversation the leading spirit was induced to sign the pledge. This name—as the other names I had then the pleasure of seeing entered into my book—I valued because of the owner's individual worth, but more because of his social and *Christian influence*. I had reason to believe that neither of these dear friends could put a bushel upon the light they received on any subject; and after events soon proved that they did not hide their convictions touching this point. I could not help noticing the emotion of this friend when he took the pen in hand. The effort was such as we may see one make when he is struggling between two opinions; but is led to adopt the one to which he ultimately adheres, because of the appearance of some new and sudden flash of evidence in its favour.   Before this he was *almost* a practical abstainer, but he did not till then see it to be his duty to be one altogether.   Those who attended these meetings,—seeing that their leader spoke out with a marked freedom of speech in relation to drink, and the necessity of abstaining from it,—the more readily opened their own lips as regards their experience.   At one of their meetings, a poor victim of strong drink ventured to tell how he had been thereby ruined, and how he had been blessed with peace and happiness since he signed the pledge.   The next speaker did not agree with the pledge-taking.   This induced the leader to speak —to declare that though long a very moderate drinker, now he did not only feel it a duty to abstain because of his relation to his fellow-creatures, but was also convinced that God demanded of him the course he had taken.   This gave courage to the rest, and one after another spoke each from his or her experience or observation, confirming all he said.   And the number brought to seek a Saviour through signing the pledge, and thereby being led to use the means blessed to their souls, was most astonishing, even to the total abstainers.

But I would not only have us think of the drinking habits, because their extinction would help to promote the best of our useful movements, but also because the adoption of total abstinence increases our chances of usefulness.   Happily examples of this are plentiful amongst those who have resolved to do what in them lies in behalf of the falling and the fallen—such as that dear lady, the author of "Haste to the Rescue."   These, and other cheering facts, would of themselves have induced me to think of the drinking habits, and to aid the temperance movement, even if I had not been convinced of the danger of the drink and the drinking habits.   Personally they never injured me; from my boyhood I have been enabled to resist all temptation to comply with these habits, so much so, that at present I do not know the taste of alcoholic drinks; but who that has seen life has not marked the insinuating nature of alcoholic drinks, and their fearful tendency when brought in contact with the human system in connexion with the drinking customs? I have thought of all this, and I can most sincerely thank God for the result. It is not in me to judge others harshly, to say how they should act in this respect, but surely no Christian will blame me if I ask that the Divine injunction—" It is good neither to eat flesh, nor to drink wine, nor *anything* whereby thy brother stumbleth, or is offended, or is made weak "—be carried into practice, at least so far as strong drink goes.

IV. WE CAN THINK OF THEIR BODILY HEALTH.

Let not this be forgotten. To the mind, unenlightened by the Spirit of God, it is easier to believe in that which is seen than in what is not seen; and hence we can secure the good favour of the people readier by attending to the wants of the body than by speaking of what more directly pertains to the interest of the soul. But a higher object even than this ought to induce us to think of the bodily health of those whom we are anxious to benefit. The body, as well as the soul, was made by God— wonderfully made—and the interest of the former is inseparably connected with that of the latter. Perhaps this will be admitted by many, but some will ask, " How are we to manifest our interest in their bodily health ? " By parliamentary and municipal action, such as amending our Public Health Acts, and whatever relates to our sanitary defects? Well, I believe in legislative force, because I have thereby been enabled in such matters to do for the people what they could not have done for themselves; but there is another, a stronger kind of action—I refer to personal duties, to individual efforts. In this book, I have avoided politics as I have avoided theology ; because, since the date referred to at its commencement, I have neither mixed myself up with politicians nor theologians, as such; but surely I can venture the statement, " that it is the duty of the state, or organised body, to protect itself, by restraining or suppressing whatever is injurious to the health and morals of the people." It is on this principle that my sympathies most heartily go out towards the idea that legislative interference, in relation to the traffic in strong drink, is compatible with the demands of justice and the claims of commerce. Nothing is more evident to me than this sad fact, that that traffic has been enabled to fix its fangs in the very vitals of society; and that it is the duty of the state—that is, that society organised—to see that this viper does not sap its foundation. But, after all is said and done, what is called the " prohibition" movement is simply the legitimate re-sult of the judicious development of the " persuasion" movement. The teaching of the people, the reasoning with them, and the proof by practice, must precede. It is true, that there are those connected with the former movement who believe, or at least act as if they did believe, that " the *moderate* use of alcoholic drink is beneficial; " but it must be admitted that a large number, if not all, even of such, have thus entered their influence in be-behalf of society because of the light, and the truth brought to light, by those who not only believe that the traffic is injurious and tyrannous, but who also felt sure that strong drink is mis-chievous to the individual, and hence, to the nation,—that is, when brought in contact with the human system, as is done by those who act according to our ruinous drinking habits.

And the same stands good in relation to the sanitary duties of governing bodies and private individuals. The people must be taught before they can bring the laws of health to bear favour-ably upon themselves. Touching this, as other important points, error has been advancing, and habits have been becoming a second nature, and both thus combined become too strong for the individual, and hence the state, or union of individuals, must come in; but the most that the best laws can do is to help the people to help themselves. Really what can the people do, when not only surrounded by hosts of unavoidable circumstances, but set down in the midst of darkness, mental and often physical? Let in the light to the minds and the dwellings.

To help in this way, the Sanitary Association is doing much, and to good purpose. The nation, but especially the poorer classes of society, are greatly indebted to the earnest ladies connected with this association, in which there are such active workers as the Hon. Mrs W. F. Cowper. By tracts, classes, lectures, and other means, it is diffusing knowledge, and leading to practices which are telling, and must continue to tell, in favour of health, but the matter must not be left even in such good hands. We must aid. The temperance reformer must become a sanitary reformer, if he expects either to reach his highest point or maintain his ground. These ladies naturally and properly look to the Bible women for help, but why not look to the clergyman, the minister, the evangelist, the missionary,— not merely for countenance, for good wishes, but for more active help, open, direct work, in this direction?

It is an observable fact that many whose duty it is to visit those who are crushed behind the leading thoroughfare of this great metropolis, become stooped and depressed. A melancholy, far from being sweet, seems to envelope a very large proportion of them. Now, those who know what they meet with, what they hear and see, need not ask the reason why. One reason of this sadness is the conscious want of success. This again starts another large question, Why this want of success? One reason is, many do not seem to know the wants and feelings of the poor, and many of the poor in turn do not understand the sentiments and phrases of the visitors. But by a little light thrown in upon the subject, both would understand that piety and dirt are generally disagreeable companions; that cleanliness is next to godliness; that our temporal good is immediately connected with our spiritual welfare. Let us be sure of this—the grand object of visitation and of preaching will be promoted by thinking of the bodily health of those we seek to help.

V. We can be Kind in Judging.

"Judge not,"—that is, do not censure harshly,—is the injunction of Jesus, who never judged "according to the seeing of the eye or hearing of the ear;" who never gave sentence merely according to outward appearance. To do otherwise is to bring us under the charge of being partial in ourselves, of having "become judges of evil thoughts," that is, influenced in judgment by evil thoughts. "Let us not therefore judge one another any more; but judge this rather, that no man put a stumbling-block, or an occasion to fall in his brother's way."

I am constrained to offer this hint because my experience has long since convinced me that in London, as elsewhere, rash and harsh judging has done much, and is doing much, to widen the breach that is between what are called the well-disposed and evil-disposed; not only so, but to rouse and strengthen the consequent unchristian feelings which too frequently stand up between these classes. Many even of those who wished to be classed amongst the well-disposed, do not only judge all—whom *they* are pleased to designate the evil-disposed—rashly and harshly, but also after a wholesale manner. An instance will illustrate my meaning better than a long explanation.

The labourer, it must be admitted, is too often set down by many as not only rough as well as ignorant, but also as only a very small step, if at all, removed from theftdom, even from that hideous and multiplied form of murderous scoundrelism which makes our high-ways, our by-ways, and our streets so dangerous. With not a few, rough hands and ferocious passions are regarded as inseparable, and, in the estimation of others, "the labourer" and "the ruffian" are synonymous terms. This impression, as well as the mode of conveying it, is very common, but very cruel. It is true, that some of them may have been brought up in our "guilt gardens," and may have suffered by the unfavourable circumstances or culpable neglect of their parents; but is it not something commendable to see such prefer the pick to the "jemmy," the spade to the "life-preserver?" Is there not room for hoping the best? There is; and yet many so speak of them, and some act towards them, as to lead them to the undisguised conviction that they are looked upon by many of their fellow-creatures as cursed, *because* they are "labourers;" as ruffians, because they do the rough work, and have to "rough it;" as having black hearts, because they may have hard hands; as having dark minds, because they may have dirty feet. Only think of the fearful, hardening effects of this upon the mind of the "labourer" and his family. This effect presses upon his mind, and is often coupled with the conviction that he, more than all others, feels the force of the saying,—"The harder the work, the less the pay." Again, add to these the tendencies of his gipsy life, here to-day and away to-morrow, uncertain of work, of food, of home,—sure of nothing but the feeling that he is looked down upon as a dangerous fellow. Is this not likely to drive from him all sense of human feeling and of social responsibility? It has; and some do yield to the mighty and galling pressure, and say, or rather act as if they said, "Let us be what we are said to be, 'it is a pity to have the word without the worship.'" And having once given way; having succumbed to the fearful force of the adversity and all the other crushing circumstances which almost always surround such a desperate life; having given way to a wild self, and selfish will, they run headlong into reckless ferocity, to ruin and death.

Now, what has been said of this large and useful portion of the community, has reference to the words and deeds of many in regard to their opinion of the working-classes as a body. I know it is true we speak of the *dignity* of labour, and labour is now more and more being recognised as honourable. It was, I think, the celebrated Dr Chalmers who said, " We believe it to be in reserve for society, that workmen will at length share more equally than they do at present, with capitalists and proprietors of the soil, in the comforts and even the elegancies of life." To believe in this, is to have much encouragement to persevere; but what I know, compels me sometimes to regard the phrase—— " *dignity of labour* "——as sounding better at Exeter Hall than in the field, or where the hard-worked, the heartless and weary labourer toils. I feel keen on this and all such points. Often have I wept with and for the noble sinews of our nation, those designated the working-classes; and the tears have been all the more bitter when I thought that noble men and worthy women were being judged harshly *because* they earned their bread by the sweat of their brow. The democracy which I love is that which seeks not to bring any man *down* from a legitimate and honourable position, but which brings *up* those who are below the standard to the places they are entitled to occupy. Let us shake hands with mankind as man, and embrace the Christian wherever found. " God hath made of one blood all nations of men." He is the Father; why then not love one another as brethren? He is our Saviour; why not then rejoice together as the redeemed? If the Holy Spirit applied to *us* the redemption planned by the Father, and purchased by the Son, may the same not be the case with *others?* What were we *in the sight of God?* Sinners. Are they——those who are so judged——more? No. Let us not only take heed to the injunction, " Speak not evil one of another, brethren; " but let us be guarded lest it may be thus said of any of us, " Thou art inexcusable, O man, whosoever thou art that judgest; for wherein thou judgest another, thou condemnest thyself; for thou that judgest doest the same things."

Startle not at this. It is the warning voice of the righteous, the just Judge of all the earth; and He has said, " To whom much is given, of him much shall be required." *Much is given;*

let those who judge harshly only think of that, and see what has helped to make them what they are. Think of the advantages of the geniuses of antiquity—its poetry and history, its delineation of human nature and analogies of human character, not only engendering, but fostering the intuitive penetration and eloquent utterance of the divine gift, so as to enable the favoured one not only to perceive and apprehend ideas, but also to give a full and forcible utterance to them. And think of this, added to the advantages which the present day gives to those brought under the inspiring influence of enlightening and developing science, of modern and improved literature, of purified sanctified art. And when all this, by the Divine Teacher, through the Divine volume, enters deeper into the heart and conscience, what may we not look for! Yet how few, even of those thus favoured, come up to the standard! how many fall far, far below it!

What, then, can we look for from those who know but little, if anything, of science, literature, and art—their enlightenment, influence, and inspiration?—of those who are comparative strangers to the Holy Bible, which gives light to the soul and joy to the heart, which tells for good on the taste and in-intellect, the walk and conversation?—of those who have been not only deprived of these elevating and sacred influences, but who have been born and bred in the midst of influences of quite an opposite kind? And, alas! this is the sad condition of a very large mass of the London population. Go where we may, we meet with many who are not only in the midst of such adverse influences, but who have at last been overpowered, and hence have given way, and suffering themselves to be tossed about by every whiff of adversity, at which before they could have snapped their fingers in defiance; many of whom vice had made capture, are being whirled into the dirtiest pools of festering corruption—even against former tastes and present conviction, wallowing in filthy mires, and becoming so besmeared, that all traces of manliness are lost—the features of the devil standing out in bold relief.   It is most painful, accutely painful, to one whose moral feelings are quickened, to behold such hideous spectacles of guilt and misery as are visible in London; but thank God and good friends, whilst many have yielded—who perhaps have only bent after the back was broken—who have been reduced to apparent regardlessness after seeing no way of escape—there are many who have borne up and struggled on in a manner truly noble, with a heroism truly Christian, and who are yet heroes in the strife.   There is something ennobling in meeting with those engaged in this grand but severe battle; but my heart is filled with downright sadness when I think that even these are, by some, judged rashly and harshly, and I feel the more keenly when I think that the results of such false judgment may be to cause these heroes to fail, and perhaps to fall, after fighting so long and so bravely in the unequal strife. Oh, let us be kind in judging!   Let us pray and watch that, in all our labours, we are constrained by the love of Christ.   More especially in all such work, though we were able to speak with the tongues of men and of angels, and have not that love, we become "as sounding brass;" even though we were rich, and gave all our GOODS *to feed the poor;* though, for their sakes, we were to expose ourselves to danger, and have not that love, " it profiteth nothing."   That love " is kind, is not easily provoked, *thinketh no evil.*"

> To the *pained* speak mildly,
> Oh, treat the poor kindly.
>   All on to the rescue,
>   The Saviour still calls you.
> While *want* reigns so wildly,
> Oh, treat the poor kindly.

CONCLUSION.

FIND I must bring this book to a close. It is much larger than I originally meant, and yet I feel an increasing desire to continue. The manuscript from which these pages have been selected is yet considerable, but my purpose, for the present, is served; namely, to answer as briefly as possible questions such as these: *Where God, in His providence, had led me? How I had been preserved by His kindness? The work in which I had been engaged? In what measure I had been successful in that work, and how?*

Though I have not altogether passed unnoticed

> " The things of fame that do renown this city,"

yet it must be evident that I have looked more closely into

> " The deeds of shame that bring disgrace and pity."

For this I offer no apology. The nature of my duties led me at once into the midst of that which suggests the *frailty* rather than the *glory* of man. The interesting monuments and things of curiosity, the statuary and paintings,—all of which abound in London,—are to me objects of attraction, but " human wrecks in city ruins " * claim my first attention; and the closer I

---

* This is the title I proposed to give to a work to which I devoted some attention in Edinburgh. In the last page of " Life Story" it is said to be in course of preparation, and so it was; but when I came to London, and found the field of observation so much enlarged, I saw the necessity of altering my plans so as to extend to South as well as North Britain, and perhaps to Ireland. If spared, I hope to be able to develop these plans, soas to make an interesting and useful volume, entitled " Human Wrecks in City Ruins."

look into the loving and lovable, the simple and sublime, the tender and sweet life of Jesus; the more I know of the spirit of the Master, the more I feel the force of His truth and the influence of His love, I am the more convinced that He has led me to choose the "*better* part." The former I despise not, nor do I seek to bring them *down* from their proper place; but I am anxious to be the humble means in Providence of helping to lift *up* the latter.

· A "human wreck," what an aspect! and how many such there are! We hear of this being an age of improvement, and so it is; that not only the few but the many are progressing, and there is some truth in this. We hear and read of men and women—and at times meet with some—who are the embodiment of untold virtues; men whose noble souls are set in the glorious effulgence of heaven-inspired light; women whose tender hearts throb out true sympathy and real benevolence; men and women who work for the good of man, to the glory of God, whose valuable labours raise them as a "light set upon a hill that cannot be hid." Yes; but against all this glorious, because God-like, effort to rise there is a pressure, a crushing, an extinguishing pressure which indicates the power of selfishness, and bespeaks the ingenuity of wickedness. There are in our midst aspirations high and holy; a desire that every bodily power and mental faculty be developed and improved, that the heart be renewed, softened, kept alive and rendered susceptible of favourable impressions and noble emotions; but there are also the evil serpents which creep in everywhere, and go deep down to the very core of society, sucking its heart's blood, abstracting from man all that is manly, tearing from woman all that is womanly, and making the boy or girl everything but a child—a happy, a beautiful, a promising child. Ah, to look on such creatures, already horrible, and to think what they may become, what they suffer, who would not weep for such, and strive to help such?

It is because I have seen such, because I am aware of the

danger such are in, and because I know that such may be rescued, that I have, in imperfect imitation of my Saviour, sought them, and tried to lead them to Him, that I humbly joined with those who anxiously

> "Long for some moments, in this busy life,
>   When they may know and feel that they have been
>   Themselves the givers and the dealers out
>   Of some small blessings; have been kind to those
>   Who needed kindness."

But never—so far as I can judge—were my best wishes, touching this point, more amply gratified than now; never was I more anxious than now *to* SEEK *that those found may be* SAVED from present degradation and future misery; never with more truth, never with stronger faith, could I say,

> " The Lord that built the earth and skies is my perpetual aid."

Truly, " God moves in a mysterious way, His wonders to perform." The closing of this book—"My Life and Labours"—brings before my mind, as vivid as ever, the revising of the other—"Life Story;" not on a table, for we had sold the last one for bread; not on a chair, for there was none,—a pair of old bellows, which none would purchase, served as my writing-desk, my seat being the gathered-up " shake down" upon which, at night, we tried to rest our weary limbs. I think no shame to say it, for ours was honest, struggling poverty. But God has blessed that little book, and I have written this one, believing that He will bless it too. Nay, He has not only blessed that book, but He even blessed the poverty which was one of the direct causes of bringing it out. Do not mistake me. It is said that poverty is a blessing, but I think few who really know anything of its penalties and its hindrance will desire such a blessing. The poverty here referred to comes by or through man,—God may and does permit it; but the blessing, when there is any, comes from Him. In His mysterious providence He overrules, and in His mercy often brings a blessing out of poverty,

T

in the same way that good may spring from sources we least expect. If we, in faith, ask His aid in poverty, as in other afflictions, He will kindly send help,—such as by wisely directing our thoughts to the fleeting nature of all things earthly, and the stability of all things heavenly, and so graciously and beneficially affect our present position and future destiny. This is my personal experience, and it agrees with my observation in London as elsewhere; hence, I think the request, " Give me neither poverty nor riches," is a prayer the most of us would likely ask after careful reflection. The medium state is the preferable, because it is that in which the greatest happiness and usefulness may be found. It must be evident that the poverty which crushes to the ground, and sometimes under it, is not desirable ; nor are the riches that prevent the possessor from entering heaven. Whatever may be the theory, the practice proves that, as a rule, such poverty is a powerful obstacle to usefulness and to improvement. It is true, some daring minds may bear up against its all but overwhelming sway, and so tower above their circumstances; but, alas! how many sink beneath the swelling flood, unpitied and unknown; but if unknown, certainly not unfelt, for if they rise not, they sink; and if they sink, others go down with them.

Oh, let us for such work and pray in the spirit and after the manner of Him who,

> " Though now ascended up on high,
> Still bends on earth a brother's eye."

And now, one word more. I would not be doing justice to my humble home, or rather to those who adorn it and make it pleasant,—to the sweet " buds of promise" and their dear mother,—did I not say that which I am certain is the truth, namely, whatever have been my difficulties in the world, whatever my struggles with life, whatever may have been the nature of the duties I have had to perform, whatever the responsibilities I have had to sustain, whatever dangers I have had to encounter, in whatever spirit I have gone up to them, whether that of courage or kindness, I owe much of the strength and success to the fact that I have been happy in my "sweet home;" for home, enlivened and beautified with such precious gems as God has given me, is sweet, be it ever so poor. My home influences have gone forth with me, and the love, counsel, kindness, and care have been, and are, such as to help me to speak and act with cheerfulness and energy. The poet has said—

> " To make a happy fireside clime
>   For weans and wife,
> That 's the true pathos and sublime
>   Of human life."

And if I have a desire stronger than another, next to that of helping the helpless, of strengthening the weak, and raising the fallen in the name of God, it is to see my home made comfortable, my loved-ones happy. For this I have laboured and waited; for this I shall labour and wait. It is sometime since, in my heartfelt gratitude to God, and to " Maggie," I penned the little poem, in which are these lines,—

> " The earth, the sea, the spangled skies,
>   Have no such gems for me."

And to this day I feel the same, and well I might. If ever one was blessed with a heroic helpmate, I have been. My prayer is, that I may be enabled in some measure to be worthy of such a noble gift—of all the gifts with which God has blessed me.

www.ingramcontent.com/pod-product-compliance
Lightning Source LLC
Chambersburg PA
CBHW080549090426
42735CB00016B/3194